**Other Books by Stephen W. Garber, Ph.D.,
Marianne Daniels Garber, Ph.D.,
and Robyn Freedman Spizman**

If Your Child Is Hyperactive, Inattentive, Impulsive, Distractible . . .
Helping the Add/Hyperactive Child

Good Behavior

Monsters Under the Bed
and Other Childhood Fears

MONSTERS UNDER THE BED AND OTHER CHILDHOOD FEARS

*Helping Your Child Overcome
Anxieties, Fears, and Phobias*

**Stephen W. Garber, Ph.D.,
Marianne Daniels Garber, Ph.D.,
& Robyn Freedman Spizman**

VILLARD BOOKS
New York
1993

The names of individuals involved in examples and experiences used in this book have been changed. We have interchanged the pronouns used, alternating gender. In most cases, the pronouns could have been easily exchanged. When reading the information and incidents, feel comfortable to think of the children you know best.

Library of Congress Cataloging-in-Publication Data
Garber, Stephen W.
    Monsters under the bed and other childhood fears : helping your
child overcome anxieties, fears, and phobias / by Stephen W. Garber,
Marianne Daniels Garber, and Robyn Freedman Spizman.
        p.   cm.
    Includes bibliographical references and index.
    ISBN 978-0-812-99222-9
    1. Fear in children. 2. Child rearing. I. Garber, Marianne
Daniels. II. Spizman, Robyn Freedman. III. Title.
BF723.F4G37 1993
649'.1—dc20   92-56812

Manufactured in the United States of America on acid-free paper

146484122

To every child
who has ever been frightened and to every
parent who has responded to the cry
"Mommy, Daddy, I'm scared"

ACKNOWLEDGMENTS

A very special thank-you to those individuals who have contributed in some way to this book:

Our families, Amy, Adam, Arielle, and Aubrey Garber, and Justin and Ali Spizman, who fearlessly put up with busy days and nights and support us in everything we do, especially Robyn's husband Willy, who contributed tirelessly in so many ways to this project; our parents, Rooks and Dan Daniels, Gerry and Al Garber, Phyllis and Jack Freedman, and Gus and the late Regina Spizman, who taught us to put aside our fears; Doris Dozier and Bettye Storne, without whom we would get nothing done; our office staff, especially Merilee Kelley, Elaine Tavani, Cathy Jones, and Marilynn Foster, whose logistical support is invaluable; our colleagues at the Behavioral Institute of Atlanta who provided encouragement and clinical support so that we could complete this book, and the staff at Borders Book Shop, Oxford Book Store, and Chapter 11, who assisted us in finding appropriate books for children.

As always, a special word of gratitude to our literary agent, Meredith Bernstein, and our publisher, Diane Reverand, for their continued support and encouragement. We are especially indepted to our editor, Emily Bestler, whose insight, skill, and charm keep us on track, to Amelia Sheldon for always being ready to get an answer, and to Nancy Inglis and Mary O'Connor, who read the copy with an eagle eye.

Finally, thank you, Kat Anderson: Your wonderful artistic talent and whimsical eye bring each fear to life in this book.

CONTENTS

Contents

INTRODUCTION

"Mommeee, Daddeeee . . . I'm scared." What do you do when your child awakens from a nightmare . . . shies away from an approaching animal . . . won't climb a ladder . . . shivers with fear because of an approaching storm . . . clutches at your leg when it is time for you to say good-bye?

What parent hasn't been in one of these situations? How do you react? How do you know if your child's fear will naturally fade? When do you intervene? It is difficult to know how to respond to a fear. Do you empathize or ignore it? Placate or push?

It's impossible for adults to remember what it's like to be a child. We know that dreams are not real and that nothing lurks under the bed, but to a child these fears are very real. No matter how many times you say, "There are no monsters in the closet," your child is unlikely to believe you. When you say, "That's just the wind blowing," your child may still hear the footsteps of an intruder outside the window.

This book is about how to respond to your child's fears. Most children experience fears of the dark, strangers, unidentified noises, and numerous other things for a short time and then they pass. By supporting your child and filling in the gaps in her knowledge, you can minimize most of the normal childhood fears many children experience. By preparing your child in advance for the new situations she must meet, you may be able to avoid new fears.

You would probably like your child to retain a little fear. Healthy fear makes your child cautious when she walks across the street, keeps him from opening the door to a stranger when you are not home, and spurs your child on to a better performance when she speaks before a crowd. Sometimes, however, fears become so intense that they disrupt a child's life. Fears like these prevent some children from going to new places, interacting with peers, trying a new activity, or doing the things other children easily do.

When a child doesn't overcome a fear, it can grow and spread. In our clinic and others across the country, therapists see many children and adolescents whose fears have escalated beyond the norm. These youngsters won't spend the night away from home, are so afraid of the dark they sleep with the lights on and the radio playing all night, cannot approach a doctor's office without feeling panic, get sick before giving an oral presentation, and avoid heights, elevators, water, dogs, cats, bugs, and a multitude of other things that scare them.

Even if your child's fears are not that severe now, you can't assume that they will go away with age. Children are often masters at hiding their fear, and unresolved fears can last well beyond childhood. Many of the millions of adults who have persistent paralyzing fears can attest to that. Their fears of heights, speaking in public, animals, elevators, and other situations were rooted in childhood experiences.

A study conducted by the National Institute of Mental Health recently reported that anxiety disorders—including fears, phobias, and panic attacks—are the number-one mental health problem in the country. The goal must be to help your child overcome his fears so he won't become one of these statistics.

Monsters Under the Bed is designed to help you understand, minimize, prevent, and overcome your child's fears. In Chapter 1, "Understanding and Responding to Your Child's Fear," you will gain an understanding of fear, which fears are normal, and when fears become phobias. You'll learn how to respond to your child's fear in order to minimize it and when to intervene with stronger measures. In Chapter 2, "Coping with Fear," you will learn the techniques to identify your child's fear and control the physical, mental, and behavioral reactions to it. These are lifelong skills that can take the fear out of fear. Chapter 3, "Overcoming Fear," presents the steps that will permit your child to overcome strong fears or ones that have lasted too long. Using four kinds of experiences involving imagination, information, observation, and exposure, you will learn how to desensitize your child's fears.

The rest of *Monsters Under the Bed* is devoted to helping you work with your child to conquer specific fears. Applying the information presented in Chapters 1 through 3, subsequent chapters deal with earliest childhood fears and fears of animals, illness, weather, separation, social events, transportation, school, heights, claustrophobia, crime, and death.

After reading the first three chapters, turn to the chapter on your child's specific fear. If your child's particular fear is not included, turn to a similar fear. For example, if your child is afraid of hurricanes, use the discussion in Chapter 3 and the steps outlined in the section on thunderstorms to design a plan for your situation. In each fear section you will find the information you need to help your child.

Monsters Under the Bed guides you through the steps to overcome the childhood fears that many children experience so that you are comfortable in responding to your child. Overcoming fear takes time and patience, but the payoffs for your child can last a lifetime. Now, when your child calls out, "Mommy, Daddy, I'm scared, there's a monster under the bed" or clings to you in fear, you will know how to respond.

Monsters Under the Bed
and Other Childhood Fears

1

UNDERSTANDING AND RESPONDING TO YOUR CHILD'S FEAR

What childhood fears are normal? Why do some fears come and go? What's the best way to respond to your child's fears?

When your child is scared all he wants to do is get away from the situation. He doesn't know why his heart is pounding or his legs feel so funny; he just knows he doesn't like the sensations. He certainly doesn't realize that the more he avoids his fear, the more it's likely to grow.

The better you understand childhood fears, the better prepared you'll be to respond to your child when he's frightened.

Understanding Childhood Fear

1. Childhood is a time of many fears. Numerous research studies have found that between the ages of two and six children have more than four fears, while between the ages of six and twelve they experience an average of seven different fears. It's fair to say that your child is as likely as any other youngster to be frightened by animals, scared of heights, and terrified of separating from you. If you're buying your three-year-old a night light, you are not alone. And if your child hates it when you leave him with even the best baby-sitter in town, other parents can commiserate. Your son might have as many fears as your daughter, but he won't admit it publicly—the research commonly concludes that girls have more fears than boys. Very early in life boys appear to be subject to male stereotyping and reluctant to admit they are less than macho. Boys may have more fears about their future, reflecting increased performance pressures that society may place on males, but as roles in society change, girls, too, may feel increased performance anxiety.

The hopeful news is you can expect your child's fears to decrease with age. Researchers have found that although children experience a number of significant fears during childhood, the number of children reporting fears decreases by age eleven. Be prepared, though, for fear to raise its head again in preadolescence. Studies indicate that the number of fears reported spikes for preteens and then decreases in adolescence. However, don't assume that adolescents don't have fears. Fears of personal safety and imaginary creatures might decrease, but school and social fears can intensify. Teens are especially traumatized by any type of public embarrassment. Also, adolescents who suppressed childhood fears may suddenly manifest anxiety under stress or when confronted with a new situation. A long-hidden fear of heights may show up on a trip to an amusement park or even at the neighborhood swimming pool. So don't presume that your nonchalant teenager is necessarily fear-free no matter how confident he seems.

2. Most fears are developmental. Fears of falling and loud noises are the only fears children have at birth. The emergence of other common fears parallels a child's increasing awareness of the world around him. Parents often comment on how freely infants can be passed from one set of arms to another. Before the age of five or six months, your baby is likely to coo and smile at almost any face that is twelve to twenty inches in front of her. Once she learns to recognize familiar faces, she may develop a fear of strangers.

Early childhood fears center on your child's environment. That's the world he knows. Fears during this period include misgivings about animals, the weather, and strange objects such as vacuum cleaners, machines, fire engines, and trucks. As a youngster gains more knowledge and understanding of real-world phenomena, a growing imagination takes over. Fears of the dark, ghosts, monsters, and the supernatural come to the forefront and can be stimulated by what your child sees on television or a few gory ghost stories told by an older sibling or friend.

Exposure to real-world dangers also intensifies fears. Recent studies of inner-city youth indicate they have a large incidence of fears of specific events in their environment, such as crime and shootings. Other children who do not live in high crime areas can also develop these fears when they hear about the terrible things that happen in our world today.

Looking over the list that follows, you can see that some fears come and go, only to reappear later. Your child might be afraid of the dark at two, fearless at three, and scared again at four years of age. Other fears don't simply reappear; they change form. A young child's fear of the dark might become a fear of burglars when he is older.

Over the years, as your child's world broadens, so do his fears. Whereas before, his fears centered on home and family, in preadolescence, your child is likely to worry about what others think. Fears of school and other social situations take precedence. Along with fears about her future, what her friends think will plague your youngster through the teen years.

CHILDHOOD FEARS

0–6 months   Loss of support, loud noises;

7–12 months   Fear of strangers, fear of sudden, unexpected, and looming objects;

1 year   Separation from parent, toilet, injury, strangers;

2 years   A multitude of fears, including loud noises (vacuum cleaners, sirens/alarms, trucks, and

thunder), animals (e.g., large dogs), the dark, separation from parent, large objects/machines, change in personal environment;

3 years	Masks, dark, animals, separation from parent;
4 years	Separation from parent, animals, dark, noises (including at night);
5 years	Animals, "bad" people, dark, separation from parent, bodily harm;
6 years	Supernatural beings, (e.g., ghosts, witches, "Darth Vader"), bodily injuries, thunder and lightning, dark, sleeping or staying alone, separation from parent;
7–8 years	Supernatural beings, dark, fears based on media events, staying alone, bodily injury;
9–12 years	Tests and examinations in school, school performance, bodily injury, physical appearance, thunder and lightning, death, dark (low percentage).

Sources: Ilg and Ames, 1955; Jerslid and Homes, 1935a; Kellerman, 1981, Lapouse and Monk, 1959; Scarr and Salaptek, 1970; in Morris and Kratochwill, 1983.

3. Some children are more prone than others to have fears. Kelly is a lively, independent eight-year-old who has a keen sense of humor. She has many friends, and adults always comment on how confident she is. Many people who think they know Kelly, would be surprised to learn that she has many fears. She cannot watch a scary movie or hear a violent news story without it influencing her dreams—or nightmares. Her parents routinely monitor what she watches; her imagination is vivid and she must be frequently reassured about the noises she hears in the night. To make things worse, Kelly's six-year-old sister isn't bothered by anything she sees or hears. In fact, she doesn't seem to have any significant fears. Even though these two girls share the same parents and environment, they are very different.

This example of two sisters illustrates how personality characteristics greatly contribute to a child's tendency to be fearful. Psychologists and others who study children frequently note how differently children respond to traumatic events. One child who hears the sounds of a distant battle can be terrorized for years. Another who spent many nights in a bomb shelter may come out with few if any fears. Some children appear to be more conditionable than others. While psychologists have not identified all the contributing factors; shy, sensitive, inhibited children seem to be more prone to develop a variety of fears; as do children, like Kelly, who are very impressionable or who have very strong imaginations. A person who is nervous and worries a lot is likely to develop more fears than someone who is calm.

If your child's personality fits one of these patterns, he may develop one fear after another. He may also be more likely to have a fear that lasts. You will, therefore, have to work doubly hard to help your child overcome particular fears and learn how to relax.

4. Unconfronted fears can last. Although many fears will disappear as quickly as they came, some persist and become ingrained. Fears that continue beyond the usual age that most of your child's peers have overcome them are likely to grow in strength if they are not confronted. Ask any one of the twenty-five million adults in this country who won't fly on airplanes if his fear has lessened because he hasn't been on a plane. What about the people who are afraid of snakes? Are they less frightened of snakes because they never see one? Probably not. Nor would a fear of elevators lessen if you always took the stairs.

Fears that are not confronted not only last, they can also spread. Your child might begin with a fear of slides. That's not too bad if it stops there. How many slides will she have to slide down as a teen or adult? How difficult will it be to avoid a slide? The problem is that your child's fear of slides can spread to other heights. If she is too frightened to climb the ladder on a slide, it is likely she will have trouble climbing other ladders, or even playing on a jungle gym. Eventually she might have trouble climbing open staircases. The same fear might lead to a fear of riding in an open elevator, walking across a bridge, or standing near a window in a skyscraper. Fears that spread are hard to avoid.

Sometimes a fear seems so mild, you might wonder why it is necessary to intervene. Even though a child is not avoiding the situation, he might suffer silently. On the other hand, your child might have a fear that he doesn't have to contend with very often, such as a fear of airplanes. Unless your family frequently travels by air, your child may only deal with his fear once a year—if that often. Of course, that's now. What about later, when his fear of planes hasn't gone away?

Other children might endure periods of intense fear followed by periods of time when a fear subsides. Unfortunately, that doesn't automatically mean it has disappeared. It, too, might be incubating only to show up later in life. Many adult fears began in childhood. Unconfronted, the fears temporarily go undercover. Sam came to the clinic because of a fear of cats that began when he was a young boy. His family was kind and understanding, so they helped him avoid cats. When children who had pet cats invited him to play, he gave an excuse. If the family was taking a walk and saw a cat approaching, everyone crossed the street to help Sam escape the feline. Actually, the young man thought his fear faded during his college years. He didn't run into many cats on campus. Out of school, he bought a small house and built a nice deck on the back. Everything was great until a nice lady who bred Siamese kittens moved in next door. Suddenly, Sam was faced with a next-door neighbor who had a backyard full of kittens. Gripped by panic, he never used the deck again and eventually sold his house.

Obviously, Sam's fear had not disappeared. There are hundreds of other cases of adults whose fears began in childhood and later disrupted their adult lives. When psychologists began to study fears like these, a pattern emerged. Fears of animals, weather, accidents, heights, enclosures, the dark, doctors, and medical procedures often begin in childhood. Fears of transportation, public speaking, meeting people, and other social fears frequently have their birth in adolescence. Of course, there are exceptions. A very shy child might develop a fear of speaking in public long before adolescence. A teenager who was never afraid of shots as a child might have a serious illness that leaves her scared of blood and needles.

5. Fears can turn into phobias. Adults frequently assume that children don't have phobias. That's not true. A child's fear may become so intense that it interrupts his daily life. When that occurs, the fear has escalated into a phobia. Unlike many childhood fears, a phobia is not simply a strong fear that will go away in a few weeks or few months. By definition, a phobia is an intense irrational fear that is out of proportion to any real danger. It cannot be reasoned away and the child does not have the conscious control to overcome it.

There are two parts to a phobic reaction. The first is the intense irrational fear; the second is avoidance. A child might get anxious thinking about something she fears. Tina's bee phobia is a perfect example. Tina was ten years old when she came to the clinic. She wouldn't play in her own backyard and ate inside when the family barbecued. It took awhile for her parents to make the connection between the child's stomachaches and her avoidance of the outdoors because Tina had never been stung by a bee. Her brother had and he was allergic to bee stings—but he still loved the outdoors. Tina's avoidance of bees reinforced her phobia. As long as she never came into contact with a bee, she couldn't overcome her fear, and every time she avoided the situation, she added another layer to her fear of bees. By the time Tina came to the clinic, she insisted on wearing long sleeves in the summer. She never went into a garden or swung in the park in the spring. In warm weather, she remained outdoors only as long as was necessary to get from one place to the next. Her fears had spread beyond just bees. If she saw a wasp or another flying insect she could not instantly identify she panicked, hyperventilated, and her heart pounded in her ears. Just the thought of going back outside would trigger the same reaction.

To determine if your child's fear has lasted longer than the norm, review the chart that follows, remembering that any chart is only a guide. Talk to other parents about their children's fears. Teachers, having known so many children, are also a good source of information. Keep in mind that each child is different. Some children develop fears earlier than usual. That might simply be a sign that your child is more aware of the world around him than his peers are. As long as he copes with his fear by the time his friends do, don't worry. If your child has more fears than his peers, but gets over them one after another, that also may be normal for your youngster. If, however, your child develops intense fears that prevent him from doing many of the things his peers do fairly easily, then you must help your child overcome them. Understanding what is normal will alert you to fears that last beyond the usual time frame.

WHAT'S NORMAL, WHAT'S NOT

Normal	*Not Normal*
Develops fears at the usual age, like peers.	Develops fears that are not age-appropriate, for example, a fear of monsters at age 12.
Develops fears at earlier ages than peers, but they fade away at the same time they do for peers.	Has fears that develop early and last long past the usual age.
Develops a number of fears during childhood and overcomes each.	Denies all fears. Hides any anxieties.
Has fears that come and go.	Gets stuck on a particular fear.
Shows anticipatory anxiety.	Worries even when not going to have to encounter the fear.
Gets nervous and experiences a number of anxiety symptoms.	Passes out (unless in relation to seeing blood). Gets hysterical.
Admits that fear is irrational but can't be talked out of it.	Really thinks someone or something is out to get him.
Has fears but with support can at least try to approach and eventually overcome fear.	Totally avoids and will not try to approach fear even with support.
Is shy. Doesn't like to talk in front of class.	Avoids people. Will not talk to others even after knowing them for awhile.
Gets nervous before going to school or taking texts.	Refuses or resists going to school because of anxiety.
Shows separation anxiety.	Refuses to spend the night out as same age peers easily do.

Responding to Your Child's Fears

Your child is going to be frightened by one thing or another over the years. If you are alert to the most common childhood fears, you can almost predict what might frighten your child. By preparing your child for new situations you can sometimes prevent an intense reaction. At the very least, by responding appropriately you can minimize many childhood fears. Keep these suggestions in mind as you interact with your child.

1. Never belittle your child's fear. Adults tend to downplay children's fears with comments such as, "That's silly; there's nothing to be afraid of—it's a little dog," or "Come on, that's ridiculous, there's no such thing as a ghost." Never tease your child about a fear—she's liable to go underground. Out of sight, though, is not out of mind. On the contrary, it is the perfect way to incubate a phobia that can emerge full-blown years from now. One woman who came to our clinic was scolded as a child for being afraid of heights. Now she has trouble flying and can't go above the fifth floor in a building. Children need to know that you take them seriously.

2. Don't force your child to confront a fear. There's a danger to exposing a child "all at once" to a fear. If for some reason the child's fear doesn't dissipate, it's likely to become firmly entrenched and even more resistant to change. If you force your child to pet the nice doggie when she continues to panic, her fear cannot disappear. As a result she's likely to be even more frightened of dogs on the next occasion.

3. Don't cater to a fear. The story of Sam, who was afraid of cats, is a case in point. His parents meant well when they protected him from cats. Unfortunately, every time they led Sam out of a cat's way, they reinforced his fear. Contriving situations to bypass your child's fear will not help him overcome it. Many families find themselves avoiding situations, taking over responsibilities, and inadvertently helping a child maintain a fear. The only way to overcome a fear is to confront it. Fear peaks and then ebbs if you wait long enough. Be your child's best support as he confronts his fear.

4. Don't overreact. This is especially true when you are also afraid of the feared object or situation. Children are supreme readers of body language. While your words are saying, "Everything is okay," your hand tightly clutched on the child's arm and the tremor in your voice communicate a different message. In the process, your child learns there is something to fear.

5. Prepare your child for new experiences. When you know that your child will be exposed to a new situation that might be frightening—any new situation produces some anxiety—prepare her for it. Introduce her to the experience through books, movies, and pretend experiences before she must confront the real thing. When Jessica was going to have her tonsils out, her parents were a little frightened, so they knew their child was likely to be also. To prepare her for the situation, they read books about going to the hospital and played hospital at home. They visited the hospital several days before Jessica was to be admitted. The child saw a room like the one she would have and met some of the nurses on her floor. She had an opportunity to ask as many questions as she wanted. On the day she entered the hospital, Jessica helped her mom pack her bag. She included in her suitcase a blanket and pillow from her bed as well as a few special toys. Her mother stayed with her at the hospital, and they talked a lot about what would be happening over the next few hours. Jessica was certainly a little nervous about having her tonsils out, but she made it through the surgery and her hospital stay with flying colors. She coped with her fears and beat them.

6. Help your child cope with fear. When they are scared, children don't understand what they are feeling. They might think something is wrong with them, but they certainly don't know what to do to help themselves feel better. In the rest of this book, you will learn skills to help your child cope with and overcome his fear. When your child has an intense fear, even if it is age-appropriate, you can use these skills to help him face his fear and overcome it. If your child is fear-prone, as you deal with each fear, you can enhance and reinforce your child's coping skills so he is able to control his anxiety and be less frightened.

The suggestions given in this book can help overcome many of the fears your child may encounter. However, there are several points to keep in mind. First, as you work with your child, realize that it takes time to get over a fear. The process requires patience. There will be times when things do not go as you planned. Step back and try again. Your child needs your support as he confronts the deepest of emotions. Second, if your child's fear is so strong that the exercises seem to worsen his fear, if your child develops a severe phobia, or if you simply have questions about your child's reactions, seek professional advice to help your child.

2

COPING

WITH FEAR

Four-year-old Caroline was too scared to climb the ladder on the slide at school. She felt quivery on the inside and her heart beat fast. She knew other children played on the slide and enjoyed it, but it wasn't fun for her. She was afraid she'd fall off it and skin her knees and elbows. She couldn't imagine herself safely perched on the top of the slide. When she went outside she played on the swings or in the doll house. When the rest of her friends climbed the slide, Caroline played alone.

Caroline's dad explained to her that her feelings were a natural reaction to being frightened. He helped her practice stepping up one rung of a ladder at a time, yet it took weeks for her to feel comfortable enough to climb the first few rungs of the slide at school, and the whole school year to make it to the top. Her classmates applauded when she finally made it down the slide the first time. Caroline's confidence soared and she was well on her way to overcoming not only her fear of the slide but also fears of other heights.

Like all fears, Caroline's has three parts. The first is the physical reaction that occurs when the mind senses danger. Caroline's heart beat faster; she felt shaky and even a little dizzy. The second is what a person says to herself about a fear. Caroline said to herself, "I'll fall and hurt myself on the slide." She couldn't imagine herself safely perched on the landing ready to take a ride. The last aspect of fear is a person's natural tendency to avoid the perceived danger. Caroline just didn't slide. She played on other playground equipment instead.

Breaking Fear into Its Parts

Understanding the fear reaction provides solutions to controlling fear. In this chapter, you will learn techniques to combat each part of the fear response. Relaxation techniques counteract the physical sensations that accompany fear. By providing information and using your child's imagination to create new positive mental pictures, you change what your child says to himself as he confronts his fear. And finally by pinpointing and providing a means to measure fear, you will be ready to break down your child's fear into steps he can manage.

The Physical Aspects of Fear

Perceived danger triggers in the body what is commonly called the *fight-or-flight response*. Imagine that you are taking a walk alone in your neighborhood late one evening. You instinctively freeze when you hear something in the bushes. After a brief silence there is another sound. Your heart pounds in your ears, you begin to hyperventilate, and your muscles tense. Suddenly, something rushes out of the bushes toward you. A few involuntary utterances escape from your throat, and you take off without waiting to see who or what made the noise. When you look back and see a small cat under the street light you feel both relieved and a little foolish. Nevertheless, you still feel a little shaky as you quickly complete your walk home.

If you had actually been attacked by an animal or person, all of your energy would have been focused on fighting off the predator. If the danger was inescapable and overwhelming you might even have fainted, which is similar to what happens when an animal "plays possum" to convince a foe it is already dead.

Explain to your child that fear is always accompanied by physical reactions. An older child will be interested in knowing what happens to the body and why he feels the way he does when he is frightened. A younger child needs to know that the feelings she experiences are normal and won't hurt her.

Use examples from your own life to explain the fear sensations your child feels. Caroline said she felt funny in her legs and her knees shook. Perhaps your have felt similar sensations in your legs when you made an important presentation or speech. Or, you could use a favorite movie to make your point. For example, in the film *Bambi* the deer freezes, trembles, and then flees from danger—both man and the forest fire.

A list of the most common symptoms of fear follows. Use the information to explain what is happening in your child's body when he is scared. Once your child understands the physical reactions to fear he will be more receptive to learning the relaxation techniques that counter them.

Each of the reactions you will explain to your child is a normal response to fear. If, however, as you read the list, you have any concerns about your child's heart racing, feelings of shortness of breath, or any other symptoms your child experiences, discuss them with your child's physician before proceeding. These symptoms are also present in other conditions that require medical or psychological care. Once you know that your child is in excellent health, you will feel confident when you tell her that each reaction is a normal part of the fear response.

Pounding Heart Fear makes the heart beat faster, pumping more blood to the rest of the body, so that we are ready to run or fight if the danger is real.

Butterflies in the Stomach When your child is scared, the blood drains away from her stomach and moves into her arms and legs so that she can run faster or fight harder.

Fast Breathing or the Feeling of Shortness of Breath Like a deer, a frightened person often breathes faster to get more oxygen into the body. Tell your child that more oxygen gives her the energy to run faster and further or fight harder.

Lightheadedness or Dizziness Rapid, shallow breathing often makes people dizzy. Remind your child how he feels when he blows up a balloon or a raft. It may feel like he is going to pass out but he won't. Explain to your child that anyone can make himself faint if he stands too quickly or too long while holding his breath, and that some people faint when they see blood. People rarely faint from fear unless it is very sudden and intense.

Shaking or Trembling Feeling Explain that these feelings come from tension that builds in the muscles of the arms and legs. Unless the tension is released in some way, your child is likely to feel shaky even after the danger has passed.

Clammy Hands, Sweating These reactions are part of the body's effort to cool itself as it expends extra energy in response to fear. Remind your child how it feels when she splashes water on herself during the hot summer. As the water evaporates it cools the skin. Sweating works the same way. It is the body's internal sprinkler system. Your child might be embarrassed if others see her perspire, but when she understands it is a natural process it will bother her less. Explain that dogs can't sweat and that is why they pant when they are hot.

Tingling in the Hands and/or Feet Tingling hands and feet are caused by blood flowing away from these areas and into the bigger muscles in the arms and legs. Rapid breathing contributes to these sensations. Remind your child about how it feels when his foot or leg "goes to sleep," and how these sensations fade when the blood returns.

Tightness in the Chest Have your child tense her arms and upper body. Notice how the muscles in the chest also feel tense. Explain to your child that this also occurs when she gets ready to run or fight. If your child complains of tightening in her chest even when she is not scared or it continues beyond the actual occurrence of the fear, you should discuss the symptom with your child's physician to eliminate any medical concerns.

Feeling as if Time Slows Down or Things Seem Strange
When a person is very frightened, all of his senses are heightened. Things might seem to be happening in slow motion or even look a little funny as the senses prepare to take in all available information. Explain to your child how this protects him and permits him to act effectively.

Dry Mouth/Lump in the Throat You can probably remember a time when you felt a lump in your throat or your mouth went dry before you had to speak. Explain to your child that cavemen yelled and screamed when they were met by danger; they also weren't interested in eating at that moment. Civilized man stifles that natural reaction so we sometimes feel a lump in the throat instead.

The Cognitive Aspect of Fear

You and your three-year-old visit a friend's home. The friend's large golden retriever is barking loudly and wagging its tail. You don't perceive the dog as a threat. Upon seeing the animal, you instantly think, "Goldens are so friendly." You know that the wagging tail and bark are simply ways the dog says hello. Your child, on the other hand, sees a large dog straining to get at him. He doesn't think the dog looks friendly. His thoughts are something more akin to "That dog wants to eat me." Your child might have an image in his mind of the dog biting his hand or snapping viciously at him. The next thing you know, your child is screaming in terror and trying to hide behind you or flee. It is your child's perception of the situation and the accompanying thoughts and images that set off a fear response.

If your child's fear is very strong or has lasted a long while, he's repeated scary statements to himself many times. Like grooves in an old, worn-out record, these fear-producing statements run deep. They are automatic thoughts that pop up everytime the fear situation arises. Over time, these fearful thoughts can spread to other similar situations. A child who is frightened by one type of dog might think that other dogs and even cats will also attack him.

It takes time to replace these automatic, negative fear-producing thoughts with more positive ones. Countering each negative thought and image is an essential aspect of overcoming fear. To accomplish it, you will provide your child with new information to correct misconceptions and make the unknown less fearful. You will help your child create a list of positive coping statements about the feared object or situation and replace the old frightening images with positive scenes of your child successfully coping with his fear.

The Behavioral Aspect of Fear

When your child is afraid, all he wants to do is get out of the situation as quickly as possible and never face it again. That's a natural reaction to fear; you have probably felt that way yourself. There are a lot of scary situations that adults rightfully hope to avoid permanently. Unfortunately, if your child runs away from his child-hood fears and successfully avoids them before he learns to cope with them, those fears are likely to remain with him for a long time, perhaps into adulthood. What's worse, as we've said, those fears that are not confronted tend to spread, so that a child who is afraid of one breed of dog is likely to become alarmed by all dogs. A child who is afraid of reading in front of class may become fearful of giving any type of public speech or even answering questions in class.

Of course, it is scary to confront a fear. What your child needs to know is that fear is like a fever—it will break. If your child stays in the situation, her fear will peak and then lessen. Remember four-year-old Caroline who was afraid of slides. Climbing up each new rung on the ladder created fear, but after awhile she got used to standing on each new step and her fear subsided. By meeting her fear, *one tiny step at a time*, Caroline was able to overcome it.

To overcome any fear, your child must counteract each of the three aspects of fear: the physical reaction, the cognitive images that promote the fear, and the behavioral tendency to avoid a frightening situation. In the rest of this chapter, you will learn coping techniques designed to combat each aspect of fear. Relaxation techniques help your child remain calm when he feels anxious. Your child will learn how to slow his breathing and relax the muscles of his body to counter the physical aspects of fear. Furnishing your child with new information permits him to replace his negative fear-producing thoughts with positive statements about the perceived fear. Pretending and imagining himself successfully coping with the fear also introduces new positive images to your child's mind that counter the ones that foster fear. Finally, the pinpointing and measuring techniques permit you to break down your child's fear into manageable steps so that your child can stay in each situation long enough for her fear to subside.

Teaching Your Child How to Relax

One of the most effective ways to counter fear is to relax. The body automatically reacts to fear, but the relaxation response is not automatic. Most of us have to learn how to relax. When you come home from the office, drive for an hour in rush-hour traffic, or finish the tasks of a busy day, it takes a while for the body to wind down. You can help it along by listening to quiet music, watching an entertaining television show, pleasantly conversing with a friend, or simply sitting down and putting your feet up. It is also possible to teach your body a new response so that with practice, you can relax on cue.

Use the following exercises to teach your body what it feels like to relax. You will learn how to slow your breathing, release the tension in the limbs and muscles of your body, and promote other calming feelings. Once you are familiar with the exercises, you can teach them to your child. As your child gains skill in using the relaxation techniques, he can use them to control the physical sensations that make him feel frightened.

To get the best results from the relaxation exercises, your child must practice them at times when he is not frightened. Since children don't like to practice anything, the following suggestions will be helpful:

1. Practice with your child. More than any declaration, your action will show your child how important you think these skills are. Besides, you will benefit from the relaxation techniques, too. In addition to countering fear, the relaxation exercises will minimize everyday stress, help you to fall asleep, and help you to remain calm when you are tense or angry.

2. Select practice times that do not compete with other things your child would like to do. Your child will not welcome your suggestion to practice in the middle of his favorite television show. Although you will see quicker results if he practices every day, the long-term effect is what's important. This is a skill you want your child to feel good about and to use. If he practices only several times a week, that's fine. Think of the relaxation technique as a lifelong skill—once it's learned, both of you will have it forever.

3. Praise and reward your child for practicing. Praise your child for cooperating as she learns the skills, and reward her for practicing them later. Chapter 3 includes a discussion of appropriate ways to use praise and rewards to motivate your child.

Use the chart that follows to reward your child for practicing the relaxation skills more often each week or for maintaining his practice schedule. For example, if your child practices two times the first week, he earns a reward. Then set a goal of three practice sessions for the next week. When your child meets or beats his goal, he earns an extra reward. Continue to reward your child until he reaches a realistic goal of, perhaps, four or five sessions per week. Continue to praise his efforts. The ultimate reward comes when your child understands and feels the benefits of these techniques, but until that kicks in, reinforcement is essential.

RELAXATION TRAINING CENTER

WEEKS ↓	DAYS→ MON	TUES	WED	THURS	FRI	SAT	SUN	TOTAL	GOAL
1									
2									
3									
4									
5									

4. Make arrangements so that you and your child will not be interrupted while practicing the relaxation skills. Unplug the phone and put a "Do Not Disturb" sign on the door. Ask your spouse or a friend to take care of siblings, let them practice, too, or occupy them with an activity while you are busy.

5. Pick a comfortable spot where you can stretch out. A bed, the floor, or even a sofa will work.

You are ready to begin. Before teaching the exercises to your child, read through the directions and try the motions yourself.

Caution: If you or your child has any back problems or other medical conditions that you think might be aggravated by doing these exercises, consult with your physician before beginning. If any of the exercises cause any discomfort or pain, stop. Don't over tense any muscle. The idea is to feel the tension, not strain a muscle.

Belly Breathing

When your child becomes tense or anxious, he probably "shortens his breath," inhaling in short, rapid breaths with the upper part of his chest. Shallow breathing like this contributes to feelings of tightness in the chest and neck as well as a feeling of lightheadedness. To counter that response, your child must learn to breathe from the diaphragm. Help him visualize the action by labeling it "belly breathing."

Belly Up Have your child lie flat on her back with her arms by her sides and her legs straight. Show her how to put one hand over

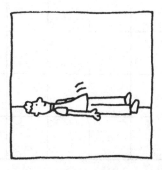

her belly button and the other hand on her chest. Observe your child breathing naturally. What happens to her hands when she inhales and exhales? If she is breathing correctly for relaxation, the hand on her stomach, rather than the one on her chest, should move up when she inhales and down when she exhales.

To teach your child how to breathe correctly, have her imagine her stomach is a balloon that she must fill with air as she inhales. Explain to your child that this will happen naturally when she inhales correctly; she does not need to push her stomach out or arch her back. Place a book on her stomach so she can see the motion easily.

If your child has difficulty mastering the motion, reassure her that "it will come." Newborn babies breathe this way; your child might do the same as she sleeps. However, when you do it on purpose, it takes a little while to get the knack of it.

Encourage your child to practice belly breathing for a few minutes every day until the skill develops. Lavishly praise her for cooperating and working to master this skill.

Breathing Slowly Once your child learns to inhale with his belly rising, have him place both hands on his navel. As he breathes in and out, ask him to count aloud slowly so that it takes longer to exhale than to inhale. Instruct your child to count to three as he inhales and then to five as he exhales. Over time your child can increase the counts so that his breathing slows even further. If your child begins to tense and grit his teeth as he struggles to do this, counter the action by instructing him to open his mouth slightly.

Next, when your child practices, slowly say the word "relax" and have him repeat it with you when he exhales. Exaggerate the word "relax" so it lasts the whole time he slowly exhales. Frequently pairing the word "relax" with slow, easy breathing will make the word a cue that induces calm feelings. Have your child continue to practice pairing the word and controlled exhaling until he can do it easily.

Belly Breathing Sitting and Standing Once your child can easily belly breathe lying down, have her practice in other positions, such as sitting or standing, so that she learns to use the skill anywhere she is. If your child has difficulty transferring the skill to new positions, have her practice the breathing while reclining with one pillow beneath her back. Increase the pillows to two, three, and so forth until she is able to breathe correctly as she sits upright. Praise your child for each accomplishment and remind her to pair belly breathing with the word "relax" whenever she practices.

Deep-Muscle Relaxation

Progressive muscle relaxation was originally developed by Dr. Edmond Jacobson. You can instruct your child how to do it or make your own tape from the script that follows so that your child can practice when you are unavailable. A commercially prepared tape of this relaxation regime, entitled, "Good Behavior Made Easy Relaxation Trainer" is also available from The Institute for Living Skills, P.O. Box 1461 Fallbrook, CA 92028 (1-800-886-2767).

Before teaching these exercises to your child, however, practice them yourself so that you make a smooth transition from one exercise to the next, progressively tensing and relaxing each muscle group in the body. When you are instructed to tense a muscle, do not cramp it. Simply tighten it enough to feel the tension and then quickly release the tension so feelings of relaxation flow in.

Puppet Arms and Legs Begin by explaining to your child that when he moves his arms or legs, the muscles in the limbs tighten and relax. Have your child pretend he is a marionette; when the string on his arm is pulled, his arm moves. Pretend to pull the string attached to his leg; what happens? If you let go of the string, the leg drops. Have your child extend his arms in front of him, hold them there until they feel heavy, and then drop them by his sides all at once as though the puppet string was suddenly cut. Your child should drop the limbs as if they are dead weight rather than easing them into position or throwing them down. Repeat this exercise until your child understands how to make his arms and legs go limp and drop.

• **Teach your child how to relax the hands.** Instruct your child to lie on a flat surface, such as the bed or floor, and to begin belly breathing. With his arms lying by his sides, palms down, ask him to focus on his *right* hand. Without lifting the arm, have your child spread his fingers, and point them toward the ceiling. Instruct your child to hold his hand in this position and count to

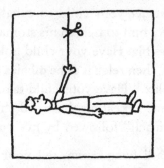

eight, then to slowly inhale and exhale, saying the word "relax" and letting his hand drop suddenly as though the puppet strings were cut. Repeat the exercise with the right hand two times. Do the same exercise with the left hand two times.

• **Teach your child to relax the arms.** Direct your child to make a fist and lift his arm a few inches off the surface as though held by a marionette string. Instruct your child to hold his arm taut for a count of ten; to take a deep breath; and, pretending that the string is cut, to open the hand and let the arm drop suddenly as he exhales and says the word "relax." Repeat the exercise alternating right and left arms until the activity is completed two times with each side.

• **Teach your child to relax the legs. (If you or your child has back problems, skip this exercise.)** Have your child focus on his legs, again, pretending that each leg has a string tied to it. Tell your child to lift his straight left leg slightly off the surface and hold it in position. Instruct your child to count 1, 2, 3, 4, inhale, 5, 6, 7, 8, exhale, and drop the leg at once as though the strings were cut as he says the word "relax." Repeat the same motions two times on each side. Praise your child for cooperating and doing the exercise correctly.

Steel Stomach Instruct your child to exhale fully so that his stomach sinks in. Direct him to tighten his stomach muscles so that they are as tight as possible. Have your child hold this "steel stomach" for a count of ten, then relax it as he inhales a slow belly breath and says the word "relax." Have your child take in five more easy belly breaths, each time repeating the word "relax." Repeat the sequence of "steel stomach" followed by five belly breaths.

Shoulder Shrug Still lying down, tell your child to raise his shoulders slowly toward his ears, tightening the muscles in his shoulders and neck without hurting himself. Have him hold a comfortable shrug for a count of ten; then inhale a slow, easy belly breath and drop his shoulders as he exhales, saying the word "relax." After five relaxed belly breaths have him repeat the shoulder shrug and five relaxed belly breaths.

Wide-Mouth Yawn Give your child permission to yawn as wide as he can without covering his mouth. If he is yawning properly, he will naturally squint. With his mouth open wide, first instruct him to inhale and then to let his jaw relax as he exhales so that his mouth closes naturally. Have your child breathe naturally for a few seconds before repeating the yawn. This exercise will relax the muscles in the jaw and around the eyes. Try it yourself to see the effect.

Clown Smile Now, have your child clench his teeth slightly, press his lips together, and smile "from ear to ear." Instruct your child to slowly breathe in through his nose, then exhale, drop his mouth open and repeat the word relax, then take several belly breaths. Have your child repeat the clown smile and the relaxed belly breathing.

Fantasy Trip Once your child has relaxed all the parts of his body, have him continue to lie quietly doing belly breathing. Begin to describe a fantasy scene that incorporates one of your child's favorite places. For example, if your child enjoys the beach, take a fantasy trip there. In a soothing voice, describe the warm feel of the sun on his body as he lies on the shore and the sound of the waves as they ebb and flow. Continue the fantasy until your child's mind as well as his body are relaxed.

Mini-Relaxer Over the next days and weeks, your child should practice the relaxation exercises so that he knows how it feels to be relaxed. After pairing the word "relax" so often with this relaxed state your child should be able to calm himself by taking a belly breath and thinking the word "relax." To enhance this effect, teach your child a mini–relaxation exercise:

Instruct your child to smile to himself, clench his teeth a little, and smile. The smile doesn't have to be as pronounced as it is for the clown smile, nor should it be obvious to an onlooker. Suggest your child practice this in front of a mirror so he will be comfortable using the technique in public. Once your child has mastered the smile, have him inhale through his nose, hold it, think the word "relax," and then exhale, letting his mouth drop open a little and the tension escape all the way from the top of his head to his toes. Have your child repeat this exercise with you until he gets the knack and reports feeling his whole body relax.

The mini-relaxer is a very good technique that your child can use whenever he feels tense or anxious. Praise and reward him for using this new skill. Model it by doing the mini-relaxation yourself whenever you feel stressed.

Teaching Your
Child Positive Self-Talk

Behind every fear there is a series of scary thoughts and images. Children say things to themselves that either create a fear or make an existing one worse. Add a runaway imagination, and panic is a heartbeat away. There are three methods, which we will reiterate throughout this book, to counteract your child's negative thoughts about the feared situation.

1. Correct misconceptions. Some of the things that children say to themselves are derived from misconceptions. One preschooler who came to the clinic had been kidded by her grandmother that she was so thin that a strong wind could blow her away. After hearing this comment, the child would not go outside whenever it was the least bit cloudy or windy. Her fear could not be overcome until the underlying misconception was discovered and corrected.

Arm your child with facts that enlarge her information base and correct misconceptions. Each fear section makes numerous suggestions about types of information that could be helpful and how to find it. Keep your explanations simple and appropriate for your child's age and interest. Of course, avoid presenting any facts that might increase her concerns.

2. Create positive statements. Information is also valuable for creating positive statements your child can use to reassure herself when she begins to feel anxious. In each fear section, several positive statements are suggested to start your child's list. To make the new thoughts automatic, your child must practice them often. Write the countering statements on a series of three-by-five cards so your child can take them wherever she goes. If she can't read, draw pictures to prompt her positive memory. For example, you might draw a waving hand on a dog's tail to remind your child to repeat to himself, "Dogs wag their tails to say hello." As an alternative, tape-record the positive thoughts, first in your voice and then in your child's, so she can listen to them at various times of the day.

3. Create positive images to counteract scary ones. Imagination can work for or against your child. Help her to imagine herself successfully coping with her fear. After practicing the relaxation techniques, lead your child through an imaginary scene in which she successfully contends with the fear. For example, if your child is afraid of small, hyper dogs, you would describe a scene with a small friendly dog, wagging its tail and playing in the yard. You would include images of your child petting the dog, throwing a stick to the dog, and playing happily with the animal. Tailor the fantasy to your child's particular fears, describing in detail your child successfully coping with various aspects of the situations. Any description you use should always end on a positive note with your child imagining herself coping well with the situation.

Teaching Your Child How to Measure Fear

Thus far, we have presented techniques to counteract physical sensations and fear-producing thoughts and images. To overcome a fear, though, its behavioral aspect must also be met and conquered. To do so all at once is too frightening. Instead, the fear must be broken down into manageable pieces, and your child must be able to give you feedback so that she doesn't become so scared that she balks. Chapter 3, "Overcoming Fear," presents a hierarchy of experiences that your child will work through until she confronts her fear directly. However, to design a hierarchy that specifically addresses your child's fear, you must know exactly what frightens her. In order to rank your child's fears, there must be a way to measure the child's level of fear.

Most children think a person is either afraid of something or not. All-or-none thinking is not helpful, since it tends to make fears seem bigger than life. In reality, there are degrees of fear. Your child might be a little bit afraid of standing on a stepladder, more scared of jumping off the low diving board, and terrified of climbing up the ladder to the high dive. Practicing a speech for your family might be nerve-racking and a bit scary, but it's much less frightening than standing in front of the class or an auditorium filled with your peers.

Learning to distinguish between different levels of fear is a very important coping tool. By being able to measure her fear, your child can communicate how frightened she is. Sharing this information makes your child feel less alone and it alerts you to when your child is too frightened to continue or comfortable enough to contend with the next level of fear. With an added sense of control, your child is likely to be able to stay longer in a feared situation so that her fear actually has time to drop. Realizing that fear decreases if you stay with it is one of the most important lessons your child will learn.

There are a number of ways for your child to measure fear. Select the one that will be the easiest for your child to use.

1. Use words. Certainly, words provide one method. Words like frightened, scared, terrified, petrified, paralyzed, and panicked are enlightening and descriptive. If you choose this approach find as many fear words as possible and use many examples to define them so that you both agree on the meaning of the descriptors.

2. Rank the fear. For older children and some younger ones who think mathematically, a ranking system based on a scale of zero to ten with ten being the worst imaginable panic can be very effective. This scale was originally developed by Dr. Joseph Wolpe and is called the Subject Units of Discomfort Scale (SUDS). Emphasize that the D in SUDS stands for discomfort and not disaster by always asking your child how *uncomfortable* a certain situation makes him feel. This is a significant distinction. From this point of view, all your child has to do to overcome his fear is to get a little more "comfortable" in each situation. For example, if your child is afraid of the dark, he has only to get more comfortable in a slightly dimmer room to succeed. The goal of getting comfortable is less intimidating to a child than a goal of getting over the fear.

The SUDS scale is subjective. Your child cannot be right or wrong, but it will be more useful if you anchor the numbers to some actual experiences. When Craig's parents taught him to rate his fear, they first discussed the different kinds of experiences that frightened him and how he felt in each. Craig got butterflies in his stomach when his teacher called on him to answer a question. Craig and his parents decided that rated a three. When he had to read aloud, he noticed his hands felt sweaty and his heart beat faster; that got a five. When Craig had to stand up and read an oral book report, his hands and knees started to shake; that was labeled an eight. Since making a speech sent him into a panic, it unquestionably rated a ten.To help your child rate his fears, draw a scale like Craig's. Use your child's

CRAIG'S 0–10 SCALE

comments to give meaning to the numbers and practice using the scale.

3. Use a visual cue. The SUDS scale is not appropriate for very young children for obvious reasons, and many older children also prefer other measurement tools. A nonnumerical visual display provides an alternative. In the same way that someone who went fishing might show you the size of the fish he caught, your child can also show the size of his fear. Hands held close together mean a small amount of fear or discomfort; hands spread as far apart as your child can reach indicate a huge amount of discomfort and fear. After you describe this method to your child, have him demonstrate how fearful he thinks he might be in a variety of situations.

A second approach also works well. Your child might indicate with a gesture how "filled up" he is with fear. Up to his knees means a little frightened or uncomfortable, up to the stomach could indicate halfway, up to the neck very scared, and up to the top of his head would mean petrified. This approach provides an easy verbal or visual shorthand for your child that he can indicate with motions and words: "Mom! It's at my ankles and rising fast."

Once your child is able to measure her fear, use the technique to help her show you what frightens her. Over time your child will

recognize that she experiences different levels of fear and anxiety. When it is no longer an all-or-nothing feeling, your child has taken a big step toward overcoming her fear.

Pinpointing What Frightens Your Child

Maybe you think you know what frightens your child. How specifically can you pinpoint your child's fear? Is she afraid of all dogs or only big ones? Do large fluffy dogs scare her as much as shorthaired types? What about old dogs or very frisky ones? Ted's parents were surprised to discover he wasn't afraid of being bitten by a dog. He was, however, horrified by the thought of being licked by one. Reassuring Ted that a small, gentle dog would not hurt him would not have helped him overcome his fear. Janice was afraid of storms—but not all storms, only the ones she heard about through weather alerts. Wayne was afraid of doctors who wore white coats because he associated them with hospitals.

Fears are very specific. Your child's fear is likely to be as individual and unique as he is. Before you can help your child overcome his fear, you must know exactly what frightens him. The following suggestions will aid your detective work:

- Observe your child. You don't have to be Sherlock Holmes to use your powers of observation. For a week or two, use a Fear Diary similar to the one shown below to take notes about your child's fear. Observe what your child avoids and what he reacts to. Look for patterns in what you see. This approach led Ted's mom to discover that her son was frightened of being licked by dogs. First she noticed that he was afraid of all dogs—size didn't matter. Her clue to his particular fear came, though, when she noted that her son reacted with disgust when a kitten tried to lick him.

  The father of a little girl who was afraid of thunderstorms noted that his daughter was also hesitant to go outside on a beautiful, clear, but very windy day. This insight led to the discovery that this very young child was afraid that she could be blown away from her family. After seeing *The Wizard of Oz* she became afraid that she could be blown away whenever the wind started to speed up. She was confused about the difference between a strong wind and a tornado.

• Discuss the fear with your child. Once you have observed your child and have some guesses about what is bothering her, check out your hypotheses. Pick a time when your child is not frightened. Being as specific as you can, review your observations with your child: "Remember when we were at Joey's house and you pulled away from his puppy when it tried to lick you? You acted the same way when Mrs. Tolliver's cat tried to lick you. Why do you think those things bothered you?"

At first your child might not know what to say, or she might resist sharing her thoughts. This is normal. Reassure your child that you want to help her overcome her fear, however long it takes. Suggest that your child help you add to the observations in the diary and talk about them periodically.

If your child is very young or reluctant to share his thoughts, use books to encourage the interactions. One child who couldn't verbalize what kinds of dogs frightened him was able to point out the types in a book that showed various breeds.

• Take a survey. A fear survey is another tool that can help you isolate your child's fear. Simply ask your child what things in a

FEAR DIARY

Date	Child's Reactions to Feared Situation or Object	Things Child Avoided Because of Fear

list of items frighten him. Select those items that are relevant and suitable for your child's age. Have older youngsters and adolescents rate all the fears, then discuss the ones that are judged to cause a fair amount of fear. You may also find it interesting to readminister the survey after your child has been working on his fears for a while.

• Put your theory to the test. By observing, discussing, and surveying your child's fears you have collected a lot of information. It's time to test your theories so you can pinpoint exactly what frightens your child, but you will need your child's help. Before beginning, explain to your child that you need his help to determine exactly what frightens him, but you promise not to force him to do anything that scares him too much. For example, if your child is afraid of the dark, ask him to show you how much darkness he can tolerate by having him close the door or use a dimmer switch to control the level of light in his room. A child who is afraid of heights might show you how high he can climb on a ladder before becoming scared. If your child is afraid of an animal, he might show you how close he can walk toward a feared animal. As your child demonstrates what frightens him, have him also report his fear level so you can identify just how afraid he actually is.

In addition to pinpointing your child's fear, you might gather some interesting facts during the process. One child who was afraid of the dark pointed out in a behavioral test that the light from the bathroom cast shadows that scared her but a light in the hall didn't.

• Specify the fear. Finally define exactly what frightens your child. Ted's mom collected this information.

General Fear: Ted is afraid of dogs.

Observations: Ted avoided all dogs and a friendly cat.

Discussion: At first, Ted couldn't say why he was afraid of dogs. It didn't seem to matter what size or type they were. When he looked at pictures of various breeds, he said that they all looked "yucky" to him. He did comment on a couple of dogs that had their tongues hanging out.

THE FEAR SURVEY

Rate your child's fear from 0 to 10 using the following.

Little to none 0,1,2,3   Moderate Fear 4,5,6   Strong Fear 7,8,9,10

	LITTLE				MODERATE			STRONG			
	0	1	2	3	4	5	6	7	8	9	10
Strangers											
Men	0	1	2	3	4	5	6	7	8	9	10
Women	0	1	2	3	4	5	6	7	8	9	10
Other children	0	1	2	3	4	5	6	7	8	9	10
Noises											
Sudden only	0	1	2	3	4	5	6	7	8	9	10
Sirens	0	1	2	3	4	5	6	7	8	9	10
Balloons popping	0	1	2	3	4	5	6	7	8	9	10
Cap guns	0	1	2	3	4	5	6	7	8	9	10
Airplanes overhead	0	1	2	3	4	5	6	7	8	9	10
Cars or trucks	0	1	2	3	4	5	6	7	8	9	10
The Dark											
Ghosts and monsters	0	1	2	3	4	5	6	7	8	9	10
Burglars and kidnappers	0	1	2	3	4	5	6	7	8	9	10
Nightmares	0	1	2	3	4	5	6	7	8	9	10
Fantasy characters											
Clowns	0	1	2	3	4	5	6	7	8	9	10
Halloween masks	0	1	2	3	4	5	6	7	8	9	10
Amusement park characters	0	1	2	3	4	5	6	7	8	9	10
Characters from scary movies	0	1	2	3	4	5	6	7	8	9	10
Separating											
Going to sleep	0	1	2	3	4	5	6	7	8	9	10
Staying with a baby-sitter	0	1	2	3	4	5	6	7	8	9	10
Going to day care/preschool	0	1	2	3	4	5	6	7	8	9	10
Spending the night out	0	1	2	3	4	5	6	7	8	9	10

	LITTLE				MODERATE			STRONG			
Going to overnight camp	0	1	2	3	4	5	6	7	8	9	10
Fear something happening to parent	0	1	2	3	4	5	6	7	8	9	10
Fear something happening to self	0	1	2	3	4	5	6	7	8	9	10
Getting lost	0	1	2	3	4	5	6	7	8	9	10
Being alone at home	0	1	2	3	4	5	6	7	8	9	10

Animals
Dogs

Big dogs	0	1	2	3	4	5	6	7	8	9	10
Little dogs	0	1	2	3	4	5	6	7	8	9	10
Specific breeds	0	1	2	3	4	5	6	7	8	9	10
Being bitten	0	1	2	3	4	5	6	7	8	9	10
Being jumped on	0	1	2	3	4	5	6	7	8	9	10
Being licked	0	1	2	3	4	5	6	7	8	9	10
Being barked at	0	1	2	3	4	5	6	7	8	9	10

Cats

Specific breeds	0	1	2	3	4	5	6	7	8	9	10
Hissing	0	1	2	3	4	5	6	7	8	9	10
Arched back	0	1	2	3	4	5	6	7	8	9	10
Being licked	0	1	2	3	4	5	6	7	8	9	10
Being scratched	0	1	2	3	4	5	6	7	8	9	10

Snakes

Outdoors only	0	1	2	3	4	5	6	7	8	9	10
In cages	0	1	2	3	4	5	6	7	8	9	10
Birds	0	1	2	3	4	5	6	7	8	9	10
Rodents (including squirrels)	0	1	2	3	4	5	6	7	8	9	10
Horses and cows	0	1	2	3	4	5	6	7	8	9	10
Other _____	0	1	2	3	4	5	6	7	8	9	10

Insects

Spiders	0	1	2	3	4	5	6	7	8	9	10
Daddy longlegs	0	1	2	3	4	5	6	7	8	9	10
Roaches	0	1	2	3	4	5	6	7	8	9	10
Ants	0	1	2	3	4	5	6	7	8	9	10
Bees	0	1	2	3	4	5	6	7	8	9	10
Wasps	0	1	2	3	4	5	6	7	8	9	10
Flies	0	1	2	3	4	5	6	7	8	9	10
Other _____	0	1	2	3	4	5	6	7	8	9	10

	LITTLE				MODERATE			STRONG			

Nature

Thunder	0	1	2	3	4	5	6	7	8	9	10
Lightning	0	1	2	3	4	5	6	7	8	9	10
Wind	0	1	2	3	4	5	6	7	8	9	10
Tornadoes	0	1	2	3	4	5	6	7	8	9	10
Hurricanes	0	1	2	3	4	5	6	7	8	9	10
Earthquakes	0	1	2	3	4	5	6	7	8	9	10

Water

Ocean	0	1	2	3	4	5	6	7	8	9	10
Lakes	0	1	2	3	4	5	6	7	8	9	10
Pools	0	1	2	3	4	5	6	7	8	9	10
Water on face	0	1	2	3	4	5	6	7	8	9	10

Transportation
Cars

Front seat	0	1	2	3	4	5	6	7	8	9	10
Back seat	0	1	2	3	4	5	6	7	8	9	10
High speeds	0	1	2	3	4	5	6	7	8	9	10
Being caught in traffic	0	1	2	3	4	5	6	7	8	9	10
Driving on expressway	0	1	2	3	4	5	6	7	8	9	10
Trains	0	1	2	3	4	5	6	7	8	9	10

Subways

All	0	1	2	3	4	5	6	7	8	9	10
Crowded only	0	1	2	3	4	5	6	7	8	9	10
Airplanes	0	1	2	3	4	5	6	7	8	9	10
All	0	1	2	3	4	5	6	7	8	9	10
Crowded only	0	1	2	3	4	5	6	7	8	9	10

Boats

Small boats	0	1	2	3	4	5	6	7	8	9	10
Large boats	0	1	2	3	4	5	6	7	8	9	10
High speeds	0	1	2	3	4	5	6	7	8	9	10
Crowded	0	1	2	3	4	5	6	7	8	9	10

Bridges

Driving on bridge	0	1	2	3	4	5	6	7	8	9	10
Walking across bridge	0	1	2	3	4	5	6	7	8	9	10
All	0	1	2	3	4	5	6	7	8	9	10
Height	0	1	2	3	4	5	6	7	8	9	10
Bridges only	0	1	2	3	4	5	6	7	8	9	10

	LITTLE				MODERATE			STRONG		

Medical

Shots	0	1	2	3	4	5	6	7	8	9	10
Finger pricked	0	1	2	3	4	5	6	7	8	9	10
Blood drawn	0	1	2	3	4	5	6	7	8	9	10
Seeing blood	0	1	2	3	4	5	6	7	8	9	10
Doctor doing exam	0	1	2	3	4	5	6	7	8	9	10
Other medical procedures	0	1	2	3	4	5	6	7	8	9	10
Throwing up	0	1	2	3	4	5	6	7	8	9	10
Passing out	0	1	2	3	4	5	6	7	8	9	10
Heart beating fast	0	1	2	3	4	5	6	7	8	9	10
Lump in throat	0	1	2	3	4	5	6	7	8	9	10
Not being able to breathe	0	1	2	3	4	5	6	7	8	9	10

Dental

Getting teeth cleaned	0	1	2	3	4	5	6	7	8	9	10
Novocaine needle	0	1	2	3	4	5	6	7	8	9	10
Cavity drilled	0	1	2	3	4	5	6	7	8	9	10
Tooth extracted	0	1	2	3	4	5	6	7	8	9	10
Other _____	0	1	2	3	4	5	6	7	8	9	10

Germs

Diseases	0	1	2	3	4	5	6	7	8	9	10
Dirt	0	1	2	3	4	5	6	7	8	9	10
Cleaners	0	1	2	3	4	5	6	7	8	9	10
Other chemicals	0	1	2	3	4	5	6	7	8	9	10

Social

Meeting adults	0	1	2	3	4	5	6	7	8	9	10
Meeting peers	0	1	2	3	4	5	6	7	8	9	10
Small groups	0	1	2	3	4	5	6	7	8	9	10
Parties	0	1	2	3	4	5	6	7	8	9	10
Blushing	0	1	2	3	4	5	6	7	8	9	10
Having sweaty hands	0	1	2	3	4	5	6	7	8	9	10
Trembling	0	1	2	3	4	5	6	7	8	9	10

School

Taking tests	0	1	2	3	4	5	6	7	8	9	10
Answering questions	0	1	2	3	4	5	6	7	8	9	10
Writing on the board	0	1	2	3	4	5	6	7	8	9	10
Giving a report or speech	0	1	2	3	4	5	6	7	8	9	10

	LITTLE				MODERATE			STRONG			
Making a mistake	0	1	2	3	4	5	6	7	8	9	10
Making a bad grade	0	1	2	3	4	5	6	7	8	9	10
Being teased	0	1	2	3	4	5	6	7	8	9	10
Bullies	0	1	2	3	4	5	6	7	8	9	10
Getting sick at school	0	1	2	3	4	5	6	7	8	9	10
Going to school	0	1	2	3	4	5	6	7	8	9	10

Claustrophobia

Crowded elevators	0	1	2	3	4	5	6	7	8	9	10
Stuck in empty elevators	0	1	2	3	4	5	6	7	8	9	10
Bathrooms, closets, other small rooms											
With the door closed	0	1	2	3	4	5	6	7	8	9	10
With door open	0	1	2	3	4	5	6	7	8	9	10
Back seats of cars	0	1	2	3	4	5	6	7	8	9	10
Crowded buses, trains, planes	0	1	2	3	4	5	6	7	8	9	10
Sitting in middle of row or in front											
Church	0	1	2	3	4	5	6	7	8	9	10
Theaters	0	1	2	3	4	5	6	7	8	9	10
Walking in crowds	0	1	2	3	4	5	6	7	8	9	10
Busy malls	0	1	2	3	4	5	6	7	8	9	10
Upper floors of buildings	0	1	2	3	4	5	6	7	8	9	10

Heights

Swings	0	1	2	3	4	5	6	7	8	9	10
Slides	0	1	2	3	4	5	6	7	8	9	10
Jungle gyms	0	1	2	3	4	5	6	7	8	9	10
Balance beams	0	1	2	3	4	5	6	7	8	9	10
Ladders	0	1	2	3	4	5	6	7	8	9	10
Diving boards	0	1	2	3	4	5	6	7	8	9	10
Balconies	0	1	2	3	4	5	6	7	8	9	10
Glass elevators	0	1	2	3	4	5	6	7	8	9	10
Ferris wheels	0	1	2	3	4	5	6	7	8	9	10
Roller coasters	0	1	2	3	4	5	6	7	8	9	10
Other amusement rides	0	1	2	3	4	5	6	7	8	9	10

	LITTLE			MODERATE			STRONG			
Death or serious injury										
Death of parent or other loved one	0	1	2	3	4	5	6	7	8	9	10
Own death	0	1	2	3	4	5	6	7	8	9	10
Seeing a dead person in coffin	0	1	2	3	4	5	6	7	8	9	10
Graveyards	0	1	2	3	4	5	6	7	8	9	10
Fire—getting burned	0	1	2	3	4	5	6	7	8	9	10
Guns and knives	0	1	2	3	4	5	6	7	8	9	10
War—being bombed	0	1	2	3	4	5	6	7	8	9	10

Questionnaire: On the fear questionnaire, Ted checked dogs and a number of other animals. He also indicated that he was afraid of germs. This led to a discussion of how he hates it when dogs lick him, especially if they try to lick his face. He said he liked most cats because they just rub against him, but he does not like cats that try to lick him.

Behavioral Test: Ted could approach a number of dogs, even those that were barking. He could not get within twenty feet of a dog that was drooling or one that was licking his little brother's hand. Ted also did not like touching trash cans or using the bathroom at the baseball stadium.

Specific Fear: Ted is afraid of being licked by dogs or other animals because they might give him germs. Ted also has a fear of germs that leads him to fear using public bathrooms.

3

OVERCOMING
FEAR

No one wants to confront a fear. It's not fun; it's scary. Your role is to help your child stay in the feared situation long enough that his fear actually decreases. Initially, your child is unlikely to believe that his fear will lessen by confronting it. As he becomes increasingly comfortable with each experience, your child will sense his success and begin to believe you.

Few things are learned in one shot. Lots of things take practice—tennis, ballet, gymnastics, handwriting, and singing, to name a few. First you must learn the necessary skills; next, you practice. Practice rarely makes perfect, but at each session you gain more control over the skills. Psychologists call the process of gradually moving toward a behavioral goal *shaping*. By slowly working through a sequence of experiences your child will be able to confront a situation she never thought possible; she will have control over her fear.

As you already know, overcoming a fear is not easy. Certainly, you already have tried to help your child. The more frightened your child is of something, the more experiences he'll need to ease himself out of the fear. Since conquering fear is hard, time-consuming work, a little motivation is in order. Keep these points in mind as you work with your child.

- Make it easier. Whatever fear you are tackling, make the process more doable by breaking the experience into small steps. You can't expect a child who is afraid of dogs to hold one—even a small puppy—first time out. She probably will look at pictures of dogs or watch a movie that stars a canine without too much trouble. After that, she'll find it easier to look through a window at a dog or stand at a comfortable distance as you pet a small, friendly dog. With each experience, your child moves one step closer to the ultimate goal. The success she gains along the way will motivate both of you to continue.

  In the remaining chapters of this book, we present the four types of experiences that will help your child overcome his fear: **Overcoming Fear Through Imagination, Overcoming Fear Through Information, Overcoming Fear Through Observation,** and **Overcoming Fear Through Exposure.** The activities for each category are presented step by step. Begin with experiences that deal with the imagination. Then proceed through those involving the acquisition of information and observations of others. In the final step, your child will confront a series of feared situations. However, we don't know your child. Your child might need every step that is outlined plus a few more you create; your child might need slightly different experiences; or your child might need fewer experiences to overcome the fear. Tailor the sessions to your child's personality and his personal fear. In addition, if you don't find your child's exact fear among those presented, select a fear in the same category as a guide and use the desensitization program described in the rest of this chapter to create a series of experiences appropriate to your child's fear.

- Measure the fear. Your child's fear measurements are important, since they will guide the pace of the experiences you present to her. When her anxiety level becomes too high, stop, help your child relax, then repeat the experience until she is comfortable in the situation. Over time, your child will report decreasing fear ratings for each experience so that she senses her progress and is ready for the next level of interaction. Progress is always motivating, so remind your child how well she is doing: "Wow, you could climb three rungs on the ladder today and your fear rating dropped to three! Do you realize a few days ago your fear rating was nine when you tried to climb one rung? That's real progress."

• Use specific positive feedback. Praise is an important motivational tool, especially when used correctly. Telling your child, "You're nice" or "That's good" is positive, but not particularly helpful. Rather than saying, "You're brave," use specific positive feedback that describes the progress he has made to motivate your child: "You should feel so good, you are patting that puppy like a pro. A few days ago you couldn't get near a dog."

Your positive feedback to your child through words and touch is crucial, so don't be afraid that you will give too much. Simply standing near your child when he approaches a fear situation provides a mountain of support. A hug, a wink, and a positive word tell him you notice his effort and the progress he is making.

• A word about rewards. We like to use rewards in a very special way to get a new behavior going. Confronting his fear is certainly a new behavior for your child, so using rewards is appropriate. Many times when parents use rewards it takes too long for a child to earn a reward, so he gives up. For rewards to be effective, keep several principles in mind:

1. **Reward initial progress every time.** With young children you can use a grab bag to reward cooperation. After your child completes an exercise, practices his relaxation skills, or takes a step toward overcoming his fear, let him reach into a grab bag filled with trinkets such as stickers, small bouncing balls, new pencils, tricks, sugarless gum and other small age-appropriate items your child would like.

2. **Use long-term rewards.** Each time your child takes a step or cooperates, award a point that accumulates for a long-term reward. If you use a grab bag, allow your child a pull from the bag and also award a point. Construct a menu of items including privileges, activities, and objects that your child would like to earn. You can also ask your child what he'd like to work for. Bailey knew exactly what he wanted to earn and his parents incorporated his wishes into the menu they created:

MENU OF REWARDS

Watch an extra television show	3 points
Time with Mom to play a game	3 points
Time with Dad in the workshop	5 points
A trip to the amusement park	25 points
A trip to a restaurant	10 points
Time to play a video game	5 points
A new baseball glove	20 points
Rent a video	8 points
Stay up one hour later on weekend	5 points

3. Use a variety of rewards. As you can see from Bailey's menu, the rewards vary in cost and type so that there are less expensive items and more expensive selections. In addition, extra time with you is a big seller, so don't underestimate the power of your attention.

• Prompt your child to use positive coping techniques. Remind your child to use the relaxation techniques and other coping skills presented in the previous chapter. Fear is an emotion that makes you feel out of control. Using the tools you have taught him—fear ratings, relaxation skills, positive self-talk, and positive imagery—returns the control to your child. He knows how to identify what he is feeling and has specific skills to calm himself. Frequently prompt your child to use these skills until he remembers to use them himself. Whenever you see your child utilizing one of these coping skills, praise his efforts.

Each of the fear sections in *Monsters Under the Bed* will help your child work through four sets of experiences to overcome his fear. By using your child's imagination, providing information, having him observe others in the feared situation, and confronting it himself, your child can overcome his fear.

Overcoming Fear Through Imagination

To a young child, the difference between fantasy and reality is a thin line at best. Big Bird and Kermit are as real as everyone else the child knows. Some children have such vivid imaginations that they actually see imaginary friends. It's not surprising that youngsters turn shadows into creatures and find a monster lurking behind their bedroom closet doors. Each creak a house makes is a burglar or kidnapper climbing the stairs.

As a child learns more about the world, new fears pop up and have to be overcome. Some children seem to be more impressionable and more affected by what they see and hear. Scary movies, rumors, and the nightly news can stimulate a child's imagination and intensify a new fear.

The imagination is a force that can work negatively or positively for your child. It can intensify anxiety, or it may be utilized to overcome fear. Children who have fears visualize themselves having difficulty in the feared situation. A child who is frightened of dogs not only imagines the biggest, meanest, and most vicious dog, but also sees himself as scared of the animal. By introducing friendly dogs who play with children through pictures and films, you begin to change your child's mind's-eye view of the animal. Helping your child first to perceive dogs as friendly animals and next to visualize himself playing with dogs are valuable steps in eliminating fear.

1. Use books to stimulate your child's imagination. It has long been recognized that fairy tales and other stories we read to our children don't just entertain them. The characters and plots have deeper meanings and educational value. They may also introduce children to a scary world. The giant in "Jack and the Beanstalk," the wicked stepmother and the witch in "Hansel and Gretel" and the villains in other tales speak to a child's deepest fears.

From going to bed to going to the dentist, contemporary stories frequently focus on issues and problems children confront daily. From books, children gather information and learn vicariously how to deal with a variety of situations. They identify with their favorite characters, laugh at their antics, and root for their successes.

Illustrations are a significant component of children's literature. In picture books, the illustrations are as important as the words in conveying the story. For our purposes, the drawings in the books you will read to your child provide a reality that is easier for him to handle. Reading about Benji, Clifford, and other friendly dogs and looking at pictures of various breeds provide a nonthreatening reintroduction to a feared animal. Drawings of bear cubs going to the dentist are less frightening than the sight of a real dental chair and instruments.

When you use a book with your child, be sure to read the book first yourself to make sure it will be appropriate for your child and that it will not elicit an intense response. As you read to your child or she reads to herself, many images and thoughts are stimulated. Encourage your child to talk about her thoughts. What would it feel like to be the character in the story? How does the character look? Encourage your child to act out the stories she reads. She will enjoy reading the stories over and over again so that the feared subject naturally becomes more familiar.

Listed at the end of the fear sections are a selection of books, organized in order of readability. Some books are designed to be read to the young child; others were written to be read by the child. However, any of the books may be useful to acquaint a child with the object of her fear. Looking at colorful illustrations of spiders or snakes can be a good starting place for a child who is afraid of these creatures. However, always preview any selection before reading it to your child to make sure the match is appropriate.

Certainly the selection of suggested books is not complete. Children's bibliographies are an excellent source of books on various topics. Two very helpful sources include *The New York Times Parent's Guide to the Best Books for Children* by Eden Ross Lipson (New York: Times Books, rev. ed., 1991) and *Choosing Books for Kids* by Joanne Oppenheim, Barbara Brenner, and Betty Boegehold (New York: Ballantine Books, 1986). In addition, ask your local librarian or bookseller for suggestions.

2. View television programs and films to increase positive images. Most children in our society spend many hours watching television and movies. The tube is like a window to the world through which children see many things, both good and bad. While children can learn a great deal by watching educational programs such as *Sesame Street*, at other times they see things that disturb them. For our purposes, the visual medium provides access to more realistic images of the things he fears than books offer. At the same time, a child knows the images cannot harm him, so that films provide an excellent means for a child to learn about the feared situation.

In each section, numerous suggestions are made about how to use films and television shows to overcome your child's fear. Seeing other people—both adults and children—play with animals, drive in cars, and watch clowns provides a new vision for a scared child. If you choose wisely and view with your child, films provide safe exposure to your child's fear.

3. Pretend with your child. Young children love to pretend. In later chapters, you will be instructed about ways to use your child's dramatic abilities to alleviate specific fears. Keep in mind that the plays you present should always end with your child successfully coping with his fear. With the youngest child, pretend exercises appear to be fanciful, nonthreatening interactions with the feared object. For example, you might pretend to be an animal that frightens your child and he becomes your trainer. Next, reverse roles so that your child takes the part of what he fears. To enhance the effect you might wear costumes or use props. Toy doctor kits make playing hospital and doctor's office more real and fun. For children who are entering preschool, playing school is the first introduction to teachers and school experiences.

Although your child might enjoy playing with you much of the time, he may resist the whole idea if you are too directive. Never force your child. Even if you only make believe for short periods of time every once in a while, it will enhance the process.

4. Use your child's imagination as a tool to overcome fear. Your child probably has a very active imagination and may even visualize in "living color" the things he fears. Sometimes a child can create a sequence of scary images that are so real that the images run in his mind, influencing his waking experiences and becoming the source of his nightmares at night.

You can utilize your child's imagination to create positive images that block frightening ones. Each fear section includes suggestions about how to use visualization to counter fear. As his positive images grow, your child will have a whole library of them that he can use to counter his fearful thoughts.

Before beginning a fantasy trip help your child get into a relaxed state, using the steps in Chapter 2. Being relaxed makes your child receptive to imagining himself in a situation that frightens him. Have your child lie down and get comfortable. With her eyes closed, have her belly breathe and repeat the word "relax," then relax each of the muscle groups in her body. For young children and those that have trouble learning this skill, substitute a back rub and play quiet music.

Once your child is relaxed, guide him through a fantasy trip that includes some of the things he fears. Make your first stories short and as nonthreatening as possible. Have your child picture himself coping positively with his fear and throw in some humor. For example, if your child is afraid of the water, describe pictures of him pouring water on your head or splashing you in the shallow end of a pool. Take fear readings as described in Chapter 2. If at any time your child's ratings go too high or you observe obvious signs of anxiety, stop the scene and help your child relax. Once your child seems comfortable, continue with the story. Always end a story on a happy note. As your child progresses make the story longer and include more fearful elements.

When appropriate, each fear section in this book includes a list of experiences that start with least fearful scenes and work up to more anxiety-producing ones. Use these as you prepare your fantasy trip or create your own.

Overcoming
Fear Through Information

What we don't know might hurt us or at least it sometimes seems that way. All of us are both curious about and afraid of the unknown. The world is full of unknowns for a child. That's fine for an infant; curiosity soon takes over. As a child develops, a little knowledge leads him to more unanswered questions: How do you know which dogs are safe to pet and which ones to stay away from? What keeps an airplane from falling? What causes lightning and how do I know it won't strike me?

Unfortunately, in their quest for information, many children gather partial answers that are likely to lead to wrong conclusions. Sometimes other children and adults foster these misconceptions in jest. Many a child has been scared by an older sibling's rendition of a ghost tale.

You will help your child overcome her fear by correcting misconceptions, filling in the gaps in her knowledge, and providing additional facts about what is feared. Each fear section outlines a sequence of activities that will provide the kinds of information that will help your child overcome her fear. Use these suggestions to provide missing information or correct the misconceptions your child has.

1. Read about it. Rather than presenting the information to your child, look for the facts together. You will be amazed by the amount of material at your fingertips. Children's magazines and weekly newspapers are excellent sources of pictures. Encyclopedias provide comprehensive material on every fear included in this book. For younger children, juvenile encyclopedias provide colorful pictures and diagrams that simplify complicated concepts. Your local librarian and bookseller can suggest reference books for almost any topic you need. Several sources we have found valuable include the following:

The World Book Encyclopedia. Chicago: World Book–Childcraft International, Inc., 1992

Childcraft: The How and Why Library. Chicago: World Book–Childcraft International, Inc., 1992

The Big Book Series: *The Big Book of Science and Technology; The Big Book of the Earth; The Big Book of Animal Life.* New York: Smithmark Publishers, Inc., 1991

The Way Things Work. David Macaulay. Boston: Houghton Mifflin, 1988.

2. Watch educational films and programs. There are many educational television programs for children. Your local library and video store are also likely to have a selection of informative documentaries.

Videotapes have the added advantage of control. You may easily stop a videotape whenever viewing it creates too much anxiety for your child. Simply rewind the tape and view the scene again. In this way, a child who is afraid of spiders, for example, can see all kinds of spiders in their natural habitats and learn about the lives of these creatures—an experience he is unlikely to have in real life. Understanding brings appreciation for these insects and a realization that spiders do not intend to harm people. Most important, with you beside her, your child can watch the material at her own pace, viewing it repeatedly until familiarity lessens her fear.

3. Help your child learn by doing. You may read about boats and watch programs about boats, but nothing will convince your child about the safety of boats like experimenting with the real thing. Determining which materials float and building model boats to see how they are constructed are valuable experiences. Playing with model boats in the "stormy" bathtub water produced by making waves with your hand shows your child how hard it is for a boat to overturn and proves that capsized vessels still float. Through hands-on learning, your child absorbs facts in an unforgettable way. Throughout the fear sections there are numerous examples of how to use experiential learning to help your child overcome fears.

4. Create a list of positive self-statements based on the facts. When you reach an impasse, what do you say to yourself? Sometimes people say, "I can't do it," then give up. Other times an inner voices says, "Stay with it," so you persevere. When your child enters a situation that frightens him, his inner voice confirms his fear. The statements he hears in his head may be based on incorrect information or misconceptions, but just the same, each thought tells your child it is correct to be afraid.

Changing your child's inner language is an important step to overcoming his fear. Based on the information you and your child collect, assist her in creating a series of positive statements that encourage the child to stay in the feared situation. The child who is afraid of boats is likely to be thinking "This boat will sink and I will drown." She can counter this negative thought and lower her anxiety by repeating to herself "This is a sturdy boat and it will float in all kinds of weather." Other positive statements reinforce this thought: "I have on a life preserver so I am safe." "The sky is clear so the weather looks good." Use the facts to arm your child with positive statements that reinforce her commitment to the situation.

Overcoming
Fear Through Observation

Children learn a great deal through observation. They take in information about the world around them and they learn from the behavior of others. The value of modeling was the subject of a number of research studies by Dr. Albert Bandura. Bandura found that when children watched other children deal confidently with feared situations, they were more confident about approaching the fear themselves. He and others also discovered that the more similar the children were, the stronger the effect. For example, having a nine-year-old boy watch other nine-year-old boys pet a dog is more effective than having a nine-year-old boy watch a nine-year-old girl play with dogs or a fourteen-year-old boy play with his dog.

Providing situations for your child to watch other children coping with the fear is a crucial part of the plan to overcome your child's fear. Several suggestions are made in each fear section about how to use observation to decrease fear. Begin by positioning your child in a safe zone—a spot where she feels safely insulated from the source of her fear. She might watch through a window from inside the house or simply stand at a comfortable distance from the object. A child who is afraid of dogs, for example, might watch from inside the house as a parent or sibling plays with a small, friendly dog on a leash; or your child might stand with another adult across the yard from where you are playing with the dog. In both cases, it is important to be able to control your child's exposure to ensure a positive outcome to the experience. Over a number of sessions, you should maintain the same level of control over the animal, as your child gradually moves closer to the dog. She can hear you interacting with the pet and you are able to give her verbal descriptions about what you see and what you are doing: "See, the doggie is friendly; he is wagging his tail, so I am petting him and scratching behind his ears. He likes that."

Once your child is comfortable watching you, he will be ready to observe siblings and peers interact with the feared object. Supervise the situation to avoid the possibility that playmates will tease your child or force her to move closer to the situation than she would like. As before, begin with observations from a safe distance and have your child move closer as she becomes comfortable.

Finally, provide opportunities for your child to notice other children naturally operating in the situation—playing with pets, riding elevators, swimming, or doing whatever it is that frightens your child. Resist making any comparisons between your child and what others are able to do.

Your child's fear ratings are your guide to how quickly you will pace your child through these experiences. If at any time your child's rating escalates above five or he becomes too uncomfortable, stop, help your child to relax, and then repeat the experience. Prompt your child to use the relaxation skills and other coping techniques discussed in Chapter 2 as he observes. Also, praise and reward your child for being willing to observe and use his skills. Talk about what you observe together and how your child feels as he watches.

Overcoming
Fear Through Exposure

By the time you reach this step your child has been indirectly exposed many times to the feared object or situation through the techniques of imagination and observation. He's learned new information and any misconceptions that added to his anxiety have been corrected. He's armed with coping skills that calm him and knows how to counter negative thoughts with positive self-talk. Each exercise puts your child one step closer to overcoming his fear, but, without direct contact with the feared object or situation, countering techniques alone rarely eliminate any fear.

Direct exposure when properly done is the key to overcoming any fear. Facing a fear, however, is never easy. So how do you get a child to face something he is afraid of? As with many other new behaviors, overcoming a fear is possible when you take it one step at a time.

Consider the way you might get into a pool on a hot summer day. Although some people jump in, get an icy shock, and then get used to the water, most of us ease our way into a pool, taking time to get used to it before plunging in.

Now think about how a child who is afraid of the water might be encouraged to get into a pool. First rule out throwing a child who is afraid of water into a pool. That approach rarely eliminates fear and can backfire; it can reinforce the fear so that it is stronger than ever before. A better approach is to provide a series of experiences that enable the child to gradually become comfortable and confident in the feared situation. A parent might sit next to the child at the edge of the pool as the child dribbles water on her face and legs and dangles her feet in the water. Over a period of sessions, the child would sit on the steps in the pool, play with a toy in the water, stand in the shallow end, and slowly immerse herself inch by inch in the water. By taking such a gradual approach the child could learn to swim without fear.

Psychologists call this process of gradually exposing a child to what he is afraid of in real life "in vivo desensitization." To better understand the process, think about how doctors "desensitize" someone to an allergy. They don't tell a sneezing and sniffling individual to stand in the middle of a field of ragweed. That approach can make the person very ill. Instead, the doctor injects a minute dose of the allergen under the person's skin and observes what happens. If the skin reaction is very strong, the physician repeats the same dosage at the next appointment. If, after a few injections, the reaction lessens, he increases the strength of the allergen in the next shot. Again, the skin's reaction guides the doctor as to how to proceed. In this manner, the body builds an immunity to the allergen.

Using a similar approach, in vivo desensitization helps a child overcome a fear. The child learns to approach the feared situation by participating in a series of experiences designed to gradually reintroduce her to the feared object. Using your child's feedback as a guide, you will work through an exercise that either indirectly or directly familiarizes your child with the feared situation. If she reports too much fear, you repeat the same experience until your child is comfortable with it.

Repetition and reinforcement are crucial elements to your child's progress. Always praise and reward your child for each interaction and remind her to use the calming techniques and other coping skills to counter anxiety.

Keep these points in mind as you work with your child:

• Design a series of experiences appropriate to your child's fear. A detailed hierarchy of the easiest to most difficult experiences is included with most of the fears presented in this book. When the order of the experiences is not relevant, then a selection of activities are presented.

Each child's fear, though, is unique. In a hierarchy of experiences with dogs, the most difficult one for your child might be petting a small, hyper terrier. For another child it might be contending with a Great Dane. You are encouraged to tailor the experiences to your child's particular situation. Some children will need a very different sequence from the one outlined.

Whatever your child's ultimate fear, work up to it by providing enough experiences in an order he can handle so that your child eases his way to the goal. Consider the example of a child who is afraid of dogs. He may start by standing twenty-five feet away from a small, calm dog held by a parent. Depending on the child's reaction, he repeats the situation or progresses to the next experience. As his fear decreases, he moves closer to the animal until he is able to pet a dog held by his parent. Eventually he will be able to hold a small leashed dog, pet larger dogs, and so forth until he no longer feels anxious when a strange dog approaches.

• Reinforce your child's cooperation. As you work through the sequence, praise and reward your child for taking each step toward overcoming her fear. Although each action might seem simple to you, it is a difficult step for your child. Reinforce her cooperation and commitment.

• Desensitization takes time. Never move too quickly or force your child to a level of interaction she's not ready for. There is a happy balance. Encourage your child to take new steps and motivate her to do so. Over time she will reach the goal and feel good about it.

• Arrange for the best possible scenario. To help your child be successful, initially control as many characteristics of each experience as necessary to ensure a happy outcome. If your child has a fear of dogs, select the smallest, friendliest, calmest dog you can find. If she is afraid of elevators, arrange to use an empty elevator that you can control. Control as many variables as you can in the situation so that you can avoid complications, problems, and any actions that might reinforce your child's fear.

4

FIRST FEARS

FEAR OF STRANGERS

Newborn babies know no strangers. Infants are happily passed from one doting relative to another. Admiring strangers who poke their heads into the baby's carriage get no reaction at all. At four to six weeks of age infants are able to focus on faces eight to twelve inches away and things begin to change. The baby begins to recognize its mother and, a little later, other frequently observed faces. Soon the baby distinguishes familiar faces from those of strangers.

By eight months of age, stranger anxiety, as it is typically known, sets in. Youngsters who used to smile at every face that greeted them might now scream at the sight of an unfamiliar face moving toward them. A child who once easily climbed into the arms of a delighted friend or relative might show extreme distress at separating from Mom or Dad for a moment. Whether it is beloved Grandma Sadie from Idaho or a new neighbor doesn't matter in the least. This reaction makes it difficult to leave a baby with a sitter or at a day-care center—even when a child has regularly experienced such separations for most of her life.

Individual differences play a role in how outgoing or shy and inhibited a particular child is. Dr. Jerome Kagan of Harvard University has spent years studying thousands of youngsters from age ten months to age ten years. In tracking these children he and his colleagues have found that the infants and toddlers who cling to their parents when they enter a room filled with other youngsters and parents playing often continue to be inhibited around strangers as they grow older. Other children who show no fear and who immediately run from their parents' side to play with a new friend rarely develop stranger anxiety.

Given the nature of the world today, having a child who "knows no stranger" is not comforting to a parent. Five-year-old Jeremy was never afraid of anyone until he became separated from his mother at the mall. He wandered through the crowd, crying and running in fear as each adult tried to help him. He was terrified when a security guard tried to calm him. Even after he was reunited with his mother, the child was frightened for some time. While he had not been particularly shy around strangers previously, afterwards he panicked when his parents tried to leave him with a baby-sitter. Trips in public were ordeals; Jeremy retreated from any stranger who approached, and clung desperately to his parents.

Occasionally a child will develop a fear of strangers at second hand. An impressionable child can be affected by media reports of crime. Overhearing others discuss a robbery may scare some children. Add some teasing by an older brother or sister, an excessive number of "be careful"'s from Mom and Dad and every stranger walking down the street becomes a potential kidnapper.

Some anxiety about strangers is normal, even helpful, for all children need to be able to distinguish true strangers from acquaintances or friends they may be meeting for the first time. But children must also learn how to interact with countless nameless people who come in and out of our lives daily—the grocery clerk, a waitress, the policeman. Dr. Kagan and other researchers have found that while this aspect of personality may be inborn, children can gradually learn to become more comfortable in a world full of people. Although it is normal for an eight-month-old to scream at the sight of a new face, this is certainly not an appropriate response for a five-year-old. If your child is not getting more at ease with strangers as time goes on, then you should begin to intervene to help him.

IMAGINATION
A healthy imagination is the source of many children's anxiety but it can also help reduce a child's fear.

1. Read books about children meeting new people and having friendly visitors in the home. There are a number of books about visiting relatives, being introduced to new people, and the "nameless" people we frequently see but don't know personally, such as the policeman, mailman, and meter maid. As you read each book, talk about the new person. How did the child in the story know the stranger was a friend? What are the people doing? How do we know they belong in the situation?

2. Pretend you are introducing your child to someone new. Take the part of the characters in the story, acting out the various roles of the people. Have your child invent his own stories for you to act out. One little boy who was afraid of repair people overcame his fear after he was given a tool box and "worker's hat." Repeat these pretend sessions until your child feels more comfortable with the thought of meeting new people and greeting them appropriately.

3. Lead your child through an imaginary scene in which he greets someone new. After practicing the relaxation exercises described in Chapter 2, describe scenes in which your child happily meets various people. Start with stories about people he knows. Picture the people as friendly but not pushy, and your child as greeting them properly and enjoying being with the new friend.

INFORMATION

Misconceptions and a lack of accurate information feeds fear. If your child understands when to be wary of strangers and how to protect himself, she will be more comfortable. Instruction is an important factor in helping your child overcome an unnatural fear of strangers.

1. Correct misconceptions. Children are afraid of people for many reasons. One little boy thought all people in uniform carried guns. Another little girl associated all young female visitors with baby-sitters. If a baby-sitter is arriving, that means Mother is leaving, hence the child's fear. Try to discover what it is about certain individuals or situations that frightens him and correct any misconceptions that cause your child's fear.

Observe any similarities among the people that frighten your child. One mother was surprised to find that her toddler reacted strongly to people who wore glasses. In this case, the fear was quickly overcome, once the child understood what the glasses were for. After they were explained and the child tried on a pair of glasses, he became more understanding.

2. Identify workers your child comes in contact with. There are many people your child sees regularly, yet he may not know them personally. They fill jobs that are important to us. Your child will be more comfortable if he understands why these people come in and out of our lives. *Mister Rogers' Neighborhood* and *Sesame Street* do a great job of explaining the jobs various people in the neighborhood have. For example, your child may hear the dogs barking at the meter man and see him as someone to fear. Explain what this man is doing, how to identify him, and how often he comes. Identifying him as the "gas man" is not very helpful; your child is likely to conjure all kinds of misconceptions about a "man of gas" unless you explain the man's job. Also describe how your child should and should not interact with this person. Waving through the window might be fine with you but you probably prefer that your child not open the door and invite the man to lunch.

As you move through the day, give your child information on people she sees and meets when you go out in public: "The grocery clerk works here every day, just like your daddy goes to his work. He probably is a daddy, too." "The mailman drives a small white truck down the street each day. He always brings the mail in the late afternoon."

3. Introduce people in ways your child can personally relate to. "Daddy's roommate from college" will probably mean nothing to your child. Show him old pictures of the two friends together as you explain that this person went to college with daddy and they shared a room. When you can, explain relationships in ways your child can personally relate to such as, "Tommy is your best friend, and Mr. Smith who is coming to dinner was daddy's friend when he was in school."

4. Teach your child about human behavior. Young children see the world from one perspective—their own. As a result they tend to misconstrue the actions of others. Someone walking quickly through the mall might appear to be chasing the child. Explain that the person is probably in a hurry. After repeated explanations and seeing the person pass, the child will realize that every person who approaches quickly is not a menace. Likewise, your child needs to understand that just because someone is unsmiling (or even frowning) doesn't mean that he's mad; nor is every smiling stranger a friend.

5. Use role-playing to prepare your child when she will meet someone new. When you will be entering situations where your child is likely to meet new people, take a few minutes to talk about who you might meet. You might say, "My Aunt Martha is coming to visit. She was so nice to me when I was a little girl. I love her just like you love your Aunt Beverly. You have met Aunt Martha before, but you were too little to remember her." If you have a picture, show it to your child.

Practice greeting Aunt Martha and other visitors. First help your child recognize cues that tell him someone is a friend. Take the role of the visitor. Be sure to make this fun and don't require too much of a response from your child. A smile or a quick hello without hiding behind you may be enough at first. The section "Meeting New People" has additional suggestions.

6. Create a series of positive statements your child can say to himself when he meets someone new. Write them on small cards so that your child can practice saying them to himself. If your child is too young to read, you can repeat them to him or even record them on a tape recorder.

OBSERVATION

For younger children it is the sudden approach of a new face that causes anxiety. Observing people in a predictable, safe way can lessen fear. In addition, watching others, especially peers, happily meet and deal with newcomers can have a lasting impact. To accomplish this, try the following.

POSITIVE SELF-TALK ABOUT STRANGERS

1. My parents know _____ .

2. This is really not a stranger to the family. I just never met him before.

3. This person has a job to do. I only have to say hello.

4. This person is just in a hurry; I have nothing to fear.

5. _____

1. Find a good place to observe people from a safe distance. It may be from your living room window or from a bench at the local mall. Ask your child to indicate how anxious she feels in the setting using the measuring system you've practiced. With you as security and knowing that it is unlikely someone will approach you, your child's ratings should decrease.

Talk to your child about the people you see. Identify children the same age and groups that look like families. Who belongs in the setting and why? Point out how people smile as they pass others or, at least, tend to their own business. As you watch, note how people greet each other and what happens when someone recognizes a friend. If you observe other interactions, point those out. In the mall you might see someone purchasing an item from a vendor or asking for directions. At home you may see joggers or children riding their bikes and the mailman delivering the mail.

EXPOSURE

There is no way to avoid running into new people or strangers, even if you stay in your house. For your child to become comfortable meeting new people, you must take control of the situation so the experiences occur gradually.

1. Avoid sudden unexpected exposure. This is especially true for very young children. Tell your child when you are going to have a visitor. Also inform your visitor that your child is uncomfortable with new people and you are working on helping him to become more comfortable. Ask the individual to maintain a little distance and not to attempt to hug or kiss your child before he is ready. This can help with the proverbial pinch on the cheek that most children dislike but which inhibited children find downright threatening.

2. Don't label your child as shy. When you feel you must explain, simply say it takes your child longer to warm up. Whenever possible let your child observe the individual's approach. Pause for a moment before opening the door to give your child a chance to adjust. Act as a buffer between your child and the new person by directing the person's entrance, where he will stand or sit, and how close he will be to your child.

3. Orchestrate the introductions. Having role-played this scene numerous times, your child will be more comfortable saying hello. Initially encourage your child to simply say hello. Afterward ask your child to rate her fear level as she met this new person. As time goes on your child is likely to become more comfortable and may naturally offer more responses. Let your child take the lead.

4. Praise and reward your child for staying in the presence of the stranger. Always praise your child for any attempts she makes to interact with new people. Remind your child to use the measuring technique to indicate how fearful she is. Being able to recognize and communicate her anxiety helps diffuse those feelings and lets you know when your child is comfortable.

5. Arrange a series of experiences. List a number of people who your child knows slightly and others who are family friends that your child has never met who are willing to help you. Arrange them in order from least to most anxiety-inspiring. At first stick with people your child knows somewhat and seems to like but still feels anxious around. Cousin Louis may be easier to tolerate than Aunt Martha.

Using your child's fear level as a guide, initiate a series of experiences with these individuals. Invite someone new to have coffee with you. Arrange to meet someone at the mall. If your child is old enough, have him buy something from the cashier as you monitor the situation from a distance.

After your child is comfortable with arranged experiences, expose him to situations in which he is likely to have to interact with a stranger. Always supervise your child, making certain he will be safe and not have a negative experience. A number of experiences are suggested at the end of this section. In addition, the section "Fear of Meeting People" will be very helpful.

SELECTION OF EXPERIENCES WITH STRANGERS

1. Nod hello to an acquaintance.
2. Wave to a policeman.
3. Say hello to someone.
4. Have a short conversation with someone.
5. Ask the librarian for help in selecting a book.
6. Make a purchase from a cashier.
7. Ask a salesperson for help.
8. Inquire about directions.
9. Get the mail from the mailman.

Books

The Berenstain Bears Learn About Strangers. Stan and Jan Berenstain. New York: Random House, 1985. Mama and Papa Bear teach the cubs about strangers.

The Case of the Hungry Stranger. Crosby Bonsall. New York: HarperCollins, 1992. Wizard and his friends solve the mystery of the missing blueberry pie and of the hungry stranger who isn't who he appears to be.

The Cat in the Hat. Dr. Seuss. New York: Random House, 1957. The original, contemporary beginning reader about a fun-loving cat "stranger" who visits the house one rainy afternoon when Mother is out and mayhem begins.

Playing It Smart: What to Do When You're on Your Own. Tova Navarra. New York: Barron's, 1989. A guide for kids. This is a helpful book that talks about many difficult situations, including encountering strangers.

The Shadowmaker. Ron Hansen. New York: Harper & Row, 1987. A stranger arrives in town bringing with him new thoughts about an old friend.

FEAR OF LOUD OR SUDDEN NOISES

A fear of loud or sudden noises is one of the few fears that children are born with. It is not at all unusual for a baby, toddler, or sometimes even a four- or five-year-old to startle and cry in reaction to a sudden loud noise. Occasionally the reaction may occur because a child is especially sensitive to sounds at certain frequency levels. Another child might be generally reactive to any sudden change in the environment. If your child repeatedly covers his ears or indicates that certain sounds hurt his ears, discuss this concern with your child's physician. In very rare cases, a physical cause may contribute to strong reactions to noises.

Most of the time, as children learn about what causes various sounds in the environment, they are less surprised by noises and may even be excited by the sound of a fire engine or ambulance. However, sometimes strong reactions persist so that a child is frightened by a particular sound or loud abrupt noises. Christie became so frightened by the sound of popping balloons that she refused to attend any more of her friend's birthday parties. Just about the time she was getting over this fear, a boy in her neighborhood received a cap pistol for Christmas. Christie was terrified by the bang and refused to play outdoors until she was desensitized to loud noises. Kevin always cowered at the roar of jets passing overhead. His fear became so intense that at five he screamed and cried when his preschool visited the airport. If your child has a similar reaction to noises that persists, use the following process to overcome it.

IMAGINATION

The first step to desensitization is to help your child understand
what causes the sounds and imagine herself not reacting to them.

1. Read picture books that show different noise-making objects. Select stories about fire engines, ambulances, dump trucks, airplanes, and other sources of noises. Animal sounds, thunder, and other naturally occurring noises are also good topics. Some suggestions are cited at the end of this section. As you read, ask your child what sounds the animals and vehicles make. Why do they make these sounds?

2. Pretend you hear sounds. When you are driving together in the car, pretend that a fire engine is coming. Take turns making various sounds. Talk about how a driver should respond and what your child should do when she hears various sounds. Have your child pretend that her play is interrupted by the sound of thunder, a shelf full of books collapsing, a siren. Have her pretend to identify the noise and act appropriately.

3. Lead your child through an imaginary experience. Sometimes older children have become very sensitive to particular sounds because of past experiences. A child who was in a very serious car crash might react strongly to the sound of squealing tires. Consider the noises that frighten your child. Practice the relaxation exercises taught in Chapter 2, and when your child is in a relaxed state begin to describe an imaginary experience like the one that frightens her, but always picture your child as successfully coping with the situation. For example, if your child is afraid of the sound of sirens, describe your child as playing happily in the yard when all of a sudden she hears the sounds of an ambulance. Picture your child as being momentarily frightened as she looks around to see the source of the sound and then, realizing she is safe and there are no signs of danger to her, continuing to play. On various occasions describe similar scenes in which your child is no longer unreasonably frightened by noises until she reports fear ratings that indicate she is no longer anxious.

INFORMATION

Understanding what makes sound and how our ears work provides valuable information your child will use as he identifies various sounds and their sources.

1. Gather information about sound and the human ear. Using various reference sources, collect information about noise. Your doctor might also be a helpful resource.

Discuss how the ear works. Alternate covering your ears and then your child's ears so that your child can learn how the ears act as catcher's mitts for sound waves. Use a model or diagram of the ear to teach your child about how the ear hears sound and the brain interprets what is heard.

Explain to your child that all sound is made of vibrations. The vibrations travel through the air to our ears and then we hear the sound. Pluck the strings of a musical instrument or a rubber band to illustrate a vibration. Have your child stop the string from vibrating. What happens to the sound? Inform your child that all sounds are made the same way. The dog's bark, a human voice, and siren are all caused by vibrations. Make a kazoo from rolled paper or use a whistle to demonstrate this point.

3. Talk about the purposes of various sounds. Why does a fire engine have a siren? Why do dogs bark? Talk to your child about the reasons for many of the loud noises that disturb her so she will understand their purpose.

4. Help your child develop positive statements she can say to herself when she feels anxious. Whenever she hears a loud noise, have her practice using positive self-talk. It may be helpful to have your child write the sentences on an index card so she can practice them when she is in very noisy situations.

POSITIVE SELF-TALK ABOUT NOISES

1. I know what this noise is; it's a _____ .
2. This noise cannot hurt me.
3. The ambulance siren alerts people that the ambulance is coming.
4. The sound will only last for a little while.
5. _____

OBSERVATION

During these experiences your child will observe how you and other children react to the loud sounds they hear.

1. Arrange situations during which your child can observe you or others making sounds. Be creative. You or a friend could beat trash cans or make other loud noises far enough away that the sounds can be identified but are not frightening. Have your child report her anxiety level as she listens to these sounds. Seeing many of the noises produced will lessen your child's fear.

2. Observe other children's reaction to noise. Talk about what other people do when they hear a siren or other loud noises. Ask friends what they do when they hear a fire engine. From a window, have your child watch as siblings or friends play with balloons. Burst the balloons with a pin. How do the children react?

EXPOSURE

To overcome her fear of noises your child must become accustomed to hearing them. Plan a series of experiences that will introduce each noise that frightens your child. The experiences listed at the end of this section will help you provide opportunities that are appropriate for your child.

1. Play recorded sounds. Make or purchase tape recordings of the sounds that frighten your child. Many sound effects records and tapes that include the sounds of thunderstorms, fireworks, sirens, aircraft taking off, and other noises are available for purchase or may be borrowed from your local library.

Explain to your child that you are going to help her get over her reactions to certain sounds. Begin with some music your child likes. Teach her how to raise and lower the volume on the recorder so that she learns how to play the music very softly and how to make it blare.

Select one of the sounds that frightens your child least. Have your child play the sound at a very low volume, listening to the noise until her fear rating indicates her fear has subsided. Next, increase the volume and repeat the process. Using her fear ratings as a guide, repeat the experience, increasing the volume and listening until your child reports a fear rating that indicates she is comfortable hearing the sounds.

Transform the activity into a kind of game by permitting your child to control the volume and timing of each sound. When your child is comfortable hearing a particular noise, proceed to the next one on the list. Continue in this manner until your child is accustomed to the sounds that frighten her.

2. Vary the recordings to surprise your child. Up until now there have been no surprises; your child has been aware of when each sound would occur. Take over the controls. Initially let her watch you so she understands how you will be making the sounds. Ask her to close her eyes and begin to work your way through the sounds as you did previously. Continue to play the noises at each level of volume until she is comfortable. Work your way up from quiet sounds to louder ones.

Now, as in a game of "musical chairs," play the recorded sounds unexpectedly. Explain to your child that you want to see whether she still reacts to the sounds. After playing some moderate tones throw in a loud one suddenly. If your child is able to tolerate this, continue until you can suddenly turn on the recording at its loudest level without it causing a strong reaction from your child.

3. Make real sounds. Make a list of sounds that frighten your child. Of the ones you can make, list them in order from the ones that are least to most frightening. Begin with a sound your child can control, such as a balloon popping or a loud bell ringing. Move about fifteen feet from your child. When she lets you know she's ready, make the sound. What is your child's fear rating when she controls the timing and distance of the noise? Continue the same activity until your child is comfortable. Move closer to your child and repeat the experience. Continue in this manner until your child's fear ratings indicate she is comfortable hearing the noise when you are standing nearby.

When your child is comfortable with one sound, proceed to another. If your child is afraid of a noise like airplanes taking off, move toward the source of the sound. Take a ride to the airport. As you drive toward the airport, put down the windows of the car, so your child can hear the airplane engines. Park in a distant parking lot and remain at that distance until the sound of the engines no longer frightens your child. Advise her that it is okay to put her hands over her ears until she feels more comfortable with the sound of the jet engines. Once your child is comfortable listening to planes taking off without placing her hands over her ears, move closer to the terminal. Eventually your child should be able to stand on an observation deck or as close to the runway as anyone else. Remember this may take some time, however, to accomplish. Be sure to praise and reinforce your child each step of the way.

Other ways of controlling exposure to sound include purchasing noisemakers such as small sirens or cap guns. Again, have your child approach these noise producers from a safe distance, using her hands over her ears to control the intensity of the sound. At each step, have your child measure her anxiety level and use it as a gauge to determine how quickly she moves closer to the source of the sound. Praise and reward your child for approaching the sound and gaining mastery over her fear. By the end of this process your child should be able to turn the siren on and off or safely shoot a cap gun.

4. Expose your child to unexpected sounds. As your child plays in the yard or enjoys activities inside, make a sound without warning. Continue to surprise your child in this manner until her fear ratings indicate she is becoming more comfortable.

5. Continue the exposure. Once your child has mastered dealing with these sounds in controlled practice situations, remind her to use her breathing skills, positive self-talk, and other coping skills to deal with unexpected noises. Praise and reward your child for successfully coping in a noisy world.

SEQUENCE OF EXPERIENCES WITH NOISES

1. Listen to known sounds on recordings.
2. Control volume and distance from sounds on recordings.
3. Listen to randomly selected recorded sounds.
4. Approach frightening sounds gradually.
5. Make sound up close.
6. Listen to unexpected sounds.

Books

I Make Music. Eloise Greenfield. New York: Black Butterfly Children's Books, 1991. A book about musical instruments and how they make their sounds. A good book for exploring how noises can be made.

The Little Engine That Could. Watty Piper. New York: Platt & Munk, 1930. The wonderful story about the little steam engine huffing and puffing and finally succeeding. A good book to noisily pretend along with while reading.

Mr. Little's Noisy Truck. Richard Fowler. New York: Grosset & Dunlap,

1989. A series of books with lift-the-flap format that provides opportunities for your child to make the sounds of various vehicles (Mr. Little's noisy fire engine, plane, boat, and car). Great opportunity to act out all the sounds.

One Fish Two Fish Red Fish Blue Fish. Dr. Seuss. New York: Random House, 1960. Noises that zany animals make.

Richard Scarry's Cars and Trucks That Go. Richard Scarry. New York: Random House, 1979. A picture book full of vehicles that make all kinds of noises.

The Very Quiet Cricket. Eric Carle. New York: Philomel Books, 1990. A wonderful picture book all about the beauty of the animal world. If your child fears strange noises in the night, this book might help point out that some noises are made by things in nature that won't ever harm you. As you turn the last page, you'll hear the cricket really chirping.

FEAR OF THE DARK

"Mommy, I want a drink of water." "Daddy, I can't go to sleep." "Mommy, turn on the hall light." "There's a monster under my bed." These may be just ploys to delay bedtime. On the other hand, these protests could be signs of a real fear of the dark. Fear of the dark is one of the most common, if not the most common, of all childhood fears.

Since man's beginnings, he searched for light, using fires to provide warmth and ward off things that lurk in the night. Today, we can instantly flick on a light; there are no saber-toothed tigers lurking in our caves, but most of us still experience some wariness as we approach a dark space. For a child, the dark seems more sinister. Even with the greatest protectors of all—Mommy and Daddy—nearby, a fear of the dark can still overwhelm a young child.

Even before two years of age some children show a fear of separating from their parents and going to sleep in a dark place. Your child might wake up in a dark room in the middle of the night and become terrified. With a vivid imagination, suddenly monsters and other creatures lurk in every shadow.

A young child knows no distinction between reality and fantasy. If your child believes there's a monster in his closet, telling him differently will not convince him. A monster "seen" at bedtime is just as real to your child as the villain chasing you through your nightmare. In fact, many children have such vivid imaginations that the monsters that disturb their sleep and the ones that camp out under the bed look the same.

Through the preschool years and beyond, a child's understanding of the world around her develops so that a fear of the dark is likely to wax and wane. Children come to realize that goblins and other creatures are fictitious, so some fears decrease, but an awareness of true-life monsters takes their place. The older child imagines that every creak of the house at night is an intruder intent on doing someone harm.

Nighttime fears may be greatly intensified by what a child is exposed to during the day. The world can be a scary place for adults, yet we underestimate how frightening it is for a child who doesn't have as much information or as many defense mechanisms as we do. For the child who is impressionable and easily influenced by what he sees, scary television shows, movies, and even news accounts of real-life horrors can have significant effects.

Never belittle your child's fear of the dark. Forcing a child to stay in a darkened room can lead to real trauma. On the other hand, don't cater to it by suggesting your child sleep in a room with all the lights on. That's not helpful either.

At the age of three, Susan began sleeping with a night-light. When that wasn't enough, her parents left on the bathroom light and later lit the lamp also. By the time we met Susan her room was as light at night as it was in the daytime, the radio played, and her Mom lay down with her. Susan, though, was still afraid.

If you find yourself following in Susan's parents' footsteps, if your child's fear of the dark has persisted over the months or is more severe than that experienced by peers, it is time to intervene. For children who are anxious about the dark, use appropriate solutions to prevent a full-fledged fear from developing.

IMAGINATION

A vivid imagination is one of the main causes of a fear of the dark. You can teach your child to channel his imagination and even use positive imagery to overcome this fear.

1. Read stories that deal with children separating from their parents, having fun at bedtime, and going to sleep. A number of books are suggested at the end of this section. Read them together at bedtime and other times of the day. Point out how content the children look in the pictures. Talk about what the characters do to counteract any fears or make themselves feel comfortable at bedtime.

2. Pretend it's bedtime. During the daylight hours, have your child pretend it is bedtime. To make it fun and more realistic, have your child put on his pajamas and have a "bedtime" snack together. While sitting on your child's bed, talk about what bothers him about bedtime. Carefully explore the room. Close the blinds, turn off the lights, even have him close his eyes. Play a memory game identifying pieces of furniture and various objects that are found in the room. Ask your child to rate his fear as he sits in the darkened room in the daytime. Repeat the daylight pretend sessions until your child is comfortable.

3. Lead your child through an imaginary bedtime experience. After practicing the relaxation exercises so that your child is relaxed, have your child lie in his bed as you tell a different kind of bedtime story. Begin to describe a typical nighttime scene with you reading a favorite bedtime story to your child as he lies peacefully by your side. Describe how you kiss your child good night and he snuggles up to his favorite toy. Continue to picture your child nestling into bed. If he hears a noise or sees a shadow, he calmly identifies what it is. Describe how your child makes up happy stories until he falls asleep without becoming scared.

At various points in the fantasy, ask your child to report his fear rating. Repeat the imaginary tales on different evenings until your child is no longer anxious listening to the scene.

INFORMATION

To a young child the dark is the unknown. In fact, young children don't understand why it gets dark or exactly when the sunlight will return. Even if your child understands about day and night, the

dark can seem to last an eternity. Although you can distinguish
various levels of darkness, your child might see only "pitch black."
Help your child understand more
about the darkness.

1. Explain night and day. Where does light come from? Using a flashlight and a ball or globe, show your child how the sun shines on part of the earth. As the earth turns, a portion of it is always in the dark. Of course, tell your child the good news—the earth never stops turning. A six- or seven-year-old might be comforted by the fact that it is always light somewhere on the planet. Using the globe, play a game of "What Time Is It Where?" Shine a flashlight on various parts of the globe and ask your child to point to a spot where it is daytime or nighttime. Identify the spots the younger child simply points to. If your child can read, have him identify the countries himself.

2. Experience sunset and daybreak. Watch a sunset together so your child can see the changing colors of the sky and the diminishing light. Watch the sun come up together so your child can experience the various shades of lightness and the beautiful colors of daybreak. On a cloudy day, show your child how the clouds dim the sky although it is still daytime. As evening approaches, explain to your child what happens when the sun slips down on the horizon, and why it gradually gets darker and darker. Remind your child that the earth is turning away from the sun as it gets darker.

3. Teach your child how the eye works. Using information from the encyclopedia or other reference texts, show your child a diagram of the eye. Have your child study your eye to see the colored iris, the clear cornea, and the dark pupil. To demonstrate how the lens of the eye, like the lens on a camera, opens and closes to let light in, look into a mirror. As you both stare at the mirror, turn a light on and off or flash a light in the mirror, so your child can see her pupils expand and contract.

4. Help your child understand how the eyes become accustomed to the dark. Many children who are afraid of the dark have no problem attending movies. If this is true of your child, use that setting to help him overcome his fear of the dark in other places. The next time you go to a movie, remind your child that it will be dark when you enter the theater. Once in the aisle, hold hands to comfort your child and remain standing until both of you can see well enough to find a seat. At various points during the movie ask your child to look around the theater and see how well he can see other theater patrons. You can recreate this effect by having your child sit with you in a darkened room. Ask your child what he can see. Wait a minute and repeat the question. Over time, point out how you are both able to see the outlines of furniture and then other objects in the darkened room.

5. Talk about the fear. If your child's fear of the dark is related to a fear of burglars or kidnapping, turn to the last section of this book for more detailed suggestions. Likewise, if in addition to being afraid of the dark, your child shows fears of separation at other times, turn to the chapter on separation anxiety for additional interventions.

6. Create a series of positive statements. Using the information you have gathered, help your child to create a number of reassuring statements about the dark. Practice saying these before bedtime.

7. Help your child practice trying to go back to sleep. Explain to your child that most of us wake up several times at night but just roll over and go back to sleep. Role-play waking up in the middle of the night and going back to sleep. Practice using positive self-talk to help him go back to sleep. Talk about the kinds of positive things he can say to himself, such as, "I am just having a

---

POSITIVE SELF-TALK ABOUT THE DARK

1. I am safe in the dark; my mom and dad are nearby.
2. The dark will go away in the morning, and it will soon be daytime.
3. The dark can't hurt me. That is just a shadow.
4. That sound is just the heater coming on.
5. _____

dream; this is not true"; "The shadows in the corner are my clothes on the chair"; or "I can go back to sleep; I just have to relax."

8. Create a nighttime kit. Include a high-powered flashlight that he can use to highlight things that scare him as well as some of his favorite books and cassette tapes. Discuss how he might use the kit before he falls asleep or should he wake up. There will be times when your child needs your assistance, but every time that he uses his flashlight, calms himself down, or looks at a book until he goes back to sleep, it's real progress.

OBSERVATION

Everyone must learn to contend with the dark. Realizing that others have accomplished this will be very helpful. To desensitize your child to the dark, you will provide a variety of types of experiences.

1. Watch others coping with darkened spaces. As naturally as possible, arrange for your child to observe both you and other family members entering and relaxing in darkened areas of your house at bedtime or other times of the day. Take a stroll at dusk. Scrounge for something in the attic or basement.

Avoid any "I can do it, why can't you?" messages. Take precautions that siblings don't tease your child about being frightened of the dark. If, however, other children in the family or any of your child's friends have gotten over a fear of the dark, ask them to share their experiences and solutions with your child. One seven-year-old girl who was afraid to go to sleep in the dark at her own home overcame her fear while spending the night out with a very close friend. Her best friend told her that she really couldn't go to sleep if there were lights on and gave her a little doll to sit on the pillow all night long. She also suggested they talk to each other in the dark until they fell asleep. It worked.

2. Watch others saying good night. If you have access to the old television series *The Waltons*, the show always ended with each

family member telling every other member good night from darkened rooms. Many movies and television shows have bedtime
scenes. Whenever you come across one, point out positive aspects
of the scene. Even when a character needs a comforter such as a
teddy bear to keep him company in the dark, talk about what
worked for the child in the scene.

EXPOSURE

*Now that your child has read about and observed others in the
dark and also learned more about it, you are ready to help him
confront his fears step by step.*

1. Play games to acclimate your child to the dark. First, play
each of the following games in the daytime. When your child indicates by her fear ratings she is comfortable, play the same game at
night.

Follow the Leader: Taking the role of the leader, have your
child follow you as you weave your way in and out of darkened areas
of the house. Move quickly through the spaces and keep it fun.
Gradually, stay longer in a dark area but be sure that your child can
see a lit exit. Next, lead your child into a darkened room and, with
the door ajar, sit down. Point out how your eyes adapt so you can
see more clearly the longer you stay in the space. When your child
reports that he is comfortable following your lead in and out of
darkened rooms, have him take the lead.

Hide-and-seek, tag, and other games: Begin each game in
the normal manner. Over time move the game from well-lit to dim
and then finally darkened areas. Have your child rate her fear at each
step and continue playing until she feels comfortable in the dark
spaces. Reverse roles so that she becomes the leader.

Approach every experience like a game and your child will gradually become increasingly relaxed in the setting. You might be surprised that your child tries to scare you in the dark.

2. Encourage your child to stay alone in the dark. Once your child is somewhat accustomed to being in the dark, encourage him to stay in the dark alone. Select a room that can be totally dimmed. Your child's bedroom is ideal. Explain to your child that you are going to teach him a new game in which he learns to stay alone in the dark. Tell him that the goal of the game is to increase the number of seconds he can stay alone in his room with the door closed and that you will mark his times on a graph. If you have a stopwatch or timer, show your child how to work it. *Together* practice walking into the room, turning off the lights, and closing the door. Have your child rehearse starting and stopping the stopwatch in the dark. If you do not have such a timer, have your child slowly count.

When your child's anxiety is at a comfortable level for the trial runs, proceed to having him stay in the dark alone. Reassuring your child that he need only stay for a few seconds, help him set a reasonable goal for his first trial. He might simply count to five the first time. Using your child's feedback to guide the experience, repeat the exercise until he is able to stay in the dark for a count of sixty. Remind your child to practice the coping skills to counter any anxiety he feels. When he reports that his fear level has increased to an uncomfortable stage, stop, help him relax, and then start with the same goal again.

Keep a record of the number of seconds your child is able to stay in the dark and reward your child for meeting or beating his previous record (see Chapter 3). Let the child turn on the lights and come out in between trials. Over a matter of a few weeks your child will be able to increase the time he can stay in the dark. Consistent practice pays off.

3. Practice staying in the dark for real situations. Don't be surprised if real experiences are more difficult for your child than the games were. Sit with your child in his room at bedtime. Cut off the lights, and gradually close the door until you are sitting together in a blackened room. Help your child identify any sights, shadows, and noises in the room that might stimulate his imagination. For example, explain how the house contracts as it cools in the evening, causing creaking and cracking sounds. Similarly, help your child identify the wind blowing branches against the house, the sounds of the furnace, the water running through the pipes, and anything else he hears. Put on your thinking caps to identify the outlines of objects and shadows in the room. Check your identification with a flashlight. Spotlight various features in the room that have frightened him before.

4. Gradually decrease the amount of light at night. Now that your child has practiced all of these techniques and has worked through various desensitizing experiences, it is time for him to deal with the dark on his own. To encourage his success, give him control over the light in the room. Place a rheostat on the wall switch or a lamp near his bed. These are easily purchased at your local hardware store. As an alternative, turn off all the lights in the child's room and control the amount of light that enters the room from the hallway by adjusting the bedroom door.

Over the days and weeks, encourage your child to slightly lower the level of light in the room every few days until the room is dark. Praise and reinforce your child for staying in the darkened room and for continuing to lower the level of light in the room. Don't get discouraged if it takes weeks or even months to accomplish the ultimate goal. As long as you and the child are noting progress and your child is gradually decreasing the amount of light in the room, you are headed in the right direction.

SELECTION OF EXPERIENCES WITH THE DARK

1. Play games such as follow the leader, hide-and-seek, and tag in dim rooms and darkened spaces.
2. Sit in a dark room with parent and have a snack.
3. Play a game with a friend or sibling in a darkened room.
4. Sit alone in a darkened room in the daytime.
5. Control light level in room at bedtime as parent sits with you.
6. Play and go to sleep in increasingly darkened room at night.

Books

Are There Spooks in the Dark? Claudia Fregosi. New York: Four Winds, 1977. A boy and girl shoo away spooks supposedly hiding in the closet and under the bed.

The Berenstain Bears in the Dark. Stan and Jan Berenstain. New York: Random House, 1982. The cubs are afraid of the dark and Papa helps them get over it. They play the shadow game and act out scary stories.

Goodnight Moon. Margaret Wise Brown. New York: Harper & Row, 1947. A rhyming story about a small rabbit who says good night to his surroundings.

Jessica and the Wolf: A Story for Children Who Have Bad Dreams. Theodore E. Lobby. New York: Magination Press, 1990. A book for parents to read to children about a little girl who has a nightmare about a wolf. She figures out a creative way to stop the wolf with her imagination.

Moonlight. Jan Ormerod. New York: Lothrop, Lee and Shepard, 1982. A little girl gets ready for bed and is tucked in, but when she is alone in the dark she is afraid. Mommy and Daddy comfort her and she finally falls asleep.

More Night. Muriel Rukeyser. New York: Harper & Row, 1981. A well-known poet for adults explores dreams and night in a way that many young children can understand.

Night Again. Karla Kuskin. Boston: Little, Brown, 1981. This book presents a bedtime ritual in poetic prose with a round picture on each blue page. (The blue color darkens as the little boy settles down to sleep.)

The Night Book. Mark Strand. New York: Clarkson Potter, 1985. The moon shows a little girl why she doesn't need to be afraid at night.

Only the Cat Saw. Ashley Wolff. New York: Dodd Mead, 1985. A poetic little story that captures night not ordinarily experienced by a child.

Shadows. John Canty. New York: Harper & Row, 1987. Benjamin learns that the "creatures" around him are really shadows.

Some of the Days of Everett Anderson. Lucille Clifton. New York: Holt, 1987. A small boy plays in the rain, feels lonely, and is afraid of the dark. One of a series of fine books.

When I'm Sleepy. Jane R. Howard. New York: Dutton, 1985. A book for younger children about how we feel when we are sleepy. This is a very reassuring and comforting book.

Who's Afraid of the Dark? Crosby Bonsall. New York: Harper & Row, 1980. A small boy gives advice to his dog who is afraid of the dark.

FEAR OF FANTASY CHARACTERS

Three-year-old Allison was excited about going to her cousin's birthday party until the clown greeted her at the door. She shrieked, clung desperately to her mother's leg, and refused to enter the house. Her mother was flabbergasted; her other children adored clowns, and Allison herself had always liked clowns on television and at the circus.

Brian's parents couldn't wait to take him to Disney World. They knew that at two he was too young for most of the park experiences but they thought he'd still have a good time—after all, he took a stuffed Mickey Mouse to bed with him every night. Everything was great as they walked down Main Street until Brian saw Mickey and Minnie walking toward him. When his parents led him closer to shake hands with the characters, his eyes got big and he wouldn't get near them. These weren't his cartoon friends. They were giants.

There's a fine line between fantasy and reality for preschool children. Most young children love watching cartoons on television and looking at pictures of their fantasy friends in a book, but when they meet life-sized versions of these characters some children panic. There are plenty of first graders who aren't sure that Cinderella isn't real. A child may love watching Big Bird on television and be petrified when he sees the huge yellow bird in person.

It is normal for a young child to be frightened by costumed characters. Over time he will learn to distinguish fantasy characters from people and animals. It took a little while, but eventually Allison even learned to like clowns. Her parents read books about clowns to her. They visited the circus but sat high up in the stands so no clowns would come too close. From this distance, she even laughed at some of the clowns' antics. Over the next few months, they played with clown dolls, watched clowns on TV, and observed clowns at the mall and fair from a distance. When she finally met a clown close up, she stood by her mom and smiled when he waved at her. If, however, your child has an intense fear of fantasy characters, you also can help him through this period.

IMAGINATION

Your child's imagination is so strong, she's sure Mickey Mouse is real. It may sound contradictory, but help your child use her imagination to control her mind.

1. Read books. Many times children first meet their favorite characters through books. This is an excellent way to introduce many beloved fantasy characters. When you know you will be visiting a place that has costumed characters, use books to introduce them to your child.

2. Watch films and television shows. Most children learn about popular fantasy characters in this manner. *Sesame Street* characters are friends to both the actors and actresses in the show and the viewers at home. As you watch together help your child distinguish the costumed figures and puppets from the real people.

Avoid movies about heroic or villainous cartoon characters that might be too intense for your child. Many films, such as *Batman* and *Dick Tracy*, that are based on favorite childhood characters are created for an adult audience and use adult themes.

3. Bring the characters into your own pretend activities. Encourage your child to include his favorite fantasy characters in imaginative play. Dressing up in hats, wigs, and masks will familiarize your child with the notion of costumes. Make masks and costumes from construction paper and colored sheets. Lay out any costume you use so that your child can see it before you put it on. Dress in front of your child.

4. Lead your child through an imaginary story in which he plays happily with the fantasy character. Lie down at naptime or bedtime with your child and tell him a story based on a fantasy character. Put your child in the story, describing how he meets the character and how much fun they have together. Have your child imagine himself playing with the figure, inviting him home, and becoming good friends with the character. Continue these stories on various occasions so that your child builds a positive library of memories.

INFORMATION

Fantasy characters are figments of someone's imagination. Take away some of the magic so your child can enjoy them.

1. Take the fantasy out of the characters. Besides reading stories about the characters, if your child is old enough, teach your child how to draw them. Books that illustrate how cartoon characters are drawn, how movies are made, how puppets work, and how actors put on costumes to play the part of fantasy characters are fun and enlightening. Many software programs teach the child how to animate or provide some motion for the figures he draws or manipulates on the screen. Although your child might not understand all of the information at first, over time his understanding of the distinctions between make-believe and real will counter many of his fears.

2. Play with puppets. Provide experiences that give your child the control. It's another chance to show your child how things work. Make a hand puppet out of a paper bag or borrow a marionette so your child can learn how it works. Many cities have puppet theaters where your child could see puppets firsthand. Explain to your child that there are various kinds of puppets, but always a human being must make the sound and the motion for the puppet.

3. Create a series of sentences your child can say to herself. Just like Dorothy taught the other characters in *The Wizard of Oz*, give your child a few helpful things to say to himself.

POSITIVE SELF-TALK ABOUT FANTASY CHARACTERS

1. This is make-believe.
2. He wants to be my friend.
3. There's a person under that costume.
4. He is being nice to other children.
5. _____

OBSERVATION

It doesn't help a lot that you will shake hands with Bozo. Children learn best from each other.

1. Watch other children interacting with fantasy characters. Watching parades on television provides a lot of opportunities for your child to observe other children interacting with clowns, cartoon characters, and other larger-than-life figures. From a distance watch other children interacting with fantasy characters. The entrance to amusement parks and seats up in the stands at the circus are safe locations for your child's viewing activities.

2. Watch siblings and friends interact with fantasy characters. When you are at the amusement park, don't force your child to walk near the costumed characters. Stand at a distance your youngster obviously feels is safe, as older siblings walk closer to the costumed figures. Listen as they converse and interact. Observe together what the character does and says. Point out things that he does like patting children on the head, giving hugs, and waving that make the character seem friendly.

EXPOSURE

Once your child understands the distinction between fantasy and reality, she will be able to get over her fear. It is time to approach a real character. Unless there is some need to push the issue, wait until natural opportunities arise to acclimate your child to the fantasy character. Always make sure you have seen the figure in print and on film before attempting to meet him in person.

1. Maintain your distance. Never force your child to touch or interact with a fantasy character. Let her know that she does not have to meet or talk to Santa, Peter Rabbit, or the clown at Cousin Stevie's birthday. Once your child gets used to the characters at a distance you can gradually move closer.

2. As your child's anxiety level decreases, move closer to the character. Take your time. Use the sequence that follows this section to design a series of experiences for your child. Using your child's fear ratings as a guide, repeat each experience until she is comfortable. Begin by simply watching the character, then moving past it, approaching it, and finally interacting with the character. Helping a child become comfortable with Santa is a good example. Josie's parents really wanted a picture of their child smiling on Santa's lap, so they spent a number of the days at the mall. Initially, they stood only as close to Santa as Josie felt comfortable with. They observed other children from that distance. They walked past Santa several times. They encouraged Josie to wave at him as she walked past his throne. After a few passes, they asked Josie if she wanted to stop. While Josie stood with her mom, she watched her dad approach the gentleman, then shake hands. Eventually Josie and her mom moved slowly toward Santa. It took several sessions. Whenever Josie reported being uncomfortable, they stopped and sometimes left for the day. On the third day Josie walked up and sat on

Santa's lap for the picture. She didn't want to talk to Santa and that was fine with her parents. Always remember to take your time. Don't force your child to shake hands and don't let Santa pull your child in for a hug. When your child is comfortable, encourage her to move another step closer. She will get there when she's ready.

SEQUENCE OF EXPERIENCES WITH FANTASY CHARACTERS

1. Play with a stuffed version of the character.
2. Read a story about the character.
3. Watch a show or movie about the character.
4. Watch the larger-than-life character from a distance.
5. Watch other children and family members interact with the character.
6. Walk past the character; wave at the character.
7. Slowly move closer to the character.
8. Stand near the character.
9. Talk to but don't touch the character.
10. Touch the character.

Books

A Bear Called Paddington. Michael Bond. Boston: Houghton Mifflin, 1962. Young Paddington, a bear from Deepest Peru, arrives in London on his own and has the good fortune to be found and adopted by the Brown family.

The Cat in the Hat. Dr. Seuss. New York: Random House, 1957. The original contemporary beginning reader. One rainy afternoon when Mother is out and there is nothing to do, that Cat in the Hat comes to visit, and mayhem ensues.

Mary Poppins. P. L. Travers. New York: Harcourt Brace Jovanovich, 1981 (revised edition). Disney's Mary Poppins is much sweeter than the original. Mary takes the children on exciting and wonderful fantasy adventures. Walt Disney's movie *Mary Poppins* is available on video.

The Mother Goose Treasury. Raymond Briggs. New York: Coward-McCann, 1966. Every child's favorite collection of rhymes and illustrations in both black-and-white and color.

Peter Pan. J. M. Barrie. These are the well-known adventures of the Darling children, the little lost boy Peter Pan, and the faithful fairy Tinkerbell.

Pippi Longstocking. Astrid Lindgren. New York: Viking, 1950. Independent Pippi is her very own boss. Her next-door neighbors, Tommy and Annika, are fascinated by Pippi's inventive and outrageous approach to life.

Snow White and the Seven Dwarfs. Translated by Randall Jarrell. New York: Farrar, Straus and Giroux, 1972. One of the best-loved fantasy tales from the brothers Grimm, rendered with great beauty by a poet and artist.

Walt Disney's Three Little Pigs. Retold by Barbara Brenner. New York: Random House, 1982. In this excellent version of an old favorite, the wolf isn't scalded to death, but is just scared off—a more humane and reasonable ending that fits a four-year-old's sensitive sense of justice.

Winnie-the-Pooh. A. A. Milne. Winnie-the-Pooh is the bear who belongs to Christopher Robin, a proper English boy of not so very long ago. Pooh, Eeyore, Piglet, Tigger, and the rest of their friends have been beloved fantasy characters for generations. Their adventures continue in *The House at Pooh Corner.*

The Wonderful Wizard of Oz. L. Frank Baum. Most children think they know the story because they've seen the film, but it is a delightful book to read aloud to children.

Yertle the Turtle and Other Stories. Dr. Seuss. New York: Random House, 1958. The fantasy characters of Dr. Seuss are destined to be favorites. In this volume, when power goes to Yertle's head, another turtle proves that even the smallest can affect the mightiest. This book also presents the woeful tale of Gertrude McFuzz, who envies others but comes to appreciate herself, and The Big Brag, a story about a boastful rabbit. Also see: *Horton Hears a Who* and *Marvin K. Mooney, Will You Please Go Now?*

5

SEPARATION FEARS

FEAR OF GOING TO SLEEP

One time that a fear of separating commonly shows itself is at bedtime. Not every child who resists going to bed is frightened; all children, given a choice, would prefer to be with Mom and Dad. There are, however, many reasons why children fear going to sleep. They may be scared of the dark or apprehensive about being alone in their rooms before they fall asleep. Some children are worried about being kidnapped or don't want to be alone with their thoughts. Still others are afraid of what might happen after they fall asleep: They might awaken and not be able to fall back asleep; they might have nightmares; they might not awaken at all. Kenneth began having difficulty falling asleep after his grandfather died. He had previously gotten over a fear of the dark, but now that fear was back and he fought bedtime. When his parents came to see us, Kenneth's mom had gotten in the habit of lying down with him at bedtime— which usually meant she fell asleep in his bed, too. Unraveling his imagination and correcting a misconception were key elements in helping Kenneth become comfortable falling asleep. A well-meaning aunt had told him that his grandfather had died in his sleep, and he decided that most people died in their sleep. After his parents corrected the information and helped Kenneth become accustomed to the dark, he was sleeping alone again within a week.

You may be aware of what frightens your child about going to sleep. If not, talk to him about it. By pinpointing your child's bedtime fear, you can help him overcome it.

IMAGINATION

Your child's imagination can be his worst enemy at bedtime. The noises he hears, the shadows he sees, and the horror stories he imagines all impede sleep. Enticing him to think more positively about bedtime and to use his imagination to control his nightly visions can be very helpful. If your child is afraid of the dark, the section on fear of the dark will also be useful.

1. Read books about children going to sleep. Many of the fears your child is experiencing are very normal. Learning that other children see monsters in their closets, don't like going to bed, and sometimes have bad dreams gives your child a new perspective on bedtime. A number of books about bedtime are listed at the end of this section. As you read these books together, talk about the fears the characters have and how they deal with them.

In addition, books provide an excellent way to help your child get ready for sleep. Reading favorite stories cuddled up in your arms is a safe, wonderful way to fall asleep. A number of bedtime books for preschoolers are listed at the end of this section. Ask your local librarian or bookseller to recommend others.

2. Pretend to go to sleep in the daytime. To build a positive image of going to sleep, incorporate the theme into playtime activities. Play "bedtime" and have your child tell you a story and pretend to put you to sleep.

In addition, pretend to go to sleep in the daytime. Include in your play actions that help you go to sleep such as getting comfortable, counting sheep, and other things you do to help yourself fall asleep.

3. Lead your child through imaginary sleep scenes. When your child is relaxed after practicing his deep-muscle relaxation skills, have him imagine a bedtime scene. Drawing upon his particular fears, guide him through an imaginary sequence in which your child gets ready for bed, listens to a beloved story, is tucked in, and receives a good-night kiss. Next have him imagine lying in bed and thinking pleasant thoughts about his day. He hears the creaking of the house and identifies the sound of his mother walking by his room. He imagines he hears a burglar, but he tells himself that his father is downstairs and the dog is outside. Finally, he drifts off to sleep and awakes in the morning. Repeat similar imaginary scenes at various times until your child reports that his anxiety level is low.

INFORMATION

Most people have very little understanding of sleep. Give your child some facts about sleep to ease his mind while he's awake.

1. Gather information about sleep. Use children's reference books and other sources to explain sleep to your child. In addition, you will find *Solve Your Child's Sleep Problems* by Dr. Richard Ferber (New York: Simon and Schuster, 1985) and *Sleepless Children: A*

Handbook for Parents by Dr. David Haslam (New York: Long Shadow Books, 1984) very helpful resources.

Explain to your child that it takes most people about twenty minutes to fall asleep. When she falls asleep her muscles relax, her breathing and heart rate slow, and she becomes unaware of what is happening around her. Your child might be surprised to learn that she changes position many times as she sleeps. Older children will be interested to know there are four kinds of sleep detected by a study of brain waves and that only during the period of sleep called rapid eye movement (REM) sleep does a person dream.

Your child should learn that everyone needs sleep. Newborn babies sleep most of the time, and most adults get along well with about eight hours of sleep. Explain to your child that children need more sleep to function well and feel good. Four-year-olds average ten to fourteen hours of sleep per night and ten-year-olds, nine to twelve hours of sleep.

Help your child determine how much sleep she needs by keeping a record of how many hours she sleeps each night and how she feels when she wakes. Using the chart that follows, keep a record of the number of hours your child sleeps, when she awakens naturally, and whether she wakes up happy or grumpy.

At the end of a week or more, review the information and calculate the average number of hours your child sleeps per night. If she appears to awaken happily with that much sleep, you are close to determining the average amount of sleep she needs to function well.

2. Distinguish real from fantasy characters. Many of the characters that frighten your child at night are the monsters that lurk in her closet and under her bed. Children younger than six have a difficult time differentiating real from unreal characters. Discuss the kinds of things that frighten your child, helping her identify the ones that are make-believe and could never hurt her.

Sit with your child in her room in the dark. Use a flashlight to identify the shapes that frighten her. The sections on fear of the dark and fear of fantasy characters have suggestions that will also help your child overcome these fears.

3. Teach your child about the importance of the relaxation exercises to help her fall asleep. Children and adults need to learn how to relax their muscles and clear their minds to fall asleep.

Day	Bedtime	Awaken	# of Hours of Sleep	Mood
Total # of Hours of Sleep				
Average # of Hours of Sleep/Night				

Practicing the relaxation exercises taught in Chapter 2 provides a skill that will help your child fall asleep.

4. Help your child create several positive sentences she can say to herself to counter any fears she has at bedtime. Use the information you've gathered to develop statements that counteract the fears she has. Remind her to practice saying these statements when she becomes anxious.

OBSERVATION

Providing opportunities for your child to watch others fall asleep and awaken will convince her that this is a natural process.

POSITIVE SELF-TALK ABOUT BEDTIME

1. My body needs to sleep now so I can have fun
tomorrow.
2. I will fall asleep and wake tomorrow.
3. Mommy and Daddy are in the next room if I need
them.
4. There are no monsters under the bed. There's no
such thing as a monster.
5. _____

---

1. Let the child watch you fall asleep. In some households this
is not very difficult. Many children reportedly don't go to sleep until
after their parents do, anyway. Or take a nap together on a warm,
sunny afternoon. After playing hard in the backyard, get out a
blanket and take a nap—or pretend to. Let your child report what
you do when you are asleep.

2. Observe babies sleeping. If you have a baby in the family,
you have a built-in model of sleep behavior. Infants sleep most of the
time and they will do it anywhere so that your child has many
opportunities to watch a younger sibling fall asleep and awaken. If
there are no babies in the family, or your friends don't have babies,
visit the viewing area of a local maternity ward and observe the
sleeping newborns. What does the baby do while she sleeps? What
does she look like? What awakens her?

3. Observe children at bedtime. The winding-down period
before bedtime prepares a child for falling asleep. Have your child
take a survey of what younger and older brothers, sisters, and
friends do to prepare for sleep. How do they get ready for bedtime?
Do they do the same thing each evening? What do they do to help
themselves fall asleep?

EXPOSURE

Help your child overcome her fear of falling sleep by using a series of activities designed to reduce her fear and ease her way into sleep. The selection of experiences at the end of the section will help you define the sequence.

1. Pretend to go to sleep in the daytime. Most people awaken several times during the night but they quickly return to sleep and don't even remember the incidents in the morning. However, some children, don't know what to do when they awaken in the middle of the night, so they call Mom or Dad.

In the daytime, pretend it's time to go to sleep. Darken your child's bedroom and get into your pajamas. As your child lies next to you, take a fear rating. Talk to her about what makes her anxious. One by one, counteract each frightening thought. Shine a flashlight on the shadows she sees in the room; identify the creaking sounds she hears; and practice using positive self-talk to contradict frightening thoughts.

Next, pretend she awakens in the middle of the night. Practice counting sheep, imagining a favorite scene, and doing the relaxation exercises to fall asleep.

2. Implement a bedtime routine. Your child will feel more secure about bedtime if a routine is established. Not only will it help her get ready for bed, but it will also clear her mind and help her be more relaxed.

Discuss bedtime with your child and together define a bedtime routine that includes a winding-down period, getting ready for bed, story time, quiet time for sharing, and bedtime. Your child might enjoy making a color wheel to highlight each period before bedtime. Divide a paper plate into five sections with a crayon and label them quiet activity, pajama time, story time, small talk, lights out. Cut out an arrow from construction paper and attach it to the center of the plate so that your child can point the arrow to each activity as he winds down to bedtime.

3. Prepare for nights when she cannot fall asleep. It happens to everyone, so be ready. Provide a "Nighttime Kit" that includes a variety of activities to pass the time and relax your child. Depending on her age, it might include a flashlight, a book, a cassette player and story tape, and a tape of the relaxation exercises presented in Chapter 2. Stretch out with your child and show her how to use the flashlight to identify unfriendly shapes she sees in the dark. Listen to the relaxation tape and practice the exercises. Listen as your child reads to you or follow along together as you listen to a story tape. As your child lies in the dark, have her rate her fear before and after she uses the PM kit. Remind her to think positive thoughts to counter any fearful ones that pop into her mind. The PM kit will also be useful in the middle of the night should she awaken.

4. Help your child fall asleep alone. If your child is afraid of falling asleep, you might have contributed to this fear by lying down with her at bedtime. To change the pattern and eradicate her fear, ask your child to set a timer for the number of seconds she can lie in bed alone. Take a fear rating and remind your child to use any of her coping skills to counteract frightening thoughts. In addition, she might read a book or play music. Return before the buzzer rings, praise your child, give her a kiss and a back rub, and set the timer for a slightly longer period. At each step of the way, take fear ratings. Continue to increase the time she spends alone at bedtime, until her fear ratings (and the fact that she falls asleep) indicate she is able to fall asleep alone.

Books

Bedtime for Frances. Russell Hoban. New York: Harper & Row, 1960. Frances is in bed singing the alphabet until she gets to T for tiger and begins worrying about whether there are any tigers in her room.

Bedtime Story. Jim Erskine. New York: Crown, 1982. Simple text and soft pictures are just right for sleepy time.

Dr. Seuss's Sleep Book. Dr. Seuss. New York: Random House, 1962. A book about sleepy time and how wonderful the night is.

Goodnight Moon. Margaret Wise Brown. New York: Harper & Row, 1947.

SEQUENCE OF EXPERIENCES WITH GOING TO SLEEP

1. With parent, pretend to go to sleep in bedroom in daytime.

2. Pretend to go to sleep alone in bedroom in daytime.

3. Pretend to go to sleep in bedroom at night.

4. Stay in bed at night for increasingly longer times until able to fall asleep easily.

5. Fall back asleep after waking in the middle of the night.

This beautifully illustrated book in rhyme form is about a small rabbit who says good night to everything around him.

Jessica and the Wolf: A Story for Children Who Have Bad Dreams. Theodore E. Lobby. New York: Magination Press, 1990. A book for parents to read to children about a little girl who has a nightmare about a scary wolf. She figures out a creative way to stop the wolf with her imagination.

Mother, Mother, I Want Another. Maria Polushkin. New York: Crown, 1988. It's bedtime and the little mouse should be going to sleep, but suddenly she wants another. Mama runs about and tries to figure out what it is she wants. The answer is charming and touching, since all the mouse wants is a kiss!

Mouse Tales. Arnold Lobel. New York: Harper & Row, 1972. Papa Mouse tells some humorous and charming bedtime stories for his little mouse children.

Patrick Goes to Bed. Geoffrey Hayes. New York: Knopf, 1985. A small book for a young child about going to bed.

Patsy Scarry's Big Bedtime Storybook. Patsy Scarry. New York: Random House, 1990. A loving, comforting collection of short stories about small creatures. Reading one each night would give a child a bedtime routine to look forward to.

Sleepy Time. Illustrated by Mary Morgan. New York: Random House, 1990. This book has wonderful pictures for young children about going to sleep.

When I'm Sleepy. Jane R. Howard. New York: Dutton, 1985. A book for younger children about how we feel when we are sleepy. This is a very reassuring and comforting book.

FEAR OF BABY-SITTERS

The first time you leave your child with a baby-sitter it's traumatic—for you as well as your child. If you are a first-time parent, it's no contest; you'll have the harder time. When you have a baby-sitter you trust, however, you will get used to leaving your child, but some children continue to have a difficult time. For two-year-old Nicki, staying with Grandma or Aunt Sylvia was acceptable, but anyone else was met with tears and screams. To overcome the problem, her mother arranged for the baby-sitter to come play with Janelle for four afternoons while the mother was there. On the first day the trio played together. On the second and third days Nicki and the sitter played as Mom worked about the house. On the fourth afternoon, Mom left the two alone for about a half hour. There were no problems after that leaving Nicki with this new friend.

For young children, this is a normal part of growing up. How you handle your child's tears will influence her reaction to baby-sitters. Many parents attempt to avoid a scene by sneaking out of the house. That's not a good idea. Your child is likely to be more frightened because she feels abandoned. A sense of trust develops when your child learns that you will not leave without saying good-bye and that you will return as you promise.

Sometimes parents prolong the leaving. That's not a good idea, either. When it is time for you to go, go. Although your child might not like being left behind, dragging your heels only reinforces him for digging in his.

Infants and toddlers are naturally afraid of strangers. As a child gets older, though, she should not have the same level of fear about staying with a baby-sitter as she did when she was a preschooler. A continuing fear of a particular baby-sitter should alert you that all might not be well when you leave home.

In this section, the approach is geared to helping the young child overcome the typical fear of being left with a baby-sitter.

IMAGINATION

Some children have a grand time with the baby-sitter. They look forward to having a baby-sitter because they know they will have someone to play with.

1. Read books about children having a wonderful time with a baby-sitter. There are many good books that deal with baby-sitters, and some are mentioned below. Choose books that deal positively with the baby-sitter. Talk about all of the fun the kids have when the baby-sitter arrives.

2. View movies and shows. Many movies and reruns of old shows feature baby-sitters and housekeepers in positive roles. View *Mary Poppins* and discuss how the children initially felt about Mary and then how they grew to love her. Were they apprehensive at first? What happened next?

3. Pretend. Incorporate into your child's pretend activities scenes of being left with the baby-sitter. Pretend she is saying good-bye to a doll and leaving her "pretend child" with a sitter. Playact enjoyable activities and how your child greets you upon returning.

4. Tell your child stories about baby-sitters. Many young children will not be able to imagine themselves with a baby-sitter. You can, however, weave a fantasy baby-sitter into your bedtime stories. When your child is relaxed before bedtime, tell him a story about a wonderful girl who comes to play. She brings a bag full of tricks and stays with your child until Mom and Dad return. Repeat such tales until your child is comfortable with the idea.

5. Lead your child through an imaginary scene. An older preschool child will be able to use her imagination when you describe positive scenes with sitters. When your child is relaxed, guide her through an imaginary scene in which she meets a baby-sitter who seems very nice. As they begin to play, you come in to say good-bye. Have your child imagine herself kissing you good-bye and waving you off with a smile on her face. Describe the games the baby-sitter plays and how much fun they have together. Picture your child as having a wonderful time and sorry to see the baby-sitter leave when you come home. Over a number of sessions continue the imaginary experiences until your child's fear ratings indicate she can comfortably imagine herself being left with a sitter.

INFORMATION

Never sneak out on your child. She'll feel abandoned. Instead
provide all the information you can about the baby-sitter
and where you will be.

1. Introduce your child to the baby-sitter in advance. Help your child feel comfortable with the sitter by making her a friend before you leave. If the sitter is someone your child has known for a long time, so much the better. Teenagers in the neighborhood, previous teachers and counselors, friends of the family, relatives, and neighbors are great resources for baby-sitters your child already knows.

2. Let your child know where you will be going, what you'll be doing, and when you will return. Create a bulletin board or post a special record created from the chart below specifically designed to give the baby-sitter and your child a visual record of where you will be and when you will return home. Include emergency numbers and other important information about the house.

Give your child a way to estimate the time of your return. Younger children can learn to measure time by comparing the time on a paper clock and the real thing. Make a clock out of construction paper or a paper plate. Fasten movable hands to the center with a brad. Set the time you will return. While you are gone, your child can compare the time you have indicated with the time on a real clock.

BABY-SITTER CHART

Child's name: _____

We will be at: _____

In the event of an emergency: _____

Pediatrician: _____

Neighbor: _____

Special advice: _____

---

3. Create a baby-sitter kit. Encourage your child to select activities to do with a sitter. In a special place, save a coloring book, an art project, or a special game reserved just for baby-sitters. Have your child bring these out when the baby-sitter arrives.

4. Create a series of positive statements she can say to herself when she feels anxious. If your child is old enough, help her use the experiences and information you have provided to develop several statements she can say to herself when she is left with a baby-sitter.

POSITIVE SELF-TALK ABOUT BABY-SITTERS

1. Ms. _____ is very nice; She will play with me.
2. Mommy and Daddy will be home soon.
3. My baby-sitter knows how to take care of me.
4. My baby-sitter knows where my mommy and daddy
    are if we need them.
5. _____

OBSERVATION

*Another way for your child to become less fearful of baby-sitters is
for your child to see friends and siblings who are having
fun with a sitter.*

1. Visit a friend or relative who is sitting for young children. If you have a relative or friend who baby-sits, arrange for your child to visit her on a baby-sitting job. This will also provide an opportunity for your child to ask questions about what a sitter does.

2. Arrange to visit your child's friends who are staying with a sitter. Explain your child's fears to friends who have young children. On an occasion when a particularly enjoyable sitter is staying with the children arrange for your child to visit for a few minutes. Let your child know in advance that no matter how much fun everyone is having you both will stay only a little while.

If your child is old enough, prompt her to ask her friends about the baby-sitters they know and what they do together. Of course, such prompting also leaves you open to the possibility that your child might some day talk with someone who didn't like a particular sitter.

EXPOSURE

*Plan a series of experiences that will help your child get used to
the sitter. Of course, you will have to pay for the baby-sitter's time,
but the money will be worth the payoff in terms of peace of mind.*

A young child will not be able to relate fear measurements as we have done with the other fears. However, watching your child through this experience should give you a pretty good feel for how comfortable your child is with the baby-sitter. Once you see your child laughing, joking, and talking freely with the sitter, you'll know it is well past the time you can leave. Be aware, however, that children can also be manipulative. They want your attention more than anything else. Give your child plenty of positive attention before you leave and when you return.

1. Invite the baby-sitter to meet your child. Arrange a play session when you will be home. This provides an opportunity for your child to meet the sitter and, just as important, for you to see the sitter in action. Show the sitter important areas of your home such as your child's room, play spaces, and the kitchen. Tell her about your child's likes and dislikes. Step to the sidelines as the baby-sitter engages your child. Slowly remove yourself from the situation, although you will remain in the house. Keep in mind that if your gut-level reaction is not good, you shouldn't hire the sitter again.

2. Hire the baby-sitter for a short stay. Tell your child well in advance that you will be leaving for a short time and that the baby-sitter will stay with her. Give your child an idea of the time she will arrive: after lunch, during a favorite television show, and so forth. Also tell your child how long you will be away, such as during lunch, long enough to play a game, or for a particular number of hours if your child has some concept of time.

When the baby-sitter arrives, don't rush out. Give them time to acclimate again, but when they are having a good time together, firmly tell your child goodbye and leave. Return as you promised.

3. Hire the baby-sitter for a longer stay. Assuming your child is progressing, proceed to an afternoon away from home. Follow the same pattern as before, and return as you promised.

Books

The Baby-Sitters Club: Kristy's Great Idea. Ann M. Martin. Scholastic, 1986. Kristy starts a baby-sitting club with her best friends. The first in a series of books for middle-grade children.

The Berenstain Bears and the Sitter. Stan and Jan Berenstain. New York: Random House, 1981. The Berenstain Bears learn all about baby-sitters.

George the Babysitter. Shirley Hughes. Englewood Cliffs, N.J.: Prentice-Hall, 1986. A delightful picture book about a regular day when the children stay with the baby-sitter while Mom's at work.

SEQUENCE OF EXPERIENCES WITH A BABY-SITTER

1. Play with sitter while parent remains at home.
2. Stay with sitter while parent leaves for a short time.
3. Stay with sitter while parent leaves for a couple of hours.
4. Stay with sitter for longer period of time.
5. Stay with a new sitter.

FEAR OF DAY CARE OR PRESCHOOL

Day care and preschool are relatively new inventions. In days gone by, infants and young children were cared for by their mothers or other members of the extended family until they entered first grade. Interest in preschool education sparked the advent of kindergarten programs for most children. In recent years, the baby-boom generation's desire to provide the best education for their children has encouraged the development of private preschool programs for children as young as two years old.

In addition to wanting a head start for their children, many families find it an economic necessity to put their children into day-care programs as soon as possible. The swelling ranks of women in the work force has necessitated new accommodations for young children so that mothers might return to work as soon as six weeks after giving birth.

As a result of these forces, the first formal separation from Mommy and Daddy for many children is much earlier than the kindergarten year. There is a continuing controversy about this trend and the quality of care and education children are receiving. If you must work, however, you must place your child in some kind of day-care program for all or part of the week or hire a housekeeper or nanny to care for your child at home. Some parents choose to enroll their children in a preschool or day-care program because of the cost or because they believe it will allow their child to socialize with other children or learn skills that pave the way for formal educational experiences.

Knowing that you are placing your child in a well-designed program conducted by caring, trained personnel with a healthy attitude toward children gives you the confidence to leave your child. When she had to return to work, Amy had a terrible time leaving her four-year-old at the day-care center. Lindsay cried and screamed. Amy just couldn't leave her sobbing daughter standing in the doorway. Leaving a pleading child whose face is streaked with tears is not easy, but you can take steps to ease your child into a new situation so that the separation will be less traumatic for you both.

There are times, however, when a child develops a sudden aversion to a program. When a child who has loved preschool or day care previously develops a fear of it or simply doesn't want to go back, there are likely to be reasons for the new reaction. There may have been some change at the school, such as a new teacher. The child might be worried because of some difficulties at home. He might have been frightened by an experience at school, or he might be avoiding a particular situation. Working your way back to a happy experience might take some time once you discover the reason.

IMAGINATION

For children who have stayed at home previously, day care and preschool are new situations. Having older brothers and sisters who attend first provides a natural introduction to school, but books, movies, and your child's own playtime activities can do the same thing.

1. Read books about preschool and day care. There are many books written about going to school and others that focus on day care and play groups. Books that focus on Mom or Dad going to work are also important choices to read to your child. Some of these books are listed at the end of this section. As you read, talk about what the children in the stories are doing and how they feel. Emphasize the interesting activities they enjoy and the fact that Mom or Dad always return to pick up the child at school.

2. Use make-believe to build a positive view of preschool.
If your child is old enough you can "play school." Every child loves
to pretend to be the teacher. Set up a pretend classroom and let your
child be your teacher. Switch roles and introduce activities such as
group time, snack time, and story time that your child would enjoy
but is unaware of.

3. Lead your child through an imaginary scene about pre-school or day care. If your child is old enough, help him imagine
going to school and having fun. At a time when your child is relaxed,
begin to describe how you take your child to the school or day-care
center. Picture other children busily playing and your child running
to greet them. Describe your child as having so much fun that he
barely has time to wave goodbye. Have your child imagine various
parts of the day, emphasizing your child and his friends as busy and
happy. Describe your child greeting you when you pick him up.
Repeat variations of these scenes on different occasions until your
child is comfortable with these imaginary experiences.

INFORMATION

*Getting the facts about the preschool and day care will help your
child feel at ease.*

1. Answer your child's questions. Remember your child's
awareness and skills grow every year. A two-year-old might have a
few questions, a three-year-old more, and an older child might add
new ones to the list he already had. It doesn't matter that your child
has been to school before; be ready for new interests and concerns.
When Jack went to the day-care center the first time, all he asked was
who was picking him up. Four-year-old Linda had quite a different
concern—she wanted to know where to find the bathroom. Most of
all, every year your child will want the nitty-gritty questions answered first. Once these are answered, everything else is likely to be
a piece of cake.

2. Talk to other children about preschool and day care.
Brothers and sisters, cousins, and friends can be very helpful when
everyone is old enough to share experiences. Getting a few facts
from a peer is sometimes more effective than all the details you can
provide. Introducing your child to another child who is at the center
or school will give her an inside source for information and provide
a built-in friend.

3. Practice positive statements. Help your child practice saying positive things about going to preschool. Make a list like the one
below and add to it. Each day read the list to your child and praise
him for repeating positive things to himself on the way to school and
when he is there.

POSITIVE SELF-TALK ABOUT
PRESCHOOL/DAY CARE

1. My teacher is nice.
2. Mommy will be back soon to get me.
3. It is fun to paint at school.
4. The playground is fun.
5. _____

OBSERVATION
*It's helpful to provide an older preschooler with an opportunity to
look around.*

1. Arrange a tour of the program your child will enter.
Prior to her first day at school, take the opportunity to show your
child around. This is easier at day-care centers that are open year-
round. Seeing the classrooms, meeting some teachers, and watching
children engaged in a variety of activities is helpful. Talk about what

the kids are doing and which classes have children the same age as your child.

2. Meet a playmate. Once you have enrolled in a program, try to arrange for your child to meet several of the children who will be in her class. Seeing a familiar face is always helpful. When possible, arrange for your child to play with another outside the school day. Having a real friend at school is a great bonus and a real icebreaker.

3. Make an observation run. Watch other children going and coming home from school. If they are picked up by van, check out the bus stop. Children are usually happy and talkative, so observe the kids as they come home from school. Young children returning from preschool often have tote bags full of the day's activities. Ask a friend to show your child what he did in school that day.

EXPOSURE

Your child's teacher at the day-care center or school has had lots of experience helping young children feel comfortable in this setting. Many preschool programs provide an orientation week during which a parent might attend school with her child one day, then leave the child for an hour the next time, working toward a full experience. Most children will adapt well under such conditions. If your child's program doesn't have a formal orientation period, use the suggestions that follow and the list of experiences at the end of this section to ease your child into the situation as you ease your way out.

If your child becomes very fearful of a preschool situation and you have assured yourself that the reasons for her concern have been alleviated and that nothing negative is happening in the classroom, use the list of experiences to reintroduce your child to the setting.

1. Plan an orientation day. Many preschool programs provide an orientation day when both child and parent must come to school.

This is a perfect opportunity for your child to get to know the classroom. The same accommodation can be made easily at a day-care center. If your preschool program does not provide such an experience, get permission to spend some time with your child in the classroom before her first day at the center.

2. Spend a short day in the classroom. Attend the center with your child. As your child becomes comfortable in the classroom, wean your way to the sidelines. When your child is actively involved in an activity, leave the classroom for a few moments by making an excuse of using the rest room. Always return as promised. After informing your child of where you will be, spend time outside the classroom, reading in the teacher's lounge or relaxing in the lobby as your child continues her stay.

3. Work your way toward leaving your child for an entire day. Many children spend long hours at day-care centers. A full-day preschool is also a long day for a young child. You might begin by leaving your child for a morning or part of a day. As your child becomes comfortable with that experience, lengthen the time she stays at the center.

Once both you and your child are comfortable in the setting, some suggestions will make the parting easier.

- Don't dillydally. When it is time to leave, go.
- Always return as promised. When your child knows that you will return on time as promised, he will be more comfortable.
- Ask for the teacher's help. If your child has difficulty separating, ask the teacher to involve her in a game or activity when it is time for you to leave.

Books

The Berenstain Bears Go to School. Stan and Jan Berenstain. New York: Random House, 1978. Sister Bear gets ready for school.
Betsy's First Day at Nursery School. Gunilla Wolde. New York: Random House, 1982. One of the Tommy and Betsy books showing children in everyday activities.
A Child Goes to School: A Storybook for Parents and Children Together. Sara Bonnet Stein. New York: Doubleday, 1978. An informal, helpful introduction in stories and photographs about going to school.
Going to Day Care. Fred Rogers. New York: G. P. Putnam's Sons, 1985.

SEQUENCE OF EXPERIENCES WITH PRESCHOOL/DAY CARE

1. Drive by the center. Observe the children playing.
2. Take a tour of the center.
3. Visit the classroom.
4. Go to center with parent; parent leaves classroom for
a few minutes at a time.
5. Stay at center alone for a short time.
6. Stay at center alone for a half day.
7. Stay at center for longer periods.

Real-life photographs of children being cared for in other people's homes and in day-care centers. "Mister Rogers" helps both parents and children understand the activities and practices.

Grover Goes to School. Dan Elliott. New York: Random House/Children's Television Workshop, 1992. This book is all about Grover's first day at school.

Harry Gets Ready for School. Harriet Ziefert. New York: Viking Penguin, 1991. Harry is a little nervous as he gets ready for school.

I'd Rather Stay Home. Carol Barkin and Elizabeth James. Milwaukee: Raintree Educational 1975. A photo essay that walks the child through the first day in school.

Little Critters' This Is My School. Mercer Mayer. New York: Western Publishing, 1990. The critters get ready for and go to school.

My Going to School Book. Freddi Felt. Memphis: F & F Publishing Company, 1987. For the young child who is beginning school. This book encourages a child to talk about his or her own experiences with parent's assistance.

Steffie and Me. Phyllis Hoffman. New York: Harper & Row, 1971. This lively and very real story of the friendship of two girls appeals to children who have had preschool experience, as much of the story takes place in the schoolroom.

Will I Have a Friend?. Miriam Cohen. New York: Macmillan, 1967. Anxiety about the first day of school ends in happiness.

FEAR OF SPENDING THE NIGHT OUT

Spending the night away from home is a treat for a lot of children. At least after the first time. They can't wait to go to Grandma's or stay up late with their best friend. Young children who still cling to security blankets and stuffed animals might think twice about bringing a favored "blankie" or "Willie the stuffed pig," but it doesn't keep them home. Most children adapt and have a good time.

Every once in a while a child will have a bad experience. She might get sick, get scared, worry that something is wrong at home, or just miss her bed. Ten-year-old Jennifer would not spend the night away from her mom when we met her. Years earlier she had spent a sleepless night at a friend's house and she was scared that it would happen again. On the one occasion she had tried to spend the night out, she called her mom and dad and asked to be picked up early.

If your child is having trouble spending the night out, you may decide not to push the issue. Your child might simply need a few more months before giving it another try. However, if your child is one of the few in his age group who refuses to spend the night at a friend's house or won't attend sleep-over parties, you may decide it is time to intervene. Otherwise, your child may grow into a preteen or teenager who also refuses to attend sleep-away camp, misses school trips, and never visits relatives. Clever excuses run thin with friends after a while and the embarrassing truth can slip out.

IMAGINATION

Your child's mind is filled with scenes of him tossing and turning all night, getting scared, and missing you. Changing those scenes to positive ones is a first step to getting her away from home for the night.

1. Read books about sleeping away from home. *Ira Sleeps Over* by Bernard Waber is a great book about a little boy spending the night at his neighbor's house. Talk about why Ira wants to go home and how he solves his problem. A list of other appropriate books is found at the end of this section. As you read the stories, talk about how the children feel being away from home and what a good time they have being with a friend.

2. Write a story about sleeping away. Turn the tables this time. Have your child dictate a story about sleeping at a friend's house. If the story tends to the negative, encourage your child to add a happy ending. Along the way you may be able to identify many of your child's fears and counter them.

3. Pretend your child is spending the night away from home. Without ever leaving home, get ready for a night out. Pack everything she would take. Role-play saying goodbye as your child goes to another room in the house to sleep for the evening. Have your child and a sibling or friend camp out in another part of the house. Supply some treats and a video for entertainment to make this feel like a real spend-the-night party.

4. Lead your child through an imaginary evening away from home. As described in Chapter 3, after your child is relaxed and lying down with her eyes closed, begin to describe a night away from home. Describe a sequence of events like the one listed at the end of this section. Begin by having your child imagine that a good friend invites him to spend the night. Have your child imagine packing for the trip and specify exactly what he would take, including any security objects. Next, picture your child driving to the friend's home and meeting his friend at the door. Describe the friends as very excited to see each other and your son so happy he rushes off to play. Walk your child through the friend's home, describing all the fun things he will see and do. Have your child imagine that he is having such fun playing with his friend that when you leave he just gives you a quick hug and runs back to fun and games. Continue the evening with your child having a wonderful time partaking of yummy treats and later calling you to relate what a wonderful time he's having and say good night. When it's bedtime, describe how his friend's parents tuck him in and say good night. Have your child imagine himself falling asleep talking to his friend. Before he knows it, it is morning and time to go home. You can even throw in the suggestion that when you come to get him he wants to play longer. Repeat positive scenes like this over a number of weeks until your child's fear ratings indicate he can comfortably imagine himself spending the night with a friend.

INFORMATION

Children sometimes are anxious about spending the night because they don't have enough information or even have misconceptions about what might happen.

1. Provide a concept for distance and time. Your child wants to know where you are and the time frame he will be away. Unless the friend lives next door, a young child will have a very difficult time conceptualizing distance. You might only be a few blocks away, but your child has little awareness of how far that is. Instead, talk to him in terms of how long it takes to get to a friend's house. Explain that if he needs you, you can be there in less time than it takes to watch his favorite show, bathe, or eat an ice-cream cone.

The older child has a greater awareness of landmarks, streets, and routes as well as a better grasp of time. Help him draw a mental picture of where he will be in relationship to your home or other known landmarks such as his school or Grandma's house. Some children might like to make a map but keep it simple, only identifying major streets and places you visit often. Over time your child can put stars on the homes where he has spent the night.

2. Provide information about what you will be doing and how to get in touch with you. While you're thinking about what fun he will have, your child might be afraid that something could happen to you while he's away. Attempt to get your child to talk about his concerns and allay any fears you uncover. Your child might also be worried that he will miss something important. Put that concern to rest. Tell your child what you will be doing and where you will be. If you are going to go out, tuck a note with the telephone number of where you can be reached in his suitcase. Also assure your child that he may call you at any time during the evening, or prearrange a special time for one telephone call to say goodnight.

3. Assure your child of safety. Kids sometimes fear that where they will be spending the night might not be as safe as home or that a friend's parents might not be as accepting as his own. Before spending the night at a friend's house, it is best if your child has visited his friend during the daytime. If the two have played together previously, then your child will be familiar with the surroundings and will have met the child's family. If this is a new friend, playing together before spending the night out will provide an opportunity for your child to scout out the situation. Seeing that his friend's parents sleep down the hall and that there's a bathroom with a light close by will relieve some anxiety. Of course, knowing that the friend's parents are understanding and will be home for the evening is also helpful.

4. Help your child create a series of positive statements that he can repeat to himself to counter anxious feelings. If your child can read, write them on an index card he can carry in his pocket. If not, have him record them into a tape recorder and play them over and over to himself as he lies in his bed.

POSITIVE SELF-TALK ABOUT SPENDING THE NIGHT OUT

1. Mom and Dad are O.K.
2. I can call them whenever I want.
3. It only takes them five minutes to get here.
4. If I want to go home I can, even if it is later.
5. I really like playing with my friend.
6. My friend's parents are nice; they understand and will help me if I ask.
7. We will stay up late and when I wake up it will be morning.
8. _____

OBSERVATION

Although observing children in your own home is not the same thing, seeing that other children might feel a bit uncomfortable and how they handle it will reassure your child.

1. Invite friends to spend the night so that your child can observe how they handle being away from home. Be sure to have friends who have spent the night happily at other people's homes before coming to yours. You want your child to see a "happy camper," not one who gets homesick. Of course, it is all right if your visitor calls home, brings a security object, or asks that the light be left on. Seeing his friend handle a little anxiety will be reassuring to your child.

2. Talk to siblings and others. Older siblings, cousins, and close friends of the family can have a big impact on your child when they share how much fun they have spending the night out. If your older child or others were once afraid of spending the night out and got over it, have them relate their experiences. Hearing this can be very encouraging.

EXPOSURE

Design a series of experiences to help your child become accustomed to spending the night away from home. Depending on your child's age and the experiences he is comfortable with, you might begin with overnight stays with grandparents or other close friends and relatives with whom your child feels totally safe. From there you can work toward experiences with friends. Adapt the sequence of experiences at the end of this section to your child's particular concerns.

1. Make a list of people with whom your child might like to spend the night. Order the names from easiest situations to most feared.

FRIENDS TO VISIT/SPEND THE NIGHT WITH
(Easiest to Most Difficult)

1.
2.
3.
4.
5.

---

2. Take several steps to help your child prepare for the sleep-over.

- Before the big night, invite the friend to spend the night at your house several times. Having fun together at your house will create positive expectations about the repeat performance at the friend's home. Be sure to keep the kids busy and happily occupied during the stay. Seeing the children play together for an extended period will also alert you to any problems the duo might have.

- Share your child's fear with the friend's parents. Their understanding and help is essential to the success of this project. A number of children who fear spending the night out select the first house to stay at on the basis of how nice the other child's parents are. Once primed about the problem, the parents might plan to take a little extra time with the children, especially at bedtime, to make sure everyone is comfortable.

- Plan what your child will do should he not be able to fall asleep. A number of children are frightened of being awake in a strange place. Provide a flashlight, a book, and, perhaps, a cassette recorder with earphones. You can prerecord a bedtime story in your own voice or supply a commercially prepared tape for your child to enjoy. Also provide a tape of the relaxation exercises described in Chapter 2. Listening to the tape will relax your child so that he can fall asleep. Remind your child to use the other coping strategies to counter any anxious feelings he has.

3. Arrange a series of sleep-away experiences. Often, it takes a number of attempts for a child who is very frightened of spending the night away from home to make it through the night. It took Jennifer, for example, five tries. On each visit to her best friend's home, she made it a little later, but no one ever complained about her late night departures. Instead, because they all understood the problem, they praised the youngster for making it until 9:00 p.m., 10:00 p.m., 11:00 p.m., and midnight. Her parents even picked her up once at 2:00 a.m. before she made it through the night. The friends slept at each other's homes for several months and then Jennifer was willing to tackle spending the night at another friend's house. This time she made it through the night on the first try.

Arrange a similar set of experiences for your child. Begin with the list below, adding to the experiences based on your child's situation and feedback you get from her. Be sure to take fear readings at each stage and encourage your child to use all of her coping techniques, especially relaxation. Start by planning for your child to spend only part of the evening at a friend's home. On subsequent occasions encourage your child to stay later with the understanding that if she cannot make it the entire night, you will bring her home. Praise your child for each stay. When she finally makes it through the night, reward her with a spend-the-night party at your house or another logical reward.

SEQUENCE OF EXPERIENCES WITH SPENDING THE NIGHT

1. Have friends over to spend the night.
2. Visit friend's home for dinner.
3. Visit friend's home for dinner and a video afterward.
4. Visit friend's home for dinner and stay until bedtime.
5. Visit friend's home and go to bed there, staying as much of the night as possible.
6. Sleep at friend's home all night.

Books

Ira Sleeps Over. Bernard Waber. Boston: Houghton Mifflin, 1973. Ira has mixed feelings about his first night away from home and bringing his security doll along.

Lester's Overnight. Kay Chorao. New York: Dutton, 1977. This book deals with those times when a child finds it hard to spend a night away from home. All little children who have felt a little homesick will sympathize with Lester.

Spot Sleeps Over. Eric Hill. New York: Putnam, 1990. Spot the dog packs up and sleeps away from home for the first time.

FEAR OF OVERNIGHT CAMP

In many parts of the country attending overnight camp is considered a summer ritual. Parents believe they must get their children out of the city to experience "nature." Although some six-year-olds go to camp for a month or more, many overnight camps provide shorter stays for their younger campers. By the time a child is nine or ten, many of his friends will be attending camp for one-month sessions.

Eleven-year-old Keisha had always had trouble separating from her parents. She had finally been able to spend the night at her best friend's home. However, when the topic of going off to camp came up, she panicked. She wanted to go with her friends but her fears stopped her. It took a carefully planned program to get her over her fears.

When a child has difficulty separating from parents, the thought of attending sleep-away camp is inconceivable. Your child must be comfortable spending the night away from home before you can consider a stay at overnight camp. Even if your child has always enjoyed spending the night with family and friends, the first time he attends sleep-away camp is likely to be difficult for both of you. There are, however, many things that you can do to help prepare your child for the big day.

IMAGINATION

If you want your child's most positive dreams about camp to come true, work on his imagination.

1. Explore books that talk about camp in a positive way. Also request pamphlets and brochures from camps that you are considering. They always highlight kids having fun and all the exciting activities that they do at the camp. Peruse the materials together, talking about what the kids are doing, what a camp looks like, and what kinds of activities your child might enjoy.

2. Watch movies that include camp scenes. Choose movies that show the positive side of camping. If a friend's children are going to camp, ask them to make a home video when they take their children or pick them up. Many of the camps in your surrounding area hold information meetings during the winter months when they show films of the camp to entice children to attend. Attend several of these so that your child will have an opportunity to watch real campers in action.

3. Simulate a camping experience. Pretend you are the counselor and set up camp at home. While this is not exactly realistic, it will still be fun. From family-style meals where you can't tell your child what to eat to mail call, try out some of the well-known camp rituals to entice your child in the fun of sleep-away camp.

4. Lead your child through fantasy trips to camp. Draw on old memories of your days as a camper or counselor. When your child is in a relaxed state, begin describing various camp experiences. Start with the fun of going shopping for new camp gear. Have your child imagine the trip to camp. If you will be taking him, describe the sites you will see and all the conversations you have about camp. If your child will be riding the bus to camp, describe who will be on the bus, the songs the counselors will teach him, and where he will stop for lunch or a snack. Always picture your child as having a great time with new friends. Once at camp, describe the way the camp looks, all the great activities he will experience—archery, swimming, horseback, campfires. Have your child imagine having fun with his cabin mates and counselors. Picture your child climbing into his bunk and talking to his bunk mate until lights-out. Finally, have your child imagine the time going so fast that he is happy to see you on the last day of camp but very sad to say good-bye to all his new friends.

INFORMATION

The more your child knows about the camp, the better he is going to feel about it.

1. Find out everything you can about the camp. Review the brochures of camps she is specifically interested in. Ask children you know to share their memories and pictures from past sessions. If many children from your area attend the camp you've selected, the camp is likely to hold a presentation for prospective campers. Your child will learn a lot listening to the directors of the camp, watching the film or slide show, and being able to ask questions. This is the perfect opportunity for your child to get the lowdown on any rumors he's heard. If your child is hesitant to ask about the "midnight raids" that scare him, you pose the question.

2. Find a buddy. If your child can attend camp with a good friend, that will provide a lot of comfort. Also ask the camp for the names of several campers who have attended the camp previously and will be returning during the session your child attends. Talking to them can be very helpful, but avoid campers who tell horror stories about the food and staff.

Even if your child is going to camp with a friend, and especially if he is not, try to establish a penpal relationship with a cabin mate. This will be one more person your child knows at camp. You may also be able to prearrange a friendly bunkmate for your child by talking to the director.

Some camps assign "big brothers" and "big sisters" to the new campers. If a friend's older sibling is attending camp, he or she might also agree to be an unofficial big brother or sister to your child.

3. Identify where your child is going. Get out the map and pinpoint exactly where the camp is located. Talk about how long it will take to get there and the type of terrain your child will see. If the camp isn't too far and is open at other times of the year, take a Sunday ride to the facility. If your child is going to a camp nearby, knowing that you can be at camp in a few hours will reassure him.

Some camps have special precamp weekends that your family can attend to get the feel of the place. Your child might also feel more comfortable if you escort her to camp, help her get settled, and then say good-bye. Some parents do better, too!

4. Answer your child's questions. Your child is likely to have a lot of questions about everything from the bathrooms to the food. And the list will get longer as new questions come to your child's mind. Answer each question that comes your way.

5. Teach your child the skills he needs. If your child doesn't know how to make a bed, fold his clothes, or sweep a cabin, start teaching him how. There are probably countless things you haven't thought of—but your child will. Ask him.

6. Plan for contact. Many camps do not allow phone calls, so children are afraid they will not hear from their family. Do more than assure your child he will receive letters. Two weeks before your child goes to camp, send a postcard with a message like the one that follows to relatives and friends:

That way you will make sure your child receives letters. In addition, provide your child with preaddressed and stamped postcards and stationary to make sure you get mail, too. If you plan to write your child every day, explain to her that the mail isn't always predictable. Hint: Mail several letters to your child before he leaves for camp, so that your camper will have mail at the very first mail call.

7. Create a series of positive statements that your child can use to counter any anxiety he feels. Children get frightened for

---

Dear _____ :
I am attending Camp _____ for the first time from
(dates _____). I know I am going to have a great
time but I will miss everybody. Please send me some
mail. My address is
  Child's Name
  Camp Address
Thank you and I'll see you after camp.
                    Signature _____

---

a variety of reasons. Help your child write a series of positive statements that contradict the unrealistic fears he has.

POSITIVE SELF-TALK ABOUT CAMP

1. My counselors will be very nice and help me.
2. If I get sick there is a nurse at camp. If I need my
parents they can come get me.
3. I know several people at camp and I will make new
friends.
4. I can use my flashlight at night and the camp grounds
are safe.
5. If I feel homesick, I can talk to my my counselors
about it. This feeling is normal and they will help
me.
6. _____

OBSERVATION

If your child is going to camp, you've probably talked about it for
years. That's an important readiness step. So is watching the

departure and arrival of siblings, cousins, and friends
who attend camps.

1. Make contact with other campers. Make it a point to write to family members and friends who go off to camp. If other sessions begin before your child goes away, be an observer at the first send-off. Be sure to take your child's fear ratings so you'll know how much work you have to do. Also make sure your child knows that a little anxiety in this situation is perfectly normal.

2. Visit the camp in session. If you have an opportunity to visit the camp your child will attend, do. Nothing will help your child feel more prepared than having been there. See the staff in action and tour the grounds. Your child might even be able to meet his counselor and see his bunk. Stay for a meal so that your child can see how that works. If there are children that will be attending a double session, your child can make some new friends before he gets to camp.

EXPOSURE

Any child will be more comfortable attending overnight camp if he has had a variety of camping experiences previously. If you have decided to send your child to sleep-away camp, and he has never attended camp before, provide these experiences yourself. Work up to an overnight experience using the sequence of experiences that follow the end of this section.

1. Get used to day camp. Most children begin their camp life at day camp. In this day and age, there is a camp for everyone. Specialty camps abound. There are camps for sports, computers, art, gymnastics, and more. Generalized programs tend to introduce children to swimming, camping, nature studies, and sports in a well-rounded manner. Your child is sure to have some preferences, but the only way he'll know what he likes is by attending camp.

2. Have a cookout. Believe it or not, you help your child get ready for camp every time you have a picnic or cookout—even if you use a gas barbecue grill. Contending with bugs and a little dirt is part of camping.

3. Spend the night outside. If your child attends day camp, an overnight experience is usually built into the program. Sleeping outdoors is one aspect of camp, however, that frightens many children. As you work through the series of camping experiences that follows, be aware of your child's level of fear. Use his ratings as a guide to pace the activities. Begin by spending a day in the great outdoors. On another occasion pitch the tent and spend the night in the backyard. Pass the time by playing games and identifying the sounds of the neighborhood. When your child makes it through that experience comfortably, move on to a night out at a local park that has camping facilities. Build a campfire and cook out over an open stove. If you get to the point that your child loves sleeping under the stars, you are almost home free! Once he has gone on an overnight with his day camp or Scout troop he will be less concerned about what he might face at regular camp.

4. Plan a sleep-away experience. Before heading to camp and a lot of strangers, plan a visit to Grandma's or another close relative's home. When your child is able to look forward to spending the night at a friend's or relative's and has gotten used to the great outdoors, he'll be more ready to tackle overnight camp. If your child has trouble sleeping away from home, he will need many more experiences before he is ready for overnight camp. The section "Spending the Night Out" should be tackled first.

5. Attend shorter camp sessions. There's a lot of difference between a one-night stay in the woods and going away for two months. Begin with a one-week camp or a specialty program your child is looking forward to attending before enrolling in more extensive programs.

Books

The Berenstain Bears Go to Camp. Stan and Jan Berenstain. New York: Random House, 1982. Experience the Bears' adventures as they go to camp.

Elmo Goes to Day Camp. Linda Hayward. New York: Random House, 1990. Elmo is a little monster who lives on Sesame Street and has fun when he attends day camp.

Just Camping Out. Mercer Mayer. New York: Western Publishing, 1989. The characters sleep out in the backyard.

Pig Pig Goes to Camp. David McPhail. New York: Dutton, 1983. Pig Pig's camp experience is so happy in a silly way that it may change some reluctant day campers' views or at the very least amuse them.

SEQUENCE OF EXPERIENCES WITH OVERNIGHT CAMP

1. Attend day camp.
2. Attend a camp cookout in the evening.
3. Sleep out in the backyard.
4. Go camping for a night with family.
5. Attend a day camp with an overnight experience.
6. Attend a one-week overnight camp.
7. Attend longer overnight camps

6

ANIMAL AND INSECT FEARS

FEAR OF DOGS AND CATS

It seems natural that children should love dogs and cats. Most do and usually the animal reciprocates the feeling. Many a pet puts up with being dragged around and having its ears pulled—as long as a small family member is doing it.

Although most children treat these pets as cuddly friends, sometimes a child suddenly treats every canine or feline as a four-legged monster. Perhaps the child has been jumped on or scratched by an animal or frightened by a dog's bark or a cat's hiss. When Janet was three, she loved all four-legged animals. She'd laugh with glee as she tried to get a hand on a favorite pet. On an outing at the park, though, a Scottie snapped at her. After that, Janet realized that not all animals were friendly, yet she did not know how to discriminate which ones she could trust. So, all four-legged creatures became a threat.

If a child is afraid of an aardvark, it's not too hard to avoid the animal, but there are millions of dogs and cats in this country alone. Many children who are frightened of these animals avoid visiting friends who have them, but you can't do that for long. Your child is bound to come into contact with a dog or cat—around the next corner, at the playground, or a relative's house. When your child won't go to a party, visit a classmate, or play outside for fear of seeing a dog or cat, then his wariness of animals has escalated to a fear that must be confronted. Even if your child is only uncomfortable around the critters, you can use the suggestions to lower your child's anxiety.

IMAGINATION

Before your child is exposed to the real animal, she must become comfortable simply thinking about cats and dogs. Start the process by exposing her to pictures of dogs and cats.

1. Look at pictures. Look at picture books that favorably feature dogs and cats. Since they are not very realistic, your child will not be threatened by the "nice doggies" and "sweet kitties" he sees in the pictures. At this stage don't dwell too heavily on the animals. This should be a pleasant experience.

2. Read books. Read stories about dogs or cats, casually focusing attention on the pictures of the animals as you discuss the plot and other story details. In passing, talk about the dog's whiskers, whether his tail is wagging, and how friendly he looks. If the animal is the hero of the storyline, talk about how he helps people. For example, in *Clifford the Small Red Puppy* by Norman Bridwell, the dog grows to be bigger than a house. In subsequent books in this series, Clifford tries to do good deeds and gets into some funny situations as he helps out his mistress. As your child looks at the pictures, ask him what he likes about the dog, how he knows Clifford is friendly, and how the children in the story react to this huge dog.

Read lengthier stories with the older child. Popular animal books that center on characters such as Lassie and Benji offer heartwarming stories that show dogs in a positive light. Again, without giving it too much attention, discuss the ways the animals show their friendliness and love of people.

3. Look at photographs. Once your child is comfortable looking at artists' renderings of cats and dogs, turn her attention to pictures of real cats and dogs. Many elementary picture books use photographs of puppies and kittens to illustrate the story. Besides picture books, reference texts on animals are a natural source of pictures of the various breeds of dogs and cats and animals of various sizes.

Carefully preview any pictures of animals before showing them to your child. Exclude any shots that show animals in aggressive postures. If your child is especially frightened of big dogs or black cats, for example, avoid those pictures initially. Beginning with the friendliest-looking animals, spend some time looking at the pictures together. Carefully expose your child to a number of photos, beginning with the ones that you think will be the least anxiety-producing and moving to others. If you know your child doesn't mind kittens or is less fearful of poodles, begin with pictures of those animals.

At various points in the exercise, ask your child to rate her fear level using one of the techniques discussed in Chapter 2. If your child becomes too anxious, wind down the session and begin again at this point on the next occasion. Remain at this level of experience until your child is comfortable looking at photographs of all types of dogs or cats.

4. Post pictures of various breeds of dogs or cats on a bulletin board or the refrigerator so that your child sees them often. Take an afternoon to cut out pictures of dogs or cats from magazines. Make a collage of the photographs and post them in a location where it will be seen often. By frequently seeing the pictures your child will become more familiar and comfortable with the animal.

5. Watch television programs and movies. Look for ones that picture dogs or cats in a positive manner. *Benji* movies and reruns of *Lassie* are good viewing choices. Even dog food and cat food commercials can provide useful scenes. If you have a video tape recorder, record commercials and television shows that have pets as positive characters for additional viewing. Take fear readings as your child watches these shows often enough to become comfortable.

6. Pretend. With a young child you can have fun pretending to be either a dog or a cat. Get down on the floor and pretend that both of you are the species your child fears. Be playful. You might even have a mock dog or cat fight as long as it doesn't get too aggressive. Have your child take the role of a dog or cat trainer who puts you through your paces. Next reverse roles and "train" your child. These make-believe sessions can help your child feel more in control while having fun.

7. Imagine. Have your child relax and then lead her through a fantasy trip as explained in the coping section of this book. Have your child imagine herself petting the animal, playing at a home where there is a pet, and throwing a stick to a dog or playing with a ball with a kitty. Describe typical situations with animals, always picturing your child as enjoying the pet. Continue with scenes such as these until your child is comfortable imagining herself interacting with the animals.

INFORMATION
The next step is to arm the child with information about the species so that she better understands the animal's actions when she meets it in the flesh.

1. Check out books that explain the behavior of dogs and cats. If you are unfamiliar with the information, become knowledgeable. Next, using the pictures that she has looked at previously, explain to your child what the animal is doing in the various pictures. Discuss what a dog is communicating when it puts its ears up or wags its tail. Explain how animals play and the meaning of the sounds they make; talk about why dogs bark and why cats purr and hiss. Also identify stalking behaviors and how the animals protect themselves. Knowledge is power; the more facts your child knows about an animal's behavior, the more he will be able to predict what an animal will do in various situations. This leads to increased confidence.

If you sense that your child is becoming uncomfortable in any of these study sessions, end the discussion for the day. Pick up at the same spot when you begin again.

2. Watch videos. Watch the television listings for shows about cats or dogs. Check out videos from your library or rent videos about animal behavior and the various breeds you are dealing with. Be sure to preview the program before you watch it with your child. Avoid any programs that contain aggressive animals, even if the other information is good. Discuss with your child what you learned from watching the program.

3. Create positive statements. Use the information that you have learned to help your child create a list of positive statements she can repeat to herself about dogs or cats. Write these on cards or tape-record for a younger child. Listed below are some sample statements. Add to the list and create ones that are specific to your situation.

POSITIVE SELF-TALK ABOUT DOGS AND CATS

1. I have never been bitten.
2. That dog is barking and wagging his tail. I know that means he is saying "Hi".
3. Cats arch their backs and hiss to scare away someone they think is going to hurt them. I am not trying to hurt that cat and he knows it.
4. If I stand still, that dog won't chase me.
5. _____

OBSERVATION

Once your child is comfortable looking at pictures and photographs of dogs and cats and has learned about animal behavior, it is time to observe others interacting with the real animal. It is important, though, that your child never becomes too anxious, so move slowly. Your child's first experiences will not take her too close to the animal, but she will observe others interacting with cats or dogs.

1. Have your child observe you. From the safety of a window, have your child observe you interacting with the animal. If you feel your child needs support, ask another family member or friend to stay with her. As your child observes, play with the dog or cat. Of course, act confidently as you handle the animal. Pet the animal, scratch behind its ears, and pick it up. Afterward ask your child to rate her fear as she watched you playing with the pet. If she is too uncomfortable, repeat this experience on subsequent days until her anxiety decreases.

2. Have your child observe others. Arrange for your child to observe someone else playing with a cat or dog. This must be a positive experience so select both the owner and animal carefully. Initially, enlist the help of an adult or older child. Later, arrange for a child who is the same age as your child to play with an animal. This exercise should take place in your yard, since your child will be more comfortable in that setting. Sit with your child as she watches from a window inside the house For the child who is very frightened of dogs and cats, it will be important to have the animal on a leash— even at this distance. In addition, select a well-disciplined animal and an owner who can control his pet easily. Later experiences may be more casual, with a child or adult playing with an unleashed animal. Again, though, do everything possible to ensure against your child observing anything she might interpret as threatening.

3. Let your child observe outside. Once your child is comfortable observing from inside the house, it is time for her to come outside. Do not push her to come close to the animal, but designate a spot at a distance where she feels safe. Begin again by having her observe you playing with the leashed animal so that it cannot get away or inadvertently scare your child. On subsequent occasions, slacken the lead so the animal can run around a bit, but retain control. Have your child use her coping skills, including relaxation and positive self-statements. With each experience, have your child rate her fear as she observes you playing with the animal. If her ratings are high, pause or repeat the experience on another day.

EXPOSURE

Your child should be ready to begin to interact with the animal. It is critical that your child feel comfortable at each step of the way before progressing.

1. Approach the animal. Start at whatever distance your child feels comfortable. Take fear readings as she gets closer to an animal that you are holding or have on a leash. If your child's fear reading gets too high, have her stop and use her coping techniques until the anxiety drops. If it stays too high, suggest that your child back up. As her fear decreases, have her move one step closer to you and the animal. Continue until she is able to stand next to you. Be sure to keep the animal under control at all times and reassure your child that you will not let the animal jump on her.

2. Pet the animal. As you hold the animal, have your child move closer to you. Pet the animal yourself so it is calm. As you hold it, ask your child to select a spot and touch the animal. For example, your child may be more comfortable if the animal is facing away from her as she lightly touches it on the back. Ask your child to repeat this several times and to rate her fear each time. As long as her fear does not escalate, continue in this manner until your child builds her confidence so that she can lightly stroke the animal. With experience, your child's anxiety level should decrease so that over a series of sessions she becomes more and more comfortable petting this animal.

3. Walk the animal. Have your child practice walking this animal on a leash. Walk beside your child, demonstrating how to control the animal. It is not important that your child become an expert at walking a dog, but it is important that she feel comfortable walking near the animal.

4. Play with a leashed animal. Have your child play with the leashed animal. You will retain control of the leash as your child interacts with the animal. Begin by asking your child to pet the animal, then playfully scratch it behind the ears. Using a retractable leash, gradually increase the length of the leash and slacken it so the animal has more freedom. Prompt your child about how to deal confidently and assertively with the animal. Demonstrate how you have control of the animal and can pull it back at any time so that your child feels comfortable. Several times during the session, ask your child to rate her fear. If at any time her rating increases, repeat the experience until she feels comfortable. If her discomfort doesn't lessen, stop the session and begin at this point on another day.

5. Play with the animal in a confined space. Begin playing with the animal together. As your child continues to play, stand back so that you become an observer. Instruct your child as to how to reward the animal with a treat for coming when it is called. This will also give your child a break as the animal enjoys its treat. If the animal is trained, prompt it to do a trick such as shaking hands or sitting.

6. Visit a pet store. Many children who have been frightened by animals find this a difficult experience because there are so many animals in one space. Others are more comfortable because the animals are in a controlled setting. Take it slowly. Initially, view the animals through the storefront window. Before entering the store, make sure no animals are running freely through the aisles. When your child is comfortable, walk through the store, interacting with the animals as your child would like.

7. Introduce your child to other animals. Over a series of sessions, introduce your child to a number of animals of various sizes and species. Do this gradually. Choose your animals carefully so that your child's newly developed confidence isn't hurt. Select calm, friendly, small animals and move toward slightly larger, more frisky ones. Start each session with the animal on a leash or being held and work to the point that your child is playing more freely with the untethered animal.

8. Take a walk. Walk with your child through the neighborhood or a park where your child might observe and meet different animals. Don't permit any animal that frightens you to approach your child. Be sure to discuss with your child various animals that you see and how he feels about them. Gradually approach those animals that your child seems to feel comfortable with. To be safe, first approach the animal yourself to be sure that it is friendly. You can also act as a go-between controlling the animal until your child is able to touch it.

9. Meet animals unexpectedly. Your child must gain experience meeting unfamiliar dogs and cats. Of course, sometimes you will come upon an animal that you both agree it is best to avoid. Demonstrate to your child how to avoid contact with animals without running away. Show her how to safely walk away from a dog when you are playing in the neighborhood or at the park. If your child becomes frightened of an animal, show her how to stand still until the animal walks away. Remind your child about how to interact with animals. Prompt your child to use the coping skills and positive self-talk whenever she becomes anxious. Continue to introduce your child cautiously to new animals. As her fear subsides, she will naturally show more confidence. If at any time, she becomes apprehensive, remind her of the ways to safely interact with the animal and repeat the learning experiences as needed.

SEQUENCE OF EXPERIENCES WITH ANIMALS

1. Approach animal from distance. Stop at each step until fear goes down, then take another step closer.
2. Pet animal while parent holds it.
3. Walk the animal on a leash, first with parent then on own.
4. Play with animal on leash outdoors.
5. Play with animal on leash in enclosed space where it is harder to get away from animal.
6. Meet other dogs or cats.
7. Walk in park and see, then meet, strangers' dogs or cats.
8. Deal with places where child might have to deal with new animals on own.

Books

Animal Sounds. Aurelius Battaglia. New York: Western Publishing, 1981. A sturdy book of illustrations of animals with the sounds that they make.

Carl's Afternoon in the Park. Alexandra Day. New York: Farrar, Straus and Giroux, 1991. A picture book of dogs playing gently with children.

The Cat. Giovanna Mantegazza. New York: St. Martin's Press, 1991. All about a cat and his behavior and what it means. These colorful illustrations are ideal for young to middle-age children.

Clifford the Small Red Puppy. Norman Bridwell. New York: Scholastic, 1972. A book about a friendly larger-than-life dog named Clifford. Part of a popular series.

Eyewitness Books—Dog. Juliette Clutton-Brock. New York: Knopf, 1991. An excellent book with realistic pictures explaining everything you need to know about dogs of many breeds. This book discusses their history and behavior.

Know Your Cat. Bruce Fogle. New York: Dorling Kindersley, 1991. An owner's guide to cat behavior for older children.

Lassie, Come Home. Eric Knight. New York: Henry Holt & Co., 1940. This is an endearing story about a collie that is loved and cherished by a young boy.

101 Dalmatians. Dodie Smith. New York: Viking, 1956. The classic story about the dedication and love a family has for their dogs.

Pat the Cat. Edith Kunhardt. New York: Western Publishing, 1984. A wonderful book for the younger child that allows her to actually feel and experience a friendly cat.

Puppies Are Like That. Jan Pfloog. Random House, 1975. A picture book all about puppies with excellent illustrations that show what puppies do and how they play and act.

Salty Dog. Gloria Rand. New York: Henry Holt & Company, 1989. A story about the heroic acts of Salty.

See How They Grow—Puppy. Angela Royston. New York: Dutton, 1991. How puppies grow up, from birth to one year. Realistic pictures of puppies as babies.

Some Swell Pup: Or Are You Sure You Want a Dog? Maurice Sendak and Matthew Margolis. Toronto: Collins Publishers, 1976. A guide to raising a puppy in comic-strip form.

Spot's Birthday Party. Eric Hill. New York: Putnam, 1990. An "open-up" mini book about Spot's family celebrating his special day.

Where's Spot? Eric Hill. New York: Putnam, 1980. An "open-up" mini book available as a full-size book about the search for a small puppy named Spot.

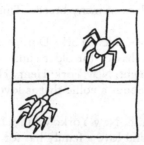

FEAR OF SPIDERS AND OTHER CRAWLING THINGS

The fact is, spiders and bugs give many of us the creeps. Just seeing the advertisements for the movie *Arachnophobia*, which means fear of spiders, was enough to scare millions of Americans. While one of your children might enjoy inhabiting the earth with all God's creatures, another may be terrified of anything that glides across the woodwork. Terry and Sandra were twins, but they were totally different in their response to bugs. Terry collected them. Sandra, however, was petrified of spiders. After being teased for years, she still recoiled in horror when she saw one. A fear of spiders and crawling creatures can prevent a child from playing outdoors, going to camp, or even relaxing indoors in a room where a spider has been spotted.

Your child might find insects fascinating when she gets to know them. At the very least, she will learn to act a little less like Little Miss Muffet. It will take time and patience to help your child overcome her fear. However, if you have a fear of bugs, it will be hard for you to help your child. Either overcome your own fear first or enlist the assistance of your spouse or a member of the family who is not disturbed by the creatures.

As you work through the program that follows, personalize the steps by substituting the particular crawler that frightens your child.

IMAGINATION

No matter how frightened your child is of insects, this is a good place to begin. Reintroduce your child to insects in a very positive way.

1. Read stories about spiders and insects. Besides Little Miss Muffet, there are a number of stories and poems that depict spiders and insects in a positive light. Think about Jiminy Cricket, Charlotte, or the Itsy Bitsy Spider. Check out the books that are listed at the end of this section and ask your local librarian to help you find others. Review each book before reading it with your child to make sure the bug is presented in a positive way that won't add to your child's fear.

2. Look at pictures. Begin with illustrations that humanize these creatures. *The Very Hungry Caterpillar* by Eric Carle is a wonderful book about a caterpillar who is hatched out of a tiny egg and eats his way through the book, becoming a beautiful butterfly in the end. Also review books that use photographs to tell the story. Talk about insects' interesting eyes, the number of legs they have, and other features that make them unique.

3. Play with toy bugs. Get plastic and rubber replicas of spiders for your child to play with. Play hide-and-seek or have a treasure hunt to search for the toy bugs under chairs and in corners where real insects might be found. Let your child and a friend search for them and see how many they can find. They may even get to the point that they tease each other with these plastic insects.

Besides playing with the toys, have your child compare the replicas with photographs of real insects. Spiders that hang by elastic cords and bounce up and down as well as mechanical ones that crawl help familiarize your child with the form of spiders and other crawling insects.

4. Lead your child through an imaginary experience with bugs. If your child has a good imagination, then just closing her eyes and imagining an insect is likely to produce anxiety. Using the techniques explained in the coping section of this book, help your child to relax. Begin to describe an imaginary scene in which your child visualizes very tiny insects that frighten her. The bugs may be dead or in a jar if that is what it takes to get a low fear reading. As her anxiety drops have her imagine the insects alive and closer to her. Picture your child playing outdoors with lightning bugs flying in the dark, having a picnic as the ants go marching by, and enjoying an afternoon playing in the park. Pause between scenes and relate a relaxing experience that is bug-free. End each fantasy trip on a positive note.

INFORMATION

Children find insects frightening because they look different and are hard to understand. Information about how insects live, what they eat, and how they interact with the rest of the environment will help your child appreciate these creatures.

1. Learn more about crawlers from books. First do a little reading yourself. Explain to your child the useful role that spiders play in the environment, especially in terms of controlling insects. Explain how the spider entraps its prey in its web. Your child will be reassured to hear that spiders do not naturally attack human beings or other mammals that are much larger than themselves. In fact, explain to your child how when a spider's web is tugged on by something that is obviously larger than an insect, the spider flees rather than attacks.

2. Look at photographs. Examine real pictures of spiders and other insects that frighten your child. The encyclopedia and other nonfiction works will be good sources for you. Study the features of these fascinating creatures that make them unique. Point out the symmetry of spiderwebs or the intricate wing structure of many flying insects.

3. Identify the insects. Look in your reference books for crawlers that you frequently see in your house or yard. Your child might call every crawler she sees a spider. Also she may think every spider is a black widow or some other poisonous bug. Help your child correctly identify the insects she sees.

4. View nature films. Films and documentaries offer an excellent way for your child to study insects in their natural habitat. Stay away from horror movies or films that emphasize poisonous spiders or rare dangerous insects. Select films that emphasize the habits and interaction patterns of these creatures. As you watch a film, summarize the information for your child. Help her to distinguish insects she should avoid and how to "live and let live" with the rest.

5. Visit the zoo or nature museum. Many zoos, nature centers, and museums have exhibits of spiders and insects. Visiting these provides an opportunity to reinforce what your child has learned. She can identify species and see the insects in action. Pay particular attention to the insects that frighten her the most.

6. Create a list of positive statements. Use the information you have learned to create a list of positive statements your child can repeat to herself to counter the fear of spiders and other crawlers.

POSITIVE SELF-TALK ABOUT INSECTS

1. Spiders and other crawlers eat bugs, not people.
2. These insects are scared of me because I am bigger than they are.
3. I can run faster than any spider or insect.
4. These little spiders and crawlers are harmless.
5. _____

OBSERVATION

*Your child sees bugs all the time, but she has probably avoided
watching them. Familiarity will make them less frightening.
Watching you and children her own age deal with crawlers will
increase your child's confidence.*

1. Watch you deal with crawlers. The easiest bugs to watch
are the ones that are found in and near your home. From a comfortable distance, have your child observe you studying an ant colony.
Since there are bound to be other insects around, interact with them
also. Over the next days and weeks, inform your child when you see
a spider, daddy longlegs, or other creature and let him see how you
deal with it.

2. Observe other children. Have your child watch as other
children interact with insects. An older sibling or another child who
is not afraid can show your child how to remove a bug from the
house safely or kill it. Seeing peers deal with crawlers without getting
frightened is one of the most effective ways to reduce your child's
anxiety. Resist the temptation to make comparisons about how
other children manage insects, and counsel the other children not to
tease or force the fearful youngster to do something he doesn't want
to do. As your child becomes more comfortable, encourage him to
move closer as he observes.

EXPOSURE

*We share the world with insects. Although your child doesn't have
to become a lover of insects, it will help her to feel more
comfortable in an environment full of bugs if she learns to*

approach them and sometimes to ignore them. As long as your child's anxiety level remains low, continue to work through the experiences. However, it is quite likely that an experience will have to be repeated on several occasions before your child becomes comfortable enough to confront a bug up close.

1. Observe an insect in a jar. Collect some insects or purchase some live insects at a bait and tackle shop. Put them in a jar that is sealed with a top, pierced with holes big enough to permit the bugs to breathe but not escape. Have your child observe the insects from a distance, slowly edging her way closer. At any point if your child's fear rating indicates she is becoming quite anxious, stop, help your child relax, and repeat the exercise. Over a number of practice sessions your child should be able to approach the jar and, perhaps, hold it.

2. Study a specimen close up. Place the specimen in a safe spot outside the jar so that your child can study it. Demonstrate how to take a pencil and gently move the insect so it can be seen from all sides. Repeat this activity until your child is comfortable "playing" with the specimens. As you work together, remind your child to use the coping skills and report fear ratings. Progress to closer encounters with the bug as her fear ratings drop.

3. Search for insects. Look around the house, garage, and other areas for bugs. Whether you and your child find any or not (you probably will) is not important. Fear is often an anticipatory response. If your child can participate comfortably in the search, that's great. Look for spiderwebs and other indications of insect life. You might also leave pieces of food on the sidewalk to attract bugs. When you come across a spiderweb, study it carefully. Determine whether it is newly spun or an old cobweb. Look for a live spider in the web and any trapped bugs.

If you discover a live spider, poke the web so that your child will see that the spider runs away when its web is disturbed. Continue to look for other insects to observe in the house and yard.

4. Teach your child how to rid an area of bugs safely. We have to live in a world with insects, but they don't have to live with you in your home. Discuss the appropriate way to remove a bug from a space. Let your child watch you brush away a cobweb, remove a bug from a room, or take steps to rid an area of insects. If your child is opposed to killing a bug, begin by teaching her to remove one from the house safely. In some ways this will be harder to do than killing the insect. Show your child how to pick up the insect on a piece of cardboard and move it outside. Have your child report her fear ratings at each step. It may take several sessions for her fear to subside enough to manage this feat.

You may believe it is important that your child learn to kill a bug. Although we'd like to think we are "one with nature," most of us have a very difficult time avoiding killing an insect at one time or another. Your child can step on it, use insecticide, or kill it with a broom. Find a suitable small insect that you think your child will be able to approach and kill with your help. If you choose to use insecticide, show your child how to spray the insect without getting any of the spray in her face.

To help your child kill a harmless bug, first let her observe you doing the deed. Over a period of days, your child should be able to do the same. Be patient and reinforce your child for any step she makes toward this ultimate goal. When your child can step on a bug, she has learned that these little creatures are not so frightening and that will keep her fear in check.

SEQUENCE OF EXPERIENCES WITH INSECTS AND SPIDERS

1. Look at bug in a jar from a distance.
2. Gradually get closer and closer to jar until able to hold it.
3. Use stick to touch dead bug in jar.
4. Use stick to touch live bug in jar.
5. Look at spiderwebs from a distance.
6. Look at spiderwebs up close.
7. Use stick to vibrate web and make spider move.
*8. Kill crawler with broom or spray.
*9. Step on a spider.

*Optional

Books

The Best Bug to Be. Dolores Johnson. New York: Macmillan, 1992. Kelly has to play a bumblebee in a school play. This book shows children dressing up in insect costumes and acting out the part.

Charlotte's Web. E. B. White. New York: Harper & Row, 1952. A story about friendship, love, life, and death. Young Wilbur, the pig, is saved from certain death by Charlotte, a very special spider.

How Many Bugs in a Box? David A. Carter. New York: Simon and Schuster, 1988. A pop-up counting book with fun interaction with bugs.

How Spider Stopped the Litterbugs. Robert Kraus. New York: Scholastic, 1991. A book about how the spider's plan saved the day at the picnic.

Keeping Minibeasts—Spiders. Chris Henwood. New York: Franklin Watts, 1988. A wonderful nature series with close-up photographs and simple text on how to care for small creatures. Series includes ants, beetles, etc.

Old Black Fly. Jim Aylesworth. New York: Henry Holt & Co., 1992. A story about a fly buzzin' around.

The Random House Book of 1001 Questions & Answers About Animals. Michelle Staple and Linda Gamlin. New York: Random House, 1990. An excellent book all about animals, with wonderful illustrations. Chock-full of facts about the curiosities of the animal kingdom, including spiders and insects.

Sam's Sandwich. David Pelham. New York: Dutton, 1990. Sam's sister wants a sandwich with everything on it. Leave it to brother Sam to give it to her plus some buggy little extras.

Start Exploring Insects. George S. Glenn, Jr. Philadelphia: Running Press, 1991. A fact-filled coloring book.

The Very Busy Spider. Eric Carle. New York: Philomel Books, 1984. A very friendly book for the younger child about a little spider.

The Very Quiet Cricket. Eric Carle. New York: Philomel Books 1990. A fabulous picture book all about the beauty of the insect world. The cricket actually chirps as you turn the last page. The special effects make this a wonderful book for children of all ages.

The World of Insects. Susanne Santoro Whayne. New York: Simon and Schuster, 1990. This book gives facts about insects. You'll learn how they live and what they eat. Realistic, beautiful illustrations make it very useful.

Worms Wiggle. David Pelham and Michael Foreman. New York: Simon and Schuster, 1988. Turning the pages "triggers" all the leaping, creeping, bouncing, pouncing, sliding, and gliding action. This book shows bugs, spiders, snakes, and more.

FEAR OF BEES AND WASPS

Most people don't like bees and wasps; a lot of us are afraid of them. Of course, most children neither understand these insects nor know how to safely interact with them. If your child has been stung or seen someone else stung, then she has even more reason to be frightened. If your child is allergic to bee stings, there is reason to be cautious. If you suspect such a reaction, check with your physician before continuing with desensitization.

Help your child get over his fear, retain a little healthy respect, and learn how to be around these insects safely by following these suggestions.

IMAGINATION

You can reintroduce your child to these insects in a safe and enjoyable way by looking at pictures, reading books, watching videos, and even using fantasy. She'll also have a chance to study these creatures in a way they would never stand still for in real life.

1. Read stories to your child that depict bees and other flying insects in a positive manner. Look at drawings and photographs of bees, wasps, and other flying insects in picture books. As you read the story, talk about the good characteristics of insects in the stories and the jobs these creatures have in nature.

2. Watch films and videos. Watch nature programs on television and check out or rent videos that show bees and other flying insects helping the environment. Help your child imagine what it would be like to be a bee flying around a beautiful garden. Again, talk about the important jobs these creatures have in nature.

3. Pretend. With very young children you can make a game out of pretending to be bees. Collect nectar from plants and do the "dance of the bees" to show other bees where the bee hive is. You can even make a pretend hive out of a blanket placed over a table and cuddle in it. Through your play explain to your child that as bees you would only sting someone who was about to hurt you or the hive.

4. Use your child's imagination. Have your child relax as explained in the coping section of this book. Lead her through a fantasy trip that includes her imagining herself playing next to pretty spring flowers. Gradually introduce bees and other flying insects flying around the garden. At first have the insects keep their distance. Take fear readings and if her rating goes up too much have the bees fly away. As your child gets use to the scenes, have the bees fly around her, but not harm her. End all imaginary trips happily.

INFORMATION

Bees and wasps are fascinating creatures. Your child sees them only as stingers on a body. Understanding the role of these insects in the environment and their special characteristics will help your child appreciate these creatures.

1. Look at pictures. Study the pictures of real bees, wasps, and other flying insects. Look for beautifully colored pictures of the different species. The encyclopedia and other reference texts will be good resources. Identify the different parts of these insects and explain the function of each. Focus on the amazing wing structure of flying insects and compare it to aircraft. Also look at the multifaceted eyes of the insects and talk about how things must appear to these creatures. This often fascinates kids so they focus less on the stinger.

2. Read about bee behavior. Study the behavior of insects such as these with your child. First focus on the contribution these insects make to the environment. Help your child understand how fascinating these creatures are. What is a queen bee? A worker bee? How do bees produce honey? Look at a wasp's nest and a beehive. These truly amazing aspects of insect society will provide a new perspective for your child. Gather information about how the insects communicate. Do bees really dance? How do they tell other members of their hive where flowers with nectar are? Finally discover why bees sting. Explain to your child that bees sting only to protect themselves or the hive. Talk about how many times your child has played outside and not been stung. Reiterate that if your child doesn't bother the bee, it probably won't bother him. How many people does he know who have actually been stung? How often do children play outside and not get stung?

3. Help your child create a list of positive statements to counter any negative thoughts she might have about bees and other insects that might sting. Put them on an index card or record them on a tape so she can practice these statements over and over.

POSITIVE SELF-TALK ABOUT BEES

1. Bees gather nectar to make honey. They sting only to protect themselves or the hive.
2. If I walk slowly a bee won't sting me.
3. I have played in this park before and never seen anyone get stung.
4. There are no beehives in my backyard.
5. _____

OBSERVATION

Your child does not need to become a bee handler to recognize where bees live and learn how to be around them.

1. Have your child observe your behavior around bees. As your child watches from a safe place, walk closer to an area where you see bees. Do nothing to purposely anger the bees, but do show your child that it is possible to be nearby without being hurt.

2. Have your child observe children playing outdoors. If your child has been avoiding outside play, have her watch a friend playing outdoors. With a window as a shield, your child should feel comfortable doing this, but remember to have her rate her anxiety level during the experience. When she is comfortable, have her observe a child safely standing in an area where she has seen bees and wasps before. Have your child talk with other children her age that are not as afraid of bees. Better yet, have your child talk to a peer who has been stung before and still plays outdoors. One little boy we know became much less worried about being stung when his best friend told him it hurt less than falling off his bike.

EXPOSURE

The last step in the process is for your child to go into situations where she might encounter bees, wasps, and other flying insects.

1. Stroll through the yard together. Without intentionally looking for bees and wasps, walk through an area where the insects might be. Ask your child to rate her fear level as she strolls along garden paths and open spaces.

2. Observe bees gathering nectar. The spring will be the best time for this activity. Together, approach a flower garden and watch the bees gathering honey, but do nothing to disturb them. Continue to watch the bees from a safe distance as they go about their jobs.

3. Play near an area with bees. Avoid hives but help your child define a reasonably safe distance from an area you have seen bees or wasps and watch their activity. Play catch or another game your child enjoys in this safe location. Continue to play as the bees do their thing in their space. Should a bee wander into your space, have your child stand still and use her coping skills until the bee flies off. Remind your child to continue to use her coping skills should she become anxious.

4. Continue to play outside. Make a list of locations that your child has avoided. One by one, cross them off the list as your child approaches the area and uses her coping skills to play naturally in the area. Praise and reward your child for playing outside and successfully managing her concerns about bees.

SEQUENCE OF EXPERIENCES WITH FLYING INSECTS

1. Play in a safe area in the yard.
2. Stroll closer to an area where there might be bees.
3. Observe bees gathering honey in the garden.
4. Play near the garden.
5. Play in various locations previously avoided.

Books

The Bee. Beth B. Norden. New York: Workman Publishing, 1991. Realistic large bee tells all about a bee. The bee is actually 3-D and larger than life.

The Best Bug to Be. Dolores Johnson. New York: Macmillan, 1992. Kelly
   has to play a bumblebee in a school play. The children dress up as their
   favorite bugs.
The Science Book. Sara Stein. New York: Workman Publishing, 1979. This
   book looks at the natural world and gives clear explanations about
   why creatures do what they do, including why bees dance.
The World of Insects. Susanne Santoro Whayne. New York: Simon and
   Schuster, 1990. Facts about insects, including bees. Learn how they
   live and what they eat. This book has beautiful, realistic illustrations.

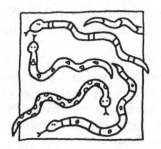

FEAR OF SNAKES

A fear of snakes is one of the most universal of all fears. In fact, there may be a biological basis for this fear. There is some evidence that the young of other species recoil at the image of snakes. However, most human children learn about snakes by watching the reaction of those around them. Infants and even toddlers don't share the adult aversion to these creatures, but one look at Mom or Dad screaming, "There's a snake—watch out!" and that's it for snakes.

Whether a fear of snakes is learned from others or not, once it develops, it usually does not go away. Cliff would not swim in the family pool after his Dad encountered a blacksnake when they were cleaning leaves out of the pool.

As you work with your child, take a deep breath and remember that getting over your own fear will contribute to your child's success. Your child may never want to own a pet snake or be a snake charmer, but if he is going to camp out, go hiking, swim in a lake, or play in the park, he'll need to overcome his fear of snakes. If your child shows a persistent fear of snakes that affects his enjoyment of the outdoors, use the following steps to desensitize him so he can deal with these creatures when he needs to.

IMAGINATION

The word "snake" probably conjures up all kinds of scary images in your child's mind. To develop more positive associations, try some of the following exercises.

1. Look at drawings and photographs of snakes. Begin with very stylized drawings of friendly-looking snakes. No fangs, please. Next, study nonthreatening photographs of various kinds of snakes. Again, avoid pictures of cobras with fangs and boas swallowing animals. Search for colorful pictures that show the beauty of snakes. Point out the intricate patterns of snake skin and tell your child how snakes use their skin as camouflage so they can avoid being killed by other animals. Younger children will enjoy the book *Hide and Snake* by Keith Baker. This author and artist reports that he used to be afraid of snakes until he painted this interactive hide-and-seek book, which camouflages snakes in a web of patterned objects.

2. Read children's books. Look for stories that have snakes as characters. Several of these are listed at the end of this section. Talk about how the snakes live and what they do.

3. Play with toy snakes. Purchase small plastic or rubber snakes. Beginning with the ones that are least realistic, encourage your child to hold the "slimy" things and play with the toys. Keep them in prominent places for several weeks so that your child becomes comfortable having them around.

INFORMATION

When your child is comfortable looking at drawings and playing with toy snakes, it's time to get the facts about snakes and correct any misconceptions he may have.

1. Read about snakes. Get the real scoop on snakes. You'll find lots of interesting facts in encyclopedias and other resources, including those listed at the end of the section. Take your child to the library so he can help select the books you will read together.

Gather information about snake habits, habitats, and benefits to the environment. Explain to your child how snakes are born, grow, and shed their skins every year. Distinguish poisonous and nonpoisonous snakes, and help your child recognize dangerous snakes. That means he is going to have to get used to seeing pictures of snakes with fangs and open mouths. If at any time your child becomes anxious and his fear ratings increase, stop, help your child relax, then repeat the experience. Continue at the same level for the next session.

2. Correct misconceptions. It's important for your child to understand that snakes bite people only in self-defense. They do not chase people for the purpose of biting them.

Find out what kinds of snakes live in your area. Over time you will help your child identify dangerous snakes in your locale and teach the correct response should she ever find such a creature. Explain to your child that the habitats of many snakes are gradually being destroyed by human development and that snakes tend to seek uninhabited areas. Armed with this information, your child will begin to realize that the likelihood of seeing a snake is less than she thinks.

3. Watch nature shows and documentaries about snakes. Attempt to preview any show in advance. If that is not possible, keep a hand on the remote control to prevent your child from viewing any frightening scenes. If, as you watch the scenes together, your child's fear measure become too high, pause until his fear decreases. Prompt your child to use the coping skills and relaxation exercises to counter anxiety.

4. Create a list of positive statements. Based on the information that you have learned, create a series of positive statements your child can repeat to himself to counter any negative thoughts about snakes. Add to the list given below based on your situation.

POSITIVE SELF-TALK ABOUT SNAKES

1. There are very few snakes around here because of all of the construction.
2. Snakes are more afraid of us than we are of them.
3. Snakes bite only if they think you are going to hurt them.
4. I can run much faster than a snake can crawl.
5. _____

OBSERVATION

To overcome his fear, your child must become acquainted with snakes. Simply observing snakes from a distance is the first step. Of course, if you have an aversion to snakes, you might want to work on your fear also.

1. Visit the zoo and pet stores. On this occasion, you will be watching other people look at snakes. If she happens to glance at a snake herself, that's fine. Don't force your child to get too close to the snake exhibits—even standing across the room from them is a good start. Without making any comparisons, talk about how comfortable the children who are studying the snakes appear to be. If you can arrange to be at the zoo or pet shop at feeding time, you may have an opportunity to watch a handler interacting with the snakes. Take fear readings and prompt your child to use the coping skills until she can comfortably be in the same location with the reptiles.

2. Watch children playing. List those places that your child has been afraid to go for fear that he might see a snake. From a safe distance, observe other children at play in the park, the yard, and wherever else your child has concerns. Point out how unlikely it is that any of these children will see or be bitten by a snake.

EXPOSURE

Arrange a sequence of experiences that permit your child to come into safe contact with snakes or situations where he might fear snakes could be.

1. Look at a dead snake. A nature center, a pet store, or even a science teacher at your local school may have such a specimen. Approaching even a dead snake is liable to be difficult for your child. Use his fear ratings as a guide to pace the experiences. First have your child look at a snake in a jar placed across the room. Over a number of sessions, your child should be able to move toward the jar and eventually hold it. Have your child turn the jar, studying the snake from every angle. Encourage him to slowly shake the jar so that the snake moves in the surrounding liquid, somewhat simulating the motions of a live snake.

2. Visit the reptile exhibit. Visit your local zoo so that your child can observe live snakes. At first your child may have to look at the snakes from a distance. Prompt your child to use the coping techniques to calm himself so that he can gradually move closer to the snake cages. Take fear readings to know how fast to progress. Although it's likely to take several practice sessions, your child should eventually be able to put his hand on the outside of the glass near a snake. Continue to observe the snakes until your child is comfortable. Remind your child that these snakes are probably larger and more diverse than the ones he would see in your locale. Utilize all the information the child has learned to identify the snakes and distinguish those that are poisonous and nonpoisonous. Repeat these exposure experiences, making each outing as much fun as possible.

3. Look for snakes outdoors. Now that your child is more knowledgeable about snakes and has been exposed to them in secure settings, go outdoors. Provide a sense of confidence as you look around your yard and in the woods for any signs of snake life such as old snake eggs or shed skins. Have your child rate his fear as you both explore the area. Even if you don't discover any signs of snakes, the experience is valuable because your child is using his new information and skills to cope with a feared animal. Remind your child to breathe slowly and to repeat his positive self-statements if he begins to feel anxious. If you do find a small garden snake, help use the pictures of snakes you collected to identify it as nonpoisonous. Consider keeping any nonpoisonous snake you find as a captive to study. If so, take good care of it and let it go after a few days. If not, show your child how the snake runs away from you since he is more scared of humans than you are of it.

4. Plan a camping experience. Before leaving, discuss what you will do on the trip and reiterate the snake facts you've learned that help your child feel safe. Talk about building a campfire to keeps snakes and animals from your campground. Take along a plastic liner to place under the tent or sleeping bag so that no snakes are able to invade your space. Your child might need to stay near you at first. Have him identify his fear level at various times during the trip. Over a period of hours and through different experiences your child should become more comfortable in settings where snakes might be sighted.

At some point during each camping trip, actively look for snakes. Finding none will reassure your child that few snakes are in the area. If you do find one, it provides an opportunity for your child to put his new skills into action.

5. Handle a harmless snake. This final step is optional. You and your child may never want to hold or touch a snake. If you do, find out when your local zoo or pet store is doing a demonstration of how to handle snakes. Often the snake keepers will demonstrate the proper way to hold harmless snakes and while doing so allow audience members to touch a reptile. Go first, then give your child a chance to touch the snake. If he chooses not to, it's no great loss. Simply watching you accomplish the feat will help lower his anxiety.

SEQUENCE OF EXPERIENCES WITH SNAKES

1. Look at pictures of snakes.
2. Play with toy snakes.
3. Look at videos of snakes.
4. Look at jar with a dead snake from a distance.
5. Get closer and closer to jar and then hold it. Swirl jar to see dead snake move.
6. From window or door, look at live snakes in glass cages at zoo or pet store.
7. Gradually get closer to cages and then touch glass.
8. Look for harmless garden snakes around the yard.
9. If you find a garden snake, either capture it or let it go.
10. Go on camping trip. Look for snakes. Take safety precautions so child knows no snake can get into the tent or sleeping bag.
11. Watch a snake handler at zoo or pet store.
12. Optional step: Touch snake that zookeeper or pet store employee is holding securely. If child wants to, allow him to hold it with supervision from the expert.

Books

Beware! These Animals Are Poison! Barbara Brenner. New York: Coward-McCann, 1980. A fascinating discussion of some hurtful creatures, including snakes. Clear text and detailed art.

The Day Jimmy's Boa Ate the Wash. Trinka Noble. New York: Dial, 1980. When Jimmy secretly brings his snake along, this turns out to be the field trip to end all field trips.

Hide and Snake. Keith Baker. New York: Harcourt Brace Jovanovich, 1991. A beautifully illustrated book about snakes and how they hide themselves.

Mrs. Peloki's Snake. Joanne Oppenheim. New York: Dodd Mead, 1980. Bedlam breaks out in the second grade when Kevin thinks he's discovered a snake in the boys' room.

The Random House Book of 1001 Questions & Answers About Animals. Michelle Staple and Linda Gamlin. New York: Random House, 1990. A wonderful book all about animals with excellent illustrations. Chockfull of facts about the curiosities of the animal kingdom, including snakes.

Snake. Mary Hoffman. New York: Scholastic, 1986. A book for young children that shows the snake in its natural surroundings and describes its life and struggle for survival.

A Snake-Lover's Diary. Barbara Brenner. New York: Harper & Row, 1970. Fictional diary with authentic photos has all the excitement of a true story. This book is very informative and accurate.

A Water Snake's Year. Doris Grove. New York: Macmillan, 1991. Information about the growth and habits of a water snake.

7

NATURE FEARS

FEAR OF THUNDERSTORMS

As soon as the first rumbles started, Denise would begin to worry. She'd cling to her mother during a thunderstorm. This response may not be unusual in your house, either. The heavens open up, thunder roars, lightning slashes across the sky, and your child runs to your side. Thunderstorms are powerful displays of the force of Mother Nature. Before infants and toddlers know what's happening, they reflexively startle and cry at the sound of thunder. As they experience more storms, learn about weather, and see the reactions of others, children can develop a fear of thunderstorms and other weather phenomena. Early-warning systems save many lives, but they also alert us to dangers that may never exist. News stories and live footage about lightning hitting people, tornado damage, and hurricane havoc impress upon us the power of these displays. It's a wonder that more children are not frightened by the weather.

If you have a weather-related fear, there's a good chance your child will develop the same fear. One mother always went to the basement of her home whenever a storm approached. Naturally her daughter SueAnn spent the time downstairs with her. Eventually the little girl previewed the weather reports and refused to go to school on days when bad weather was predicted. If you have fears of the weather, you should desensitize yourself first before trying to help your child. Otherwise, enlist the help of your spouse or a friend. Don't assume, though, that your child's fear will go away. Fear of the weather is easily reinforced and can persist through adolescence and adulthood.

IMAGINATION

Thunderstorms are frightening because of their power and the fact that we have no control over them. We do, however, maintain control over what we do during storms. Use your child's imagination to help her see herself surviving quite nicely through storms.

1. Read books that include stories about storms. Begin with stories that include weather as background rather than a plot element. Using books on the list at the end of this section and others you find, cuddle up together while reading a story that has a stormy setting. Initially, avoid stories about dangerous situations even when the characters survive. As you read, talk about how the characters continue to play and to work as it storms outside.

Next, read stories in which a storm is part of the plot. Many books use storms as themes; ask your local librarian to help you locate chapter books in which the main characters overcome any problems the storms might cause. Preview the books before reading them to your child. As you read together, discuss with your child the precautions the characters take and how they remain safe.

2. View television shows and movies that have storm scenes. Again, thunderstorms are popular plot elements. Carefully preview any scenes you select. At this point, select films like *Singin' in the Rain* in which rain and storms are part of the scenery rather than dramatic plot elements.

3. Pretend it's a rainy day. When it is sunny outside, playact a story about a stormy day. Pretend you are putting on rain gear and getting ready to go outside but it is raining so hard you decide to wait. Pretend to have a snack, but keep looking out the window to see how hard it is raining.

4. Lead your child through an imaginary storm. After doing the relaxation exercises together, lead your child through an imaginary rainy-day scene. Describe a light rain tapping on the windows building the scene until the wind is roaring and the rain is pouring. As the storm roars outside, have your child imagine himself playing a game, eating a snack, and generally enjoying some quiet time. Take your child's fear rating during the imaginary exercise. Repeat these sessions until he is comfortable simply imagining himself managing a storm quite happily.

INFORMATION

Help your child get the facts about storms. Thunderstorms are powerful forces that must be heeded. Having correct information will help your child to know when there is cause to be frightened.

1. Understand the phenomena. Gather information about storms and weather prediction. Your favorite television weatherman is likely to be a valuable resource. Many stations publish materials on storms for public use. In addition, there are numerous books written for various ages that will help you in your quest for information. Some of these are listed at the end of this section.

Discuss with your child the origin of thunder. Thunder is caused by the rapid expansion of air that is heated when lightning passes through it. There are many different sounds of thunder. The rumbling sound of thunder is caused by the part of the trunk of lightning that is farthest away; the sharp crackle of thunder occurs when lightning divides into many branches; and the loud crash of thunder is caused by the main trunk of lightning. Thunder always reaches us *after* lightning. By counting the seconds between the flash of light and the sound of thunder, you can tell how far away the storm is. If five seconds elapse between the lightning and the thunder, the storm is one mile away.

Gather facts about storms. Your child might be reassured to know that 50,000 thunderstorms occur throughout the world each day. That's 18,250,000 storms every year. Look at that number. Given that there are so many, relatively few cause any harm to people or property, and your child's chances of being hurt in a storm (as long as he acts wisely) are very slim.

Find out when most storms occur and how you can use cloud formations to predict storms. Discuss the purpose of the National Weather Service and how the information they transmit is intended to be used.

2. Make plans for severe storms. It is reasonable to have emergency procedures for severe storms. Your child will feel more comfortable knowing that the family is prepared for those occasions when there should be concern. Gather a flashlight and a battery-powered radio and place them in a specific location where they will be kept in case of a severe storm warning.

3. Make a list of positive statements your child can use to counter scary thoughts about storms. As you read through the materials help your child develop a list of reassuring facts about storms. These positive statements will become the basis of the positive self-talk he can use when he becomes frightened. For example, by counting the number of seconds between a lightning display and the clash of thunder, your child will be able to tell himself how far away the storm is.

POSITIVE SELF-TALK ABOUT THUNDERSTORMS

1. Lightning hits the highest place and I am safe inside.
2. Most storms do not cause any harm.
3. Storms pass very quickly. This storm will be over soon.
4. I saw the lightning _____ seconds before I heard the thunder, so it was _____ miles away.
5. _____

OBSERVATION

By watching you and others who are not afraid of storms, your child can become more relaxed about the weather so that he is more comfortable dealing with storms.

1. Watch your reactions to weather. Have your child watch how you react to watching the weather. When a weather alert comes on the television or weather radio, demonstrate how you listen, but don't panic. On a day where there is *distant* thunder and lightning, so that no one is placed in a dangerous setting, have your child watch from a window as you walk outside in the rain. If you have a video camera, also have someone videotape the scenes for later viewing.

2. Watch others, including siblings and peers, deal with weather. If others in the family, including siblings, are not afraid of weather, have your child observe how they react to lightning and thunder. Also point out how they react to weather reports and alerts without getting scared. Invite one of your child's nonfearful friends over so she can also model not being afraid. Monitor the situation and prevent any teasing. Don't compare your fearful child to the others. Point out that everyone's fears are different. Have your child talk to other children about how they feel about the weather.

EXPOSURE

Your child has watched simulations and viewed others contending with a storm; it is time for more direct experiences. Of course, you should do nothing that would place anyone in a dangerous situation. Storms are powerful phenomena that must be heeded. Your purpose in helping your child overcome her fear is to permit her to take proper action should a dangerous storm arise and to continue normal activities during safe but stormy weather. Use the hierarchy at the end of this section to provide a number of experiences to challenge your child's fear.

1. Mute the characteristics of the storm. Together, sit in a well-lit room, watching and listening to a storm. If your child's fear ratings are high, play some of her favorite music loud enough to block out most of the sound. When her fear ratings indicate she is comfortable, gradually turn down the music and dim the lights so that she can experience more of the storm. Next, gradually move toward the window. When your child is comfortable, turn off the lights and watch the storm from the window.

2. Plan special activities for storms. You can't predict when a storm will occur any better than the weatherman can, but you can be prepared. Get a snack and gather some rainy-day activities your child can use to distract herself during the next storm. A tape player with recorded stories and accompanying books, a game, cards, and an arts-and-crafts box are good possibilities. Have your child regularly report her fear levels. Repeat such plans for each storm until your child is able to pass the time more comfortably.

3. Continue normal activities during a storm. When a storm arises, permit your child to continue whatever she is doing, but come in the room with her. Slowly ease yourself out of the room by taking short breaks to use the restroom or get a drink of water. Have your child report her fear ratings. Continue these experiences until your child is able to remain alone while the storm rages outside. Remind your child to use her coping skills to reduce her anxiety when a storm arises.

SEQUENCES OF EXPERIENCES WITH STORMS

1. Listen to recordings of storms.
2. Listen to a real storm with loud music playing in background.
3. Listen to a real storm with very soft music playing.
4. Watch storm with lights out with parent.
5. Watch television or play a game as storm rages.
6. Continue normal activity during a storm with parent nearby.
7. Continue normal activity during a storm with parent out of room.

Books

Catch the Wind—All About Kites. Gail Gibbons. Boston: Little, Brown & Co., 1989. Have fun with the wind with kites.

Eyewitness Books—Weather. Brian Cosgrove, New York: Alfred A. Knopf, 1991. This book explains and answers questions about the weather, tornadoes, clouds, thunder, etc.

Flash, Crash, Rumble, and Roll. Franklyn M. Branley. New York: Harper & Row, 1985. This book focuses on why storms occur.

Forces of Nature. Anita Ganeri. New York: Western Publishing, 1991. How weather has shaped our world.

Thunderstorm. Mary Szilagyi. New York: Bradbury, 1985. A mother, a little girl, and their dog spend some time together during a storm.

Tornado Alert. Franklyn M. Branley. New York: HarperCollins, 1990. This book takes a close look at tornadoes.

The Weather Pop-up Book. Francis Wilson. New York: Simon and Schuster, 1987. An exciting and informative pop-up book that graphically explains in full color and three dimensions everything you'll want to know about weather.

What I Like. Catherine and Laurence Anholt. New York: G.P. Putnam's Sons, 1991. A book about children's likes and dislikes. Your child will see that other children feel the same way he does about things like thunder and lightning. Since this book suggests a variety of other dislikes, read it first.

The Wonderful Wizard of Oz. L. Frank Baum. Dorothy is whisked off to Oz when a tornado hits the Kansas farm. This classic tale is excellent for reading aloud to young children.

FEAR OF TORNADOES

The fierce winds of a tornado are the most violent found on earth. Often children who are frightened by tornadoes live in areas where they are likely to occur. Other children who simply see films of a tornado might become frightened by the whirling winds lifting up everything in its path. Anthony, a child whose house was severely damaged by a tornado that cut a swatch of destruction through his town, got over his fear after a few months, but a friend who lived outside the path of the same tornado was extremely anxious more than a year later.

When you live in a location where tornadoes are prone to occur, your child might react to the hours of televised weather warnings and tornado sightings that beep across the television set. As the tornado approaches the county you live in or even one hundreds of miles away, it's frightening to see repeated threats of a tornado. Your child, however, must be able to act wisely during an alert and enjoy her life the rest of the time. The desensitization experiences that follow are designed to help your child overcome irrational fear so that she maintains a healthy level of awareness.

IMAGINATION

*Use your child's imagination to help her combat an unreasonable
fear of tornadoes.*

1. Read books that include tornadoes in the plot. The classic story is, of course, *The Wizard of Oz* by L. Frank Baum. It's ironic that in the original version, Dorothy realizes she will be spinning in the air for a while, so she takes out a book to read. As you read various books about tornadoes, discuss the characters' reactions to the storm and how they manage the situation. Some children might share Dorothy's worries in *The Wizard of Oz* about Toto's safety. As you read the stories talk about ways to handle each of your child's concerns.

2. View pictures of tornadoes. Begin with still photographs of funnel clouds and work your way through documentaries and films that include footage of tornadoes. With each material, take fear measurements as your child studies the pictures. Continue each exercise until she can look at pictures with little anxiety.

3. Pretend you are in a tornado alert. Have your child imagine that a storm is brewing and the weather service issues a tornado warning. Pretend the lights go out and make your way around the house by flashlight. You might even go to a safe area of the house and have a snack. Remind your child to use her relaxation techniques and other coping skills as she pretends to hear the storm outside.

4. Lead your child through an imaginary tornado alert. At a time when your child is relaxed, begin to describe an imaginary evening when the wind begins to blow and storm clouds gather. Describe how the local weatherman breaks into your child's favorite television show with an important message. Continue to describe how your child becomes anxious when she hears there has been a tornado sighted in the next county and what the family does to prepare for the bad weather. Always describe your child as acting calmly and end the imaginary scene with the skies clearing and the weather alert called off.

INFORMATION

Most tornadoes last less than an hour, but the memory created lasts forever. By helping your child to understand when and how tornadoes arise, she will recognize periods when they are more likely to occur.

1. Gather information about tornadoes. Visit the library and request information from your local television weatherman or the National Weather Service. After reading the information, share pertinent facts with your child.

Tornadoes, also called twisters and cyclones, occur throughout the world, but most occur in the United States. A typical tornado travels a distance of about twenty miles at speeds from ten to twenty-five miles per hour. An unusually powerful storm may travel two hundred miles at speeds up to sixty miles per hour.

2. Provide information that helps your child distinguish when tornadoes might occur. Most tornadoes occur during the spring and early summer. About seven hundred tornadoes a year are reported; others occurring in sparsely populated areas might not be reported.

Help your child mark a map with the areas where tornadoes are likely to occur. Most tornadoes develop when a weather front passes through or in the late afternoon on hot, humid days. Large thunderclouds appear in the sky and thunder rumbles across the area. When a cloud becomes dark and dense so that rounded masses of cloud at the bottom begin to twist, it is possible for a tornado to develop. Often heavy rains and some hail accompany such a storm.

Also consider investigating books about the wind, the direction it takes across the earth, and how the wind propels the weather patterns. Also expose your child to the variety of ways that the wind can be a positive force.

3. Devise a safety plan. Your child will feel more confident if she knows how to act should a real storm arise. Some children might find it comforting to have a small weather radio nearby that he can listen to in the event the weather looks threatening. For other children who tend to dwell on the weather, this would not be a good idea.

Define the safest place in your home to go during a storm. Discuss what your child should do if a tornado warning is issued. Gather supplies for a safety kit should the lights go out or a true disaster occur. Furnish each family member with a flashlight, and practice getting to the safe room in the dark.

4. Help your child create a series of positive statements to counter her fears about tornadoes. Use the information your child has learned to contradict the fear-producing statements she makes to herself during a storm. For each negative thought, create a positive statement your child may repeat.

POSITIVE SELF-TALK ABOUT TORNADOES

1. If there is a tornado, there will be an alert.
2. I know where to go to be safe if there is a tornado coming.
3. There is a big difference between a thunderstorm and a tornado.
4. The weather is not right for tornadoes.
5. _____

OBSERVATION

Watching how others handle tornado alerts, warnings, and severe storms can help your child be less panicky.

1. Listen to weather reports together. Although this will initially increase anxiety, the more your child understands the weather report, the less likely he is to be unnecessarily alarmed. Watch newscasts together; explain the symbols on the weather map and the terminology the forecasters use. As your child becomes more comfortable, watch weather forecasts on days with more frightening weather. It is important to continue to listen to and watch weather reports until your child is able to watch accounts of tornadoes and even alerts without panic. Seeing how you react can be very helpful. Share your thoughts and explain that you feel safer knowing what is going on.

2. Observe others watching weather reports. As you watch the reports yourselves, also comment on other family members' reaction to the weatherman's forecast. What kinds of comments do they make? Do they appear frightened or anxious? Have your child ask them how fearful they are and compare it **mentally** with her own level of fear. Avoid any direct comparisons such as, "See, they're not frightened; why are you?"

EXPOSURE

Ideally, your child will never experience the power of a real tornado. The goal of the desensitization experience is to help your child identify occasions when fear is merited and she needs to act cautiously.

1. Watch films together. As you watch realistic films of storms, have your child imagine herself in the film. Play background sounds of real thunderstorms and tornadoes to enhance the effect. You may make your own audiotape of a thunderstorm, purchase a commercially produced recording, or borrow a sound-effects recording from your local library. Continue the experience until your child's fear is reduced to a comfortable level.

Remind your child to use the coping skills to reduce her anxiety level. Should she become very anxious, practice the relaxation exercises as the storm footage plays in the background. Take frequent fear ratings and continue to watch the scenes until your child's fear level subsides.

2. Practice weather safety actions on planned occasions. Tape-record a weather warning, or if you have a video camera, record a severe weather warning. It's possible your local television station has tapes of previous weather alerts that they will let you borrow when you explain your purpose. At a predetermined time, run the alert and have your child and the rest of the family role-play what they would do under those conditions. Repeat the experience until your child's fear ratings indicate that she is comfortable.

3. Role-play weather safety actions at unplanned times. Without warning your child, play the weather alert and have family members take appropriate action. Over the next weeks and months occasionally repeat such experiences until your child can respond without panic.

SEQUENCE OF EXPERIENCES WITH TORNADOES

1. Listen to the sounds of a storm and watch films on a pretty day.
2. Listen to the sounds of a storm and watch films on cloudy days.
3. Listen to the sounds of a storm and watch films on stormy days.
4. Follow safety procedures for planned drills.
5. Follow safety procedures for unplanned drills when the weather is good.
6. Follow safety procedures for unplanned drills during stormy weather.

Books

Catch the Wind—All About Kites. Gail Gibbons. Boston: Little, Brown, 1989. Have fun with the wind with kites.

Eyewitness Books—Weather. New York: Alfred A. Knopf, 1991. This book explains and answers questions about the weather, tornadoes, cloud formation, etc.

Forces of Nature. Anita Ganeri. New York: Western Publishing Company, Golden Book, 1991. How weather has shaped our world.

Tornado Alert. Franklyn M. Branley. New York: Harper Collins, 1990. This book takes a close look at learning about tornadoes.

The Wizard of Oz. L. Frank Baum. New York: Grosset & Dunlap, 1956. Dorothy is whisked off to Oz when a tornado hits the Kansas farm. This classic tale is excellent for reading aloud to young children.

FEAR OF EARTHQUAKES

Only someone who has felt an earthquake, or even a tremor, can truly relate to the lyric in the rock-and-roll song, "I feel the earth move under my feet." An earthquake, of course, is nothing to laugh at. Although the vast majority of earthquakes are not felt and do little damage, strong earthquakes do cause much damage and tragic loss of life.

Memories of earthquakes are imprinted on the minds of those who experience them or see them in the news. While all schools have fire drills, many schools also have intensive earthquake drills. Children who live in areas prone to quakes grow up surrounded by Richter scale readings, earthquake safety tips, and a full education about what to do if disaster hits. Many adults are equally fearful and naturally afraid to leave their children during warning times. All of this reinforces a child's fear.

After the most recent reports of California earthquakes, many children and adults developed phobic reactions. Every aftershock sent people into panic. Many children had difficulty sleeping, feared separating from their parents for months, and remained anxious for some time. The schools instituted counseling programs to see children through this difficult period so that their fears would not incubate and return.

You will not be able to erase all fears of earthquakes. Most children who have this fear have experienced one or live in an area where an earthquake might occur. Unfortunately, present technology cannot predict quakes effectively, so we cannot be totally prepared for these natural events. Therefore, it is doubly important to help a child feel comfortable in the situation so that she lives normally day to day and is able to act sensibly should tremors or worse occur.

IMAGINATION

Use your child's imagination as a positive force to help her work through her fear and be ready for possible occurrences.

1. Read books that have earthquakes as part of the plot. These are not easy to find for the young child. Any that you select should not be too graphic and should have happy endings.

2. View movies and television shows that have earthquakes. Preview anything you show your child in advance. Avoid viewing intense scenes of earthquakes that show people who are hurt. Taped footage of newscasts or sporting events during which tremors cause the cameras to sway but no damage is done are effective. Take frequent fear ratings as you watch the shows, repeating scenes until your child is able to watch them with little anxiety.

3. Imagine an earthquake. If your child has experienced an earthquake, she has strong memories of how she felt during it. As she lies in bed and pretends she is a asleep, shake the bed and describe a tremor. Ask your child to identify what she is experiencing so that she gains a sense of control in the situation. Have her talk about what she would do and where she would go. Continue the practice sessions until your child is comfortable talking about the situation.

INFORMATION

Earthquakes are particularly frightening because we feel a loss of control. Helping your child understand more about earthquakes will help her feel less frightened and more able to deal with the thought of an earthquake.

1. Gather information about earthquakes. Earthquakes are described as a shaking, rolling, or sudden shock of the earth's surface. According to the plate theory, the earth's surface is composed of twenty rigid plates that move slowly around each other. When the force of this movement becomes too great, the rocks rupture and shift, causing an earthquake. Most of these ruptures, or faults, lie below the earth's surface, although a few, like the San Andreas fault in California, can be seen. As you explain earthquakes to your child, be sure to distinguish earthquakes, tremors, and aftershocks.

There are many sources for information to describe earthquakes and where they are likely to occur. Begin by using an encyclopedia, reference texts, and other nonfiction sources appropriate to your child's level of understanding. A number of these are listed at the end of this section.

2. Identify where earthquakes are likely to occur. As many as one million earthquakes occur each year. Most of these are not felt and do little damage, because they occur underneath ocean surfaces. On a map locate where the major faults are. If your local paper has a weekly "Earth watch" map that highlights major environmental happenings around the world, use it to educate your child. If your child is old enough to understand it, explain the Richter scale and how the numbers indicate the strength of an earthquake. Your child will be reassured to learn that numerous shocks of the same severity she has experienced occur each week and cause little damage.

3. Educate your child about safety measures. Cities in earthquake-prone areas have strong building codes. If you live in these areas, show your child evidence of the measures to strengthen buildings and protect people from injury. Discuss the procedures your family will take in case of an earthquake. Designate a meeting area and other appropriate safety precautions to take if your family is home during a quake.

Your child is bound to worry about what to do if he is alone when a quake occurs. What is the safest place in the house or school? Who would be in charge? How would he reach his parents to know if they were all right? All of these questions should be dealt with in a preventive manner and answered so that your child feels more prepared.

4. Create an earthquake kit. Should you live in an earthquake-prone area, prepare for it by gathering supplies, including blankets, food for seventy-two hours, a first-aid kit, and other items you might need in the event of an earthquake.

5. Use the information to help your child create positive statements to counter fear-producing thoughts. Along the way you have increased your child's store of information and corrected any misconceptions she might have. Use these facts to develop statements that will increase your child's ability to cope with her fears.

POSITIVE SELF-TALK ABOUT EARTHQUAKES

1. Most earthquakes cause no damage.
2. This is probably a tremor and will end in a few seconds.
3. This building is reinforced and safe.
4. I know what to do in an earthquake.
5. _____

OBSERVATION

Most children who have a severe fear of earthquakes live in areas where strong earthquakes might occur; moreover, such children may have experienced a significant earthquake.

1. Be a model for your child. Stay calm during tremors and other activity. As with most behaviors, you are your child's best teacher. If you are calm and efficient in handling common tremors, your child is more likely to develop a calm attitude.

2. Observe and talk to other children. Have your child observe siblings and even peers during or after a tremor. Prompt your child to talk with those who seem to be handling things and yet who will still be willing to talk about feeling scared. Seeing that other children get scared but are able to talk about it while still handling things can be most helpful to your child.

EXPOSURE

We hope that neither you nor your child will ever experience a severe earthquake. Should you be caught in an earthquake, you both will be scared—and so will everyone else around you.
The goal of this section, then, is not to eradicate fear, but to help your child reach a comfort level that will permit her to act reasonably on a day-to-day basis and be able to act sensibly should an earthquake occur.

1. Prepare for earthquakes. Determine the area in your house that is most structurally sound to withstand the effects of an earthquake. Collect medical supplies, bottled water, food, and other supplies you would need in a natural disaster. Go to the designated safe area in your home. Take your child's fear ratings and continue the experience until your child is able to function in these circumstances with little anxiety.

2. During earthquake tremors, practice relaxation and other coping skills. When you are with your child during a tremor, move to a safe location and practice the coping skills. Repeat the positive phrases you have created and practice the relaxation skills. Take fear ratings so that your child can recognize the progress she has made.

Books

Forces of Nature. Anita Ganeri. New York: Western Publishing, 1991. This book is about how conditions of nature shaped our world.

The Magic School Bus Inside the Earth. Joanna Cole. New York: Scholastic, 1987. All aboard the magic school bus. Ms. Frizzle's class is off to the center of the earth. Along the way, the class learns many facts about the earth's crust and core including what causes earthquakes.

FEAR OF WATER

Water is the most common substance on earth. Three-quarters of the earth is covered with it. In fact, it's nearly impossible to get away from the stuff. So to be frightened of water is a big handicap for your child. It means that when all your child's friends are jumping in the pool, splashing water in their faces and having a wonderful time, your child is left on the sidelines. Worse than that, if a child is so frightened of the water that he is unable to swim, it is dangerous to play near water.

Many children naturally become accustomed to water through water play and bathing. At one point or another, most children will get upset about getting water in their eyes. Most of the time, if parents ignore the fuss, keep soap out of the child's eyes, and make getting wet fun, she will get over it. Some children become more frightened or have experiences in water that add to their fear. Andy never liked the water. From the time he was an infant, he cried during his bath. No matter how comfortable his mother tried to make him, he screamed. When he got older he would not go in the wading pool. Occasionally he ran through the sprinkler with his big sister. His parents were afraid he'd never get close enough to water to learn to swim. However, with great patience, a little help, and by spending many months playing with water, Andy eventually approached a pool and later learned to swim. Helping a child become more comfortable with water is a must.

IMAGINATION

Helping your child imagine herself having fun in the water is an important first step to overcoming her fear.

1. Read books with watery settings. A great deal of learning and fun occurs seaside, so it should be easy to take your child on an imaginative journey into the water by wading through books. Begin with books that focus on the characters having a pleasant time by the water. They might be playing on the sand near the shoreline, fishing in the lake, or splashing in a wading pool.

Many of your child's most beloved characters, from Big Bird to the Berenstain Bears, visit the pool or beach and love it. Older children will be enthralled by the stories of treasure hunts at sea and island adventures. A number of appropriate books are listed at the end of this article. Preview any book you select for your child to be certain there are no scary scenes with shark's fins skimming the ocean surface or children that drown.

2. Watch movies that involve the water. Search for movies that are set near the water, but avoid any scenes that might add to your child's fear. Together watch the scenes of people sitting beside the pool, playing volleyball on the shore, splashing and enjoying themselves at the pool, lake, and beach. Take your child's fear ratings. If you find that she is comfortable watching scenes like these you might include ocean scenes with stronger waves and surfers riding them.

3. Go for a pretend swim. With a young child, begin by pretending with your child that you are sunbathing by the pool. Pretend to get so hot you move over to the edge of the pool and dangle your feet in the water, then get in the pool and swim. Talk about how hot it is outside and how good the water feels.

4. Lead your child through an imaginary experience. As described in Chapter 2, have your child relax and then begin to describe a water scene that is unlikely to cause your child much discomfort. Take frequent fear measures to guide the pace as you begin to describe scenes that are more difficult for your child. For example, begin by picturing a scene of both of you sitting near the edge of a swimming pool. Next enter the pool by the steps at the shallow end of the pool. Have your child imagine herself gently splashing the water and getting her feet wet. Next, your story shifts to entering the pool further so that the water comes up to your child's waist. If your child is afraid of getting her face wet or going under water, slowly describe how she wets her face with her hands and dips into the water so her shoulders get wet. Finally picture her wetting her face and hair. Always describe your child as enjoying the experiences. Continue to use experiences with imagery until your child is comfortable imagining herself in the water.

INFORMATION

Water is really not a mystery; however, it is the most unique substance on earth. Having some facts about water and correcting any misconceptions she might have will help your child feel more comfortable.

1. Provide some helpful information about water. Begin with the basics. Your body is about two-thirds water. However, human beings are lighter than water, so that's why we can float. If you close your mouth while you are in water, it can't come in. Dogs and other animals can tread water without ever being taught. Explain to your child how he can float and tread water, too.

2. Do experiments with water. Find out what floats. Fill a sink with water and try floating a bar of soap, a glass, a rock, and so on. As your child begins to understand the concept of floating, explain that people can float also.

Provide a variety of opportunities for your child to play with water: Pour it from container to container, color it with food coloring, freeze and boil it, so that your child learns the many properties of water.

3. Teach your child water safety rules. Your child will feel more comfortable if he understands the kinds of behaviors that promote safety. When you discuss pool safety, if your child is old enough, elicit the information from him: Avoid running, you could slip and fall; never swim alone; always swim with an adult watching; never clown around by a pool; if you can't swim, wear an approved flotation device; never dive into unknown or shallow water.

4. Use all the above information to help your child create positive statements that will counter any anxious feelings he has. Your child has probably been repeating to herself many negative statements about water. Changing what she says to herself will help a child feel more confident.

POSITIVE SELF-TALK ABOUT WATER

1. I am lighter than water, so I can float.
2. A little water in my face cannot hurt.
3. Water is fun if I relax.
4. If I follow the rules I will be safe.
5. _____

OBSERVATION

Since water is something we cannot escape, children must contend with it often. Providing opportunities for your child to watch others playing in water will help ready her for more direct experiences.

1. Provide opportunities for your child to watch you in the water. Put on your bathing suit and let your child observe from the sidelines as you pour water on your face, get your hair wet, and lather up in the tub. Let your child direct where you pour the water next and let her pour some on you. If your child is not bothered by these activities, move to a pool area where she can observe you sitting on the edge of the pool, on the steps in the water, playing in shallow water, and swimming. Take your child's fear ratings, stopping at any point that she becomes very anxious. End the session and begin at that point on the next occasion.

2. Observe others swimming. There's not a safer place around a pool than next to the lifeguard. Discuss your goals with him and enlist his help. Have the lifeguard explain to your child how he keeps swimmers safe. Arrange for your child to sit in a comfortable spot next to the lifeguard as she watches children swimming in the water. Talk about how happy the kids look, what they are doing, and how well they are following the safety rules.

EXPOSURE
Your child is going to have to get wet to get over her fear of water. Plan a series of experiences to desensitize your child to the water. The sequence of experiences at the end of this section will help you tailor your sessions to your child's fear. Use your child's fear ratings as a guide to how long to remain with a particular kind of experience.

1. Begin with watery experiences in the house. If your child is scared of getting water on her face, you will begin by playing at the sink. Fill a sink with warm water and have your child wash her face. First have her use her hands. Next, add a washcloth. If having her face covered bothers her, have her keep a warm washcloth on her face for a few seconds. When she is comfortable with this action, move on to the tub. Have her splash water on her face, use a washcloth to wet her face, pour water over her head, and finally have the shower spray lightly over her head. Take your child's fear rating and repeat each experience until her fear subsides. It may take a number of sessions or even weeks for your child to decide the stuff isn't so bad.

2. Play outdoors with water. Before your child hits the pool or lake, get wet when there is no chance of drowning. Put on your bathing suits, get out the hose and run under waterfalls and through jump ropes of water. Let your child decide how fast or slowly she runs through the water. Continue to play until your child's rating and the look on her face show her comfort.

3. Plan a series of pool experiences. To give your child some privacy, begin these practice sessions at a private pool or at a time of day when there are few people bathing. If you have access to a heated pool, your child is likely to enjoy the experience more. If not, select a warm, sunny day to begin.

Using the complete list of experiences that follow this section, encourage your child to become accustomed to the water slowly. Begin by simply sitting on the edge of the pool. When she is comfortable, have her dangle her feet and then gently kick her legs in the pool. When your child's fear ratings indicate she is comfortable, have her sit in a wading pool. If no wading pool is available, have your child sit on a step in the shallow end of a regular pool or stand in very shallow water. Have her play with a few toys in the water. If your child remains very frightened, allow her to wear an approved flotation device during these practice sessions, but always make sure she can put her feet on the floor of the pool.

When your child is comfortable standing or sitting in shallow water, have her use her hands to wet her face, and then gently dribble water on herself. Have her pour water on your face and head and, when she is ready, do the same to herself. As your child becomes comfortable wetting her own face, demonstrate how to blow bubbles and suggest she give it a try. Encourage your child to wet her face and hair over the next few sessions until her fear ratings have lessened considerably. At that point, suggest that you pretend to be seals bobbing in the water and quickly duck under the water and up again. When your child has accomplished these feats, she is ready for swimming lessons.

4. Choose a swimming teacher carefully. Explain to anyone you select your child's previous difficulties with water. Many times children who have had a fear of water will do well in small group lessons where they model the other children's actions. However, unless you are certain the other children in the class are comfortable with the water and that the group is small enough so that the teacher will have plenty of time for your child, you may prefer that your child have private instruction.

5. Repeat the experiences at the beach or lake. Because your child is comfortable in a controlled watery environment such as a pool does not mean she will be comfortable in a lake or at the beach where she cannot see through the water. Repeat the same sequence of experiences at the lake or beach until your child is comfortable in those watery environs.

SEQUENCE OF EXPERIENCES WITH WATER

1. Put water on face.
2. Splash water on face.
3. Pour water over head.
4. Sit on edge of pool and dangle feet in water.
5. Sit on step in the shallow end of pool.
6. Stand in the water.
7. Get face wet.
8. Duck head under the water; blow bubbles.
9. Walk in the water.
10. Learn to float.

Books

Let's Go Swimming with Mr. Sillypants. M. K. Brown. New York: Crown, 1986. Mr. Sillypants signs up for swimming lessons.
The Magic School Bus at the Waterworks. Joanna Cole. New York: Scholastic, 1986. Another magic school bus trip, this time to the waterworks. Ms. Frizzle educates her students about water.

One Fish Two Fish Red Fish Blue Fish. Dr. Seuss. New York: Random House, 1960. Collection of verses about wild and zany fish at play and at rest in and out of the water.

Seashore Noisy Book. Margaret Wise Brown. New York: Harper & Row, 1939. If you haven't met Muffin, you've got a treat in store. Lots of interaction in this fun book.

Swimmy. Leo Lionni. New York: Pantheon, 1968. An exquisitely illustrated story of a little fish who not only looks different from other little fish, but thinks differently, too.

Water Is Wet. Penny Pollock. New York: Putnam, 1985. Simple text and candid black-and-white photographs show children using and exploring water in all its forms.

What's in the Deep. Alese and Morton Pechter. Washington, D.C.: Acropolis Books, 1991. A beautiful book about respecting and exploring the ocean.

8

TRANSPORTATION
FEARS

FEAR OF CARS

Most children love riding in the car. When your child was an infant you might have taken him for rides to lull him to sleep. As children grow older, they become aware of the dangers of the highway, but few develop a fear of automobiles until they have been in an accident. Chuck was five when he was a passenger in a car hit by another auto. His leg was broken in the accident and his mother was briefly hospitalized. Even after everyone healed, Chuck cringed when it was time to go somewhere in the car. Often he begged not to go. At first his parents let him stay home when they could. Quickly, though, they realized this was not a helpful solution to the problem.

A very sensitive child occasionally develops a fear of riding in cars because of something he has seen on a newscast or because a friend or relative has been in an accident. If your child is impressionable and affected by what he watches, you should restrict his viewing. The photographic images shown on television are very graphic and frightening even for adults. However, no matter how careful you are, if your child has a vivid imagination, something will stimulate it. One little girl was traumatized by playground accounts of a tractor-trailer rig running into several cars on the highway. The story scared the child so much that she was terrified when her family drove on the freeway for a trip.

IMAGINATION

A vivid imagination feeds a fear. Teaching your child how to control her fear and use it in a positive way is an important step in overcoming a fear.

1. Read books. It's hard to get anywhere without a car, so you will have no trouble finding books that have pictures of cars and plots that involve automobiles. In addition, there are a number of stories that have cars as characters. Use the books listed at the end of this section and others you find to help your child see an automobile in a positive light. As you read the stories, discuss why people need cars and how difficult it would be to get around without them.

2. Watch movies that involve automobiles. There are a number of movies that not only show children and families having fun in cars but actually give the cars personalities or magical properties. Classics like *The Love Bug* and *The Absent-minded Professor* that featured autos with unusual abilities are fun to watch and certainly provide a new point of view. As you watch a highway scene, count the number of cars you see. Point out how many people drive without accident each day.

3. Take pretend car trips. Place two chairs side by side and take a make-believe car trip. Assume the role of the driver and comment on what you might see on the way. Next, sit in your car while it is parked in the driveway and pretend you are taking a trip. We have worked with a number of children who overcame their fears simply by taking pretend trips in cars that go nowhere. As you "drive" along, take fear ratings; continue your trip until your child is comfortable.

4. Lead your child through an imaginary car ride. As described in Chapter 2, alternate relaxation and imagery exercises to desensitize a child to her fear. At the end of a relaxation session, begin to describe a scene that is unlikely to cause your child much discomfort. Take frequent fear measures to guide the pace as you begin to describe scenes that are more difficult for your child. For example, begin by having your child imagine a scene in which both of you are sitting in your car as you ride through the neighborhood. Next, the story shifts to a drive along a busier thoroughfare and onto the highway. If your child is afraid of large trucks, include some small trucks in your story and later large ones. End by imagining a trip on the interstate with large trucks passing you. If your child was in an accident or witnessed one, you would at some point include an accident scene. However, use your child's fear rating to guide the number of times you repeat similar experiences. If you discover that her fear remains intense you may need professional help to deal with such images. Always end your imaginary sessions with positive images that make your child feel safe.

INFORMATION

How cars work remains a mystery to most children—and many adults. Many children know very little about how a driver makes a car stop and go. Nor do they understand the rules of the road or the meaning of traffic signs. In fact, aside from the seat belts, most passengers know little about the safety features manufacturers build into their cars. With such little information, it's a wonder any child trusts that big piece of machinery. Even though your child cannot drive, understanding a little bit about how a car works will help him feel less helpless.

1. Read about cars. Gather information about how cars are built and how they work. Depending on how frightened your child is, simply looking at illustrations of cars in auto-repair manuals might be difficult. Your local library as well as your friendly mechanic or car dealer should be good sources of information. Several additional resources are listed below.

2. Build a model car. A fun way to build a positive association with automobiles is to build one. Depending on how much you both enjoy the endeavor, begin with snap-together models and work your way to more elaborate ones.

3. Take your child on a tour of your own car. Look under the hood, point out where the transmission is, and identify other parts of the motor you have studied previously. Use the dipstick to measure the oil and be sure to check the water while you are at it. Show your child how the brakes work and point out the emergency brake and the brake lights on the back of the car. For some children knowing that your car has two sets of brakes increases the feeling of security.

4. Educate your child about the rules of the road. Take a walk along a busy street. When you reach an intersection, point out how the light not only helps pedestrians, but also directs drivers. Discuss the meaning of various road signs you see and talk about how drivers must learn all the driving rules before being issued a driver's license. Take along a small composition book so that your child can make drawings of the traffic signs and become acquainted with them.

5. Identify the safety features in the car. Show your child the proper way to use a safety belt. Demonstrate how taut it becomes when sudden pressure is applied to the belt. If your car has air bags, reinforced side beams, roll bars, or other features to protect the passengers, also identify those.

6. Create a series of positive statements about cars that your child can repeat to himself to counter anxiety. Using the information you have collected, help your child construct a countering statement for each of his car fears.

POSITIVE SELF-TALK ABOUT CARS

1. Drivers must learn the safety rules to get a driver's license.
2. Most drivers drive every day without having an accident.
3. Cars are the safest way to travel.
4. This car has very strong brakes and many safety features.
5. The car is not going very fast; the driver has plenty of time to stop.

OBSERVATION

For most children the car is a source of fun and sometimes great joy. Use every opportunity you find to promote a positive association with automobiles. As you work through the experiences, take frequent fear ratings to indicate how long you need to stay with each kind of experience.

1. Introduce your child to friends who adore cars. If you have a friend who is a car enthusiast, let him show off his car to your child. Don't push her to take a ride in the car, but if your friend offers and your child accepts, let her go.

2. Watch others in cars. Sit along a parkway where you can comfortably watch a number of cars go past. Talk to your child about what she sees. How do people look? Do they look scared? What are they doing in the cars? Avoid making any comparisons between your child's behavior and that of other children you see. Simply state facts and accentuate how happy the riders look.

Play a game. Make up stories about the people you see in the cars and where they are going. For example, if you see a station wagon loaded with luggage, you might guess that the people are going to the beach or the mountains. Talk about the fun they will have and how you will have fun on the next trip you take.

3. Watch a sibling or friend take a ride. Have a sibling or a friend your child's age take a ride around the neighborhood in the family car. Watch the child get into the car and then give a blow-by-blow description of the trip. Repeat the experience until your child can comfortably watch the other child and even pretend to take his place in the car.

EXPOSURE

For exposure you will arrange a series of experiences in the car to complete the desensitization process. There should always be a licensed driver in the car with your child. Be sure your child wears her seat belt and drive slower than the speed limit, since speed is likely to be a factor in your child's fear.

Begin with experiences during which your child is completely comfortable and work your way up to experiences that make your child very uncomfortable. Take frequent fear ratings as you work your way through the series of experiences, repeating experiences at a particular level until your child's fear rating indicates she is comfortable. Prompt your child to use her relaxation skills and other coping techniques. A complete hierarchy of suggested experiences is provided at the end of this section.

1. Begin by sitting in a parked car. Have your child sit in the back seat of a car parked in your driveway. You may play music or pass the time with a game until your child is comfortable sitting in the car. Turn on the motor and repeat the experience until your child's fear rating indicates she is comfortable. As you sit in the car, take your child on a pretend trip, talking about the route you would take and what you would see.

2. Sit in a moving car. Assuring your child that you will not leave your yard, drive the car up and down your driveway. Again play music. Bring along a few of your child's favorite cassette tapes and distract her with conversation. Repeat the experience until her ratings are in a comfortable range.

3. Take short trips. With your child safely belted in the backseat, drive around your neighborhood or on quiet streets. Take short five- or ten-minute drives, diverting your child's attention by pointing out sites or playing a game. When your child's fear ratings indicate she is comfortable with these experiences, begin with short drives in more heavily trafficked areas. When your child's fears subside, move to experiences on the highway.

4. Have your child sit in the front seat and in more crowded cars. Some children are more frightened sitting in one part of the car than another or become more anxious when sitting between passengers. Once your child is comfortable with driving alone, have him sit in the front seat and then add additional passengers one at a time until his fear ratings indicate he is comfortable riding in a crowded car.

5. Continue with a series of experiences to help your child feel comfortable riding in the car. Now move your child to the backseat. Continually take fear measurements and proceed to a new experience only when your child is comfortable. With your child sitting in the back seat of a car, drive down quiet streets, and then busy ones. When your child's fear ratings are below five, try an interstate. Repeat the same sequence of experiences with your child sitting in the front seat of the car. You might also play your child's favorite music, play a game during the ride, and talk about what you see as you drive along to help your child feel more comfortable.

6. Plan longer car rides. As your child progresses, take longer car rides. Bring along games and books to keep your child busy. An idle mind in the car easily remembers old fears or creates new ones. A cassette and earphones can be a major aid to countering fear. As you drive, encourage your child to tell you anything that bothers her and remind her to use the coping skills to counter anxious thoughts and feelings.

Praise and reward your child for progress at each step of the way. It will also help if you include among your journeys trips to places your child wants to go. A surprise at the end of a ride can increase your child's motivation to overcome his fear.

Books

The ABC of Cars and Trucks. Anne Alexander. New York: Doubleday, 1971. This is an excellent book noted for clear, colorful pictures.

Amazing Cars. Trevor Lord. New York: Alfred A. Knopf, 1992. This book is a close-up look at photos of cars in amazing detail.

Baby Strawberry Book of Cars, Trucks, Trains, and Planes. Illustrated by Lawrence Di Fiori. New York: McGraw-Hill. Sturdy cardboard book with almost no text, but lively double-page spreads.

Cars and Trucks and Things That Go. Richard Scarry. New York: Western Publishing, 1974. An oversized book full of action, little dramas, and tons of details.

The Little Auto. Lois Lenski. New York: Walck, 1934. This is a small book with simple stories and pictures.

Mr. Gumpy's Motor Car. John Burningham. New York: Crowell, 1976. Mr. Gumpy takes all the animals for a zany ride.

SEQUENCE OF EXPERIENCES WITH AUTOMOBILES

1. Sit in the backseat of a parked car.
2. Sit in the backseat with the motor running.
3. Sit in the backseat of a car driving up and down a driveway.
4. Sit in the backseat of a car for short drives through the neighborhood.
5. Sit in the backseat of a car for short drives through busy streets.
6. Sit in the backseat of a car for a short drive on the interstate.
7. Sit in the front seat of a car for #1–6.
8. Sit in the backseat of a car with two other people for a series of experiences. Depending on your child's fear rating, work through a hierarchy similar to #1–7.

My *Lift-the-Flap Car Book*. Angela Royston and Colin King. New York: G. P. Putnam's Sons, 1991. Lift the flaps and this book lets your child operate the car and learn all about it. Your child will interact with every aspect, including lifting the hood and stepping on the brakes.

The Wheels on the Bus. Paul Zelinsky. New York: Dutton, 1990. The traditional song adapted and illustrated with parts of the bus that move.

FEARS OF TRAINS, SUBWAYS, AND BUSES

Trains, subways, and buses have several things in common. They are big, fast, and often very crowded vehicles. They make noises, sway suddenly, and sometimes go in dark tunnels or soar above ground. Many children love riding on trains, subways, and buses. Others don't. A child who is claustrophobic might be scared of getting stuck in a crowd. Other children feel a loss of control and fear being in the dark or going over bridges. If a child is scared of strangers, these moving boxes are full of them. And finally, although thousands of buses, train and subway cars move people safely daily, when there is an accident it haunts the airwaves for days.

In most of America's big cities, it is difficult to get around if you are afraid to ride on public transportation. Use the exercises in the sections that follow to help your child overcome his particular fear. Although trains are most often used in the examples, the experiences can be adapted easily for other forms of public transportation.

IMAGINATION
Familiarize your child with buses, trains, and subways before he has to contend with the real thing.

1. Read books that depict trains, subways, and buses in positive ways. *The Little Engine That Could* by Watty Piper is a perfect example of a story that shows a train in a positive way. In fact, the little engine sets a great example for the role of positive thinking in overcoming an obstacle. Talk with your child about the positive aspects of each mode of transportation. Discuss how the passengers look and where they might be going. Have your child imagine he is a character in the book riding on the train, bus, or subway.

2. View movies and shows that involve trains, subways, or buses. Build positive feelings about these modes of transportation by watching characters safely ride on them. Preview any films that you select to rule out any scenes of accidents or criminal acts.

3. Play make-believe. Children love to pretend. Using sets of model trains and buses, have your child imagine he is a conductor or driver. If you know someone who has an electric train, arrange to play with it.

4. Use your child's imagination. When your child is relaxed, begin to describe a ride on a train (or bus or subway). Lead your child through the station and onto the train. Picture friendly strangers who smile when your child passes and a calm enjoyable ride to a fun destination. Have your child imagine the swaying of the cars as the vehicle moves along, the noises he might hear, and the sights outside the windows. As you work your way through the imaginary journey, always depict your child as enjoying the ride. At various points during your imaginary tour, have your child report his fear levels and prompt him to use his positive coping skills to remain calm.

INFORMATION

Trains and subways are very different from buses and cars. You cannot easily see the driver, nor do you have any sense of control. Understanding how these modes of transportation operate will help your child feel more comfortable.

1. Gather information about the mode of transportation.
Using the encyclopedia and other reference texts, gather facts about trains, subways, and buses. Several suggested sources are listed at the end of this section.

Trains have a long history and played an important role in America's growth. Discuss the transition from steam locomotives to electric trains and the newer forms of trains, subways. Help your child understand where the operator sits and how each driver or conductor knows where to go.

2. Study diagrams, pictures, and models of the vehicles.
Familiarize your child with the parts of these vehicles: where the conductor sits, the exits, and the safety features. Look at pictures in books of these vehicles and note how the designs have changed over the years. If there is a local museum that houses older versions of trains, visit it.

3. Create a series of positive statements your child can use to counteract any anxiety he feels when riding in these vehicles. Talk about the facts your child has learned about modes of transportation. Help him write a positive statement for each negative thought he might have. It might be helpful to have an older child write these positive statements on a 3" × 5" card so he can practice them on trips.

POSITIVE SELF-TALK ABOUT TRAINS, BUSES, AND SUBWAYS

1. The driver of this vehicle is especially trained and licensed to drive this train [subway, bus].
2. This train is safely ridden by thousands people each year.
3. I will be able to reach where I am going safely and quickly so I can have fun.
4. The train is fun to ride. This is really neat.
5. _____

OBSERVATION

Before your child must contend with the vehicle, let him get used to seeing strangers and family members taking a ride.

1. Find a comfortable spot where your child can safely watch other people getting off and on the train. The train station is ideal because it provides an opportunity for your child to visit the location where he would also be leaving and arriving. As you watch the passengers, discuss with your child how they look and where they might be going. Have your child report his fear level as you sit in the station. Repeat the experience until your child is comfortable.

2. Watch other family members take a ride. As your child watches his friends or family get on the vehicle and then return, have him relate how he feels and suggest what the rider might be doing and feeling.

EXPOSURE

To overcome his fear, your child must meet it directly. With the bus and subway your child will be able to take a number of short rides and even get on and off the cars in order to overcome his fear. However, unless you can make other arrangements, he must take a complete ride on the train in order to have an experience. He will not be able to get off the train halfway through the trip. In the following discussion we suggest a series of experiences that will help your child overcome his fear.

As you work through the experiences, use your child's fear ratings to gauge how long to remain with an experience before moving to the next step. If your child's fear ratings are five or greater or if your child shows signs of anxiety, repeat the experience until it subsides. If you find that your child's fear is very strong and you do not see it decreasing with experience, you may need additional help from a trained professional to support this effort.

1. Plan a pretend trip. Arrange with Amtrak or your local rapid transit authority to have your child simply sit on a train, subway car, or bus. As your child enters the train and makes his way down the aisle to his seat, remind him to use his positive coping skills to remain calm. Pretend you are taking a trip across the state or to another part of the city. Describe the scenes outside your window and what the people on the vehicle are doing. Continue with the experience until your child's fear measurement is below five.

2. If your child is frightened of subways or buses, plan a series of experiences to help her become accustomed to the transportation. Use the sequence of experiences listed at the end of the article to help you plan appropriately. Begin with shorter trips on uncrowded vehicles. Permit your child to sit in a location that she finds acceptable. For example, you might begin by sitting in a seat on the aisle near an exit and work your way to the back of the vehicle. Initially, stay on the vehicle a short time, getting off at the first station. Over time, build to the point your child is able to remain on a crowded vehicle for longer periods of time.

For longer trips, suggest that your child take a toy or book to pass the time. Some children might enjoy listening to music. Remind your child to use her relaxation skills and other coping strategies to counter any anxiety she feels.

3. Plan a train trip. Begin by planning a short trip to an enjoyable destination. Have your child go with you to pick up the tickets. As you pack for the trip, also have your child select several toys or activities to take along on the trip.

Get to the train station early. Watch the other passengers arriving and talk about how they appear to feel about the trip. Arrange for your child to board the train before the bulk of the passengers. Once your child is situated, suggest he walk around the car so he feels less trapped.

As the trip begins, identify the sounds that you hear about the train. Identify the personnel and what they do. If your child begins to feel anxious, lead him through the relaxation exercises. As you approach your destination remind your child of the whine of the brakes when the train comes to a stop and how his body will feel when it is pushed into the seat as the trains roars into the station. Praise your child for a successful train ride and begin planning your next trip.

SEQUENCE OF EXPERIENCES WITH BUSES, OR SUBWAYS

1. Sit on an uncrowded bus or subway car.
2. Ride one stop on an uncrowded vehicle.
3. Ride additional stops until a destination is reached.
4. Take a round-trip ride.
5. Make the entire sequence of trips on a crowded bus or subway during rush hour.

Books

Baby Strawberry Book of Cars, Trucks, Trains, and Planes. Illustrated by Lawrence Di Fiori. New York: McGraw-Hill. Sturdy cardboard book with lots of vehicles for viewing.

Freight Train. Donald Crews. New York: Greenwillow, 1982. True-color illustrations of a freight train in action.

The Little Engine That Could. Watty Piper. New York: Platt & Munk, 1930. One of the all-time favorite books of American children. This is the story of the little engine that thought it could help deliver toys and food to the children living over the mountain.

SEQUENCE OF EXPERIENCES WITH TRAINS

1. Visit a train station and observe people leaving and arriving.
2. Spend time in the boarding area.
3. Arrange to board a parked train.
4. Sit on a parked train.
5. Purchase tickets and pack for a real trip.
6. Arrive early at the station and observe arrivals and departures.
7. Ride the train to your destination and back.

FEAR OF FLYING

Three-year-old Tara is taking her first flight to visit her grandmother. When her daddy explains to her that the tiny buildings and cars she sees out the plane's window are real, she complains, "Daddy, you are not supposed to tell stories." For Tara and other youngsters, a plane is just a long room with a bunch of seats that recline. Even though she's seen airplanes flying overhead many times, she doesn't really comprehend the fact that she is flying "way up there."

Young children rarely develop a fear of flying. Even if a child has a rough flight and her ears hurt or she gets airsick, by the time she is ready to fly again, she's forgotten it all. As children get older, they realize how high they are flying and the things that might go wrong. That's when flying can get scary. If a child is claustrophobic, being stuck in the middle seat on a crowded plane is very uncomfortable. Media accounts of air crashes alert everyone to the danger of air travel, but if you have an impressionable child then even stories of past crashes make the next flight more frightening.

If you are a fearful flyer—and twenty-five million adults in the United States are—it's impossible to hide your anxiety from your child. The message is tucked away and may affect your child later. For people who rarely travel by plane, each flight can become an ordeal. Martha Elizabeth came from a family in which almost everyone was afraid to fly. In fact, she didn't take her first plane ride until she was married and going on her honeymoon. It wasn't until years later when her six-year-old son wanted to go to DisneyWorld that she decided she would have to get some help to overcome her fear. If you have a fear of flying, you cannot help your child until you deal with your own fear. If your child is afraid of flying, you should work on desensitizing her before she reaches adulthood.

IMAGINATION

Flying stimulates many fantasies, good and bad. Your child's imagination can be both the cause of his fear of flying and a means to help him overcome it.

1. Read books about flying. For the young child, there are many books in which children have fun riding on airplanes. A number of these are listed at the conclusion to this article. For older children, adventure stories about pilots and flying can be helpful, but review any books first to omit those that might frighten your child. Several of the airlines periodically publish comic books about airplanes. Read these books to your child and discuss how much fun the characters are having. Point out the positive aspects of the flight. This may stimulate your child to talk about his feelings about flying.

2. Watch movies that include airplanes. Even films that are based on airline disasters include portions when the passengers are enjoying the flight. Carefully preview any airplane films and show only those scenes that are positive. Take frequent fear ratings as your child watches the films, repeating individual scenes until he is more comfortable.

3. Act out the stories you've read or seen. Ask your child to select his favorite stories and spend time acting them out. Put three seats together to simulate a row of an airplane. If your child is young enough to still enjoy pretending, serve him a meal "airplane style." Take turns playing pilot and air controller. Repeating such scenes will make flying seem less foreign.

4. Build a positive image. Fear is in your mind. Lead your child through new positive scenes to counter the negative images that fill his thoughts. Practice the relaxation exercises introduced in Chapter

2. With your child lying comfortably with his eyes closed, talk him through a series of scenes describing various aspects of air travel. Use the suggested sequence of airline scenes at the end of this article for additional ideas.

Begin your imaginary trip with scenes that are unlikely to threaten your child, such as packing for a trip, driving to the airport, checking in at the ticket counter, walking to the gate, and waiting to board the plane. When your child's fear rating indicates he is comfortable, picture your child standing in line to get on the plane, walking down the ramp, and getting on the plane. The next sequence might include finding his seat, buckling up, and hearing the flight attendants describe the parts of the plane and the safety exits. If your child's fear measurements permit, continue with scenes of the plane's engines starting, the plane backing up, the plane waiting on the runway to take off, the engines roaring as the plane starts down the runway, the plane taking off and climbing, the warning lights going off, and the plane flying above the clouds. Always describe your child as calm and enjoying the flight, even when your scenes indicate that the plane hits an air pocket or some clouds. In other sessions, have your child imagine himself eating on the plane, the plane banking to the left, the sound of the nose gear coming down, the captain preparing for landing, and finally, landing and safely arriving at your destination.

After each scene, take a fear reading. Use the relaxation response to counter any anxiety your child feels from imagining the sequence. If the reading indicates even moderate fear, repeat the imaginary scene until the levels drop. Continue until your child can take an imaginary flight feeling little anxiety.

If your child shows no fear during the imaginary sequences, it may mean that he is not visually oriented and this form of desensitization may not help. If, however, your child's fear remains very high during imagined scenes, you may need additional help to overcome this fear.

INFORMATION

Flying is considered the safest way to travel. Still, if you are afraid to fly, this statistic does little to ease fear. How such a large object gets off the ground and stays up in the air is a mystery to most people. Any sound or sudden motion a plane makes while you are in the air can be incorrectly identified as a sign of impending disaster. For the younger flyer, learning about how planes work builds confidence; for older youngsters and teens, understanding more about planes and flight can
help lower anxiety.

1. Gather information about planes. Read about how planes are built, powered, and fly. Encyclopedias like World Book–Childcraft's *The How and Why Library* have simple explanations for younger readers. A number of books listed below as well as reference texts that you can find at your local library are good sources of easily understood information for both younger and more mature readers.

2. Watch documentaries and other films about the history of aviation and modern airplane travel. Movies about the Wright Brothers and other aviation heroes provide background information that makes air flight less mysterious. Always preview any movies to exclude inappropriate or scary footage. Watch these with your child and discuss what you learn.

3. Arrange for a tour of the airport and an airplane. A number of airlines have educational programs that include tours of the airport, maintenance facilities, and flight simulators used to train pilots. Trips to air and space museums such as those at the the Smithsonian, Huntsville Space Center, Cape Canaveral–Kennedy Space Center, and others provide pleasant orientations to flight.

4. Build models. Another good way to learn about planes is to build model airplanes. Making paper airplanes, building plastic models, and even making or flying model aircraft familiarize your child with flight.

5. Create a series of positive statements your child can use to counter anxiety. Using the information your child has learned, define several statements about airline travel your child could use to calm herself and counter any negative thoughts she has during a flight.

POSITIVE SELF-TALK ABOUT FLYING

1. Airplanes are the safest way to travel.
2. That little bump is an air pocket and not a problem with the airplane.
3. The pilot has thousands of hours of flying experience.
4. This plane is checked out by a maintenance crew before each flight.
5. _____

OBSERVATION

Even before you go on another flight with your child, you may be able to lower his anxiety by indirect observation.

1. Watch for airplanes. Every chance you get, look for airplanes flying overhead. If you are knowledgeable about airplanes, make it a game to identify whether the plane is a military fighter or transport, small private plane, or commercial passenger plane. Talk about where you think the plane is going and who might be in it: other fathers and mothers on business trips, grandparents coming to visit, families going on vacations.

2. Watch takeoffs and landings at the airport. Park a comfortable distance from the airport terminal and watch the planes taking off and landing. Take your time so that your child becomes accustomed to the roar of their engines. Speculate on where the planes have been, where they might be going, and who might be in them. Also observe the people in the parking lots as they make their entrances and exits. Look for other children who are approximately your child's age. Do they appear excited about their trips or where they have been? Monitor your child's fear level and remind her to use her relaxation response to counter anxiety. Once her fear level has dropped you can go into the terminal.

3. Plan a series of observations. When your child is able to observe comfortably from a distance as people arrive and depart, begin a series of observations of the airport. Using the sequence of experiences outlined at the end of this article and the scenes that follow, help your child become increasingly comfortable with airplane travel.

Make your way through the airport to a departure gate. Sit at one of the departure gates of a large airline. Watch the passengers arrive and get ready to board a plane. Search for passengers who are your child's age. After the passengers board, watch the plane taking off and suggest that your child pretend she is on the plane. From the observation deck, you will have a clear view of takeoffs and landings. Frequently monitor your child's fear level and have her use relaxation exercises and positive self-talk to counter anxiety.

Take a snack along to improve the positive feelings your child has. Stay long enough for your child's fear to drop significantly. At the beginning of each trip to the airport notice if your child's initial fear reading is lower than at the start of the previous visit. Talk with her about the progress she is making. Have your child give you feedback on what she notices at the airport and what she is thinking about flying.

4. See a friend or relative off on a trip. When your child is fairly comfortable with the airport observations, see a friend off on a trip. Walk to the gate, and ask the attendant for permission to walk part of the way to the plane with the friend. Your child will know there is no possibility that she will be leaving, so if she suggests walking her friend onto the plane follow her lead.

EXPOSURE

By now your child is more familiar with airplanes and even more knowledgeable about how they work. Create a series of experiences that will lead your child to be more comfortable flying.

1. Take a mock trip. Many airlines will arrange a tour of an airplane and let your child sit on a parked airplane if you tell them you are working on getting over a fear of flying. Assure your child that the plane is not going to take off. Or, if the plane is being prepared for takeoff, assure her that you will both get off before the passengers arrive. You might be lucky enough to talk to a flight attendant or the captain of the plane. Sit with your child as far back in the plane as she is comfortable. Have your child fasten her seat belt, recline in the chair, and close her eyes. This is an excellent time to lead your child through an imaginary trip. If the captain begins to warm up the engines, it is very easy to imagine being up in the air. Take fear readings and prompt your child to use her belly breathing and relaxation exercises. Several mock flights will help prepare a frightened flyer for a real trip.

2. Plan a trip. If you can, make the destination somewhere your child really wants to go. When you book the flight, select seat assignments that your child is comfortable with. Be enthusiastic about the flight, and include your child in each step of the preparation. Get to the airport early so that your child can observe a number of other flights coming and going. Make it a game to look for other children who are also traveling. Arrange to board the plane early so that your child has time to get used to his seat. Once you are situated, it may be helpful for your child to move around; perhaps ask for permission to get on and off the plane several times so that he feels less trapped.

If your child tends to get airsick, bring along appropriate medication prescribed by your physician. Also take along a few books, toys, and tapes to keep your child occupied during the flight. One young boy we worked with who had been afraid of flying was so excited by a new hand-held video game he played with the entire trip that he hardly noticed he was in the air.

As the plane takes off, explain each of the sounds that you hear. Once the plane has leveled off and the seat belt sign is turned off, suggest your child walk around to reduce any feelings of restlessness. Pass the time by playing games. If your child becomes anxious, lead her through the relaxation exercises.

When the plane begins its approach for landing, remind your child of the sounds he will hear, especially the noise the landing gear makes when it is lowered. Talk your child through the landing by explaining what each movement means so that he does not become frightened. Once the plane has landed, praise your child for all of the coping skills he used during the flight. Have him tell you which part of the flight he liked best.

SEQUENCE OF IMAGINARY EXPERIENCES WITH FLIGHT

1. Packing for the flight.
2. Driving to the airport.
3. Checking in at the ticket counter.
4. Walking to the gate.
5. Waiting to board the plane.
6. Standing in line to get on the plane.
7. Walking down the ramp to get on the plane.
8. Finding your seats.
9. Buckling your seat belt.
10. Sitting on the plane as the doors close.
11. Sitting on the plane as it backs up and taxis on the runway.
12. Sitting in the plane as it takes off.
13. Sitting in the plane during the flight.
14. Sitting in the plane as it lands.

Books

Airplane Ride. Douglas Florian. New York: Crowell, 1984. A bright, cartoon-style adventure as a perky little biplane goes soaring over the variegated landscape, including plains and canyons.

Airport. Byron Barton. New York: Crowell, 1982. A realistic trip from arrival at the airport to takeoff.

Amazing Flying Machines. Robin Kerrod. New York: Knopf, 1992. Close-up photos of airplanes.

Baby Strawberry Book of Cars, Trucks, Trains, and Planes. Illustrated by Lawrence Di Fiori. New York: McGraw-Hill. A sturdy cardboard book with almost no text, but lively double-page spreads.

Curious George at the Airport. Margaret and H.A. Reys. Boston: Houghton Mifflin, 1987. George's curiosity has a way of getting him in some tight spots. This time he's at the airport. Fortunately for this little monkey, there's always a way out with a little help from his big friend in the yellow hat.

Curious George at the Airshow. Margaret and H.A. Reys. Boston: Houghton Mifflin, 1990. Continuing adventures of George.

Famous Flying Machines. Leon Baxter. Nashville: Ideals Publishing, 1992. A quick history of flight, with seven authentic models to make and fly.

Going on an Airplane. Fred Rogers. New York: G.P. Putnam's Sons, 1989. A sensitive book with realistic photographs of children taking a ride on an airplane. This is an excellent book showing what will happen minute by minute.

The Little Airplane. Lois Lenski, New York: Walck, 1934. A small book with simple stories and pictures.

The Smithsonian Book of Flight for Young People. Walter J. Boyne. New York: Macmillan, 1988. Beautifully illustrated history of aviation.

Super Wings. Peter Clemens and Jose Delgado. Los Angeles: RGA Publishing Group, 1991. A step-by-step paper airplane book introducing school-age children to the fascination of flight.

FEAR OF BOATS

When nine-year-old Julie went fishing with her father at the lake, a storm suddenly came up and the boat was tossed wildly. Dad was able to get back to the dock without a mishap, but ever since that incident Julie has refused to go on the family boat. Her dad figured the fear would go away with time; it didn't.

Jason has never been in a storm, but he's afraid to leave shore in a boat. He learned to swim late and still isn't a very strong swimmer. Jason heard a news account of a boat capsizing and someone drowning at the beach where his family vacations. Now he's frightened when his older brother water-skis. Jason's fear doesn't seem to be going away, either.

When a child develops a fear of boats and water that doesn't decrease, you must help him overcome it. Of course, if your child has a fear of water you must deal with that first. Knowing how to swim will naturally make your child feel more confident in the water. However, being a good swimmer and being afraid of boats are not mutually exclusive. Some youngsters are afraid of speed; others don't like being "trapped" on a boat. Still others worry about falling overboard, man-eating sharks, and getting seasick. Pinpoint what aspect of boating frightens your child and begin to work on the fear.

IMAGINATION

Your child might not have had much experience with boats. Use his imagination to help him become more familiar with boating.

1. Read books about boats. There are numerous books that vividly picture the boating experiences. For the younger reader there are stories with personified boats that become the hero of the story such as the childhood classic *Little Toot* by Hardie Gramatky. For older readers, there are adventure stories about voyages to faraway places and the more functional side of boating. Some of these books are listed below; your librarian will be able to help you find others. Preview any book you are about to use with your child to avoid stories that emphasize the dangers of boating. Only share happy stories in which everyone is safe and enjoys the experience.

As you read the stories, ask your child what he thinks it would be like to be one of the characters in the book. Discuss how the people seem to feel on the boats, what they are doing, and how cautious they are.

2. View films that include boats. Thank goodness for reruns. There are quite a few television shows that show boats and ships in a favorable light. From reruns of *Flipper* and *The Love Boat* to weekly programs on fishing, look for shows that make boating look like calm fun. The fishing shows might be a little boring unless someone in the family is an enthusiast, but they also clearly make the point that someone can sit in a boat for hours with nothing bad happening.

3. Take your child on an imaginary boat ride. As described in Chapter 2, when your child is relaxed, lead him through a very calm, pleasant boat scene. With younger children, you might even add a chorus or two of "Row, Row, Row Your Boat." Begin, for example, with your child imagining himself sitting on the dock looking at the boats in the harbor. If his fear rating is not high, describe your child getting on a boat and taking a ride around the dock. Gradually make your imaginary trips longer as your child spends more time on the boat in calm waters. After your child reaches the point that he can imagine these expeditions without much anxiety, introduce some feared elements such as choppy water, gathering storm clouds, and the rocking motion of the boat. Always describe your child as enjoying the voyage and coping well with the situation when the scene ends happily at the dock.

INFORMATION

Sometimes a child's fear of going on boats is intensified by a lack of knowledge about what causes things to float or misconceptions about how easy it is for a boat to overturn. Teaching your child more about boats and water can help to lower his anxiety.

1. Read about boats. Use the encyclopedia and other books listed below to teach your child how boats work and to identify various kinds of boats. Some information about weather prediction would also be useful.

Begin by identifying what kinds of materials float. Gather a number of materials, such as a rock, a piece of wood, a glass, a piece of soap, and so forth, and place each in a pan full of water. Which ones float? Discuss what causes material to float and what boats are made out of.

In an encyclopedia, you can also find information on the history of boating and all kinds of boats from barges to yachts. Knowing that Norsemen crossed the sea in primitive ships with no engines can make your child feel more secure about modern boats being able to make it across a lake.

2. Build or use model boats. A good way to help your child understand boats is to study their construction. Build a model boat or play with a ready-made one. Point out the important parts of the craft and practice testing it. Whichever model you select, try it out first. You wouldn't want your child to watch the model sink on its maiden voyage.

In a tub or pool let your child play with the boat in "rough seas" by making waves with his hands. That way he can learn how difficult it is to overturn small craft. Purposely turn over the boat so that your child will learn that it still floats in the water.

3. Learn about water safety. The Coast Guard has a number of booklets on water safety that will help you instruct your child about boat and water safety procedures. Taking a drown-proofing course can also add to everyone's sense of security. If you do not have a water safety vest for your child, purchase one. Of course, whenever you are on the water, practice all the safety steps. If your child goes boating with someone else, reinforce the idea that he has the right to insist on the same level of caution that you would demand.

4. Create a series of positive statements your child can use to calm himself. Based on the information about boating and water safety you have collected, help your child develop several sentences he can use to counter negative thoughts.

POSITIVE SELF-TALK ABOUT BOATING

1. My boat has been checked and is in good shape.
2. I have a life preserver and I know how to swim.
3. The water is very calm and there is no threatening weather.
4. My dad is a safe driver and I am in good hands.
5. _____

OBSERVATION

*Watching others ride safely in boats can lower your child's anxiety
before he gets on the water. As you spend time around boats,
frequently take fear readings, using them to
gauge how quickly you progress.*

1. Spend an afternoon on the dock watching other yachtsmen come and go. Talk to different boaters as they are preparing
to go out on the water, are coming in, or are working on their boats.
People love to discuss where the fish are biting, repairs they are
making to their boats, and fun places they've cruised.

2. Watch a friend take a ride. You might begin at an amusement park, watching the boat rides. Or arrange for a family member
or friend your child's age to take a ride on a boat similar to the one
your child is likely to ride on. As you and your child remain on
shore, talk about what the people on the boat are doing and how
they appear to feel about the experience. Avoid making comparisons
such as "Why don't you like to ride in boats like . . . ?"

3. Watch boats on the water. From the shore, look for other
children near your child's age. Point out the fun they are having. Let
your child talk to other kids on the dock. Ask your child what he
thinks about what he observes. Take fear ratings regularly and remind your child to use his positive coping skills to lower any anxiety
he feels.

EXPOSURE

By this point in the program your child has learned a lot about boats and water safety and has watched a number of children and adults enjoy boating experiences. To overcome his fear, your child must participate in a series of experiences involving boats.

1. Use your child's level of fear to guide you through a number of boating experiences. Never push your child to participate in an experience that he is not ready for. Instead, repeat an experience several times in one day or over a period of weeks or months until your child is comfortable. If long periods of time interrupt your child's boating opportunities, back up and begin with an activity that your child is comfortable with.

2. Plan a series of experiences that culminate in a boat trip. If your child is still extremely frightened or you want to test the waters gradually, you might select a ride at an amusement park where the boat operates on a mechanically operated track. Generally, the focus of that type of ride is on viewing a show or fantasy characters. Avoid boat rides that lead the child through scary or dark areas.

Use the sequence of boating experiences listed at the end of this article to map out your child's plan. If your child is very frightened, begin by having him sit on the dock until his fear rating indicate he is comfortable. If your child's anxiety allows, you might continue by sitting on a boat tied to the pier. Next, proceed to untie the boat and take it a short distance from the dock. Ask for frequent fear ratings to gauge how long you continue with a particular session and when you move to a another experience. Prompt your child to use the relaxation response and positive self-statements to help him cope.

For some children, how fast the boat moves through the water is of concern. Once your child is comfortable sitting on a boat that is drifting slowly, gradually throttle up. Your child might feel a greater sense of control, and thus be less frightened, if you allow him to control the engine of a motor boat. Letting your child sit in your lap and steer may reduce anxiety and add some fun to the experience. Likewise, directing the tiller of a sailboat or handling the oars of a rowboat can also be effective.

When weather is a major factor in a child's fear, be certain to listen to weather reports. Initially, avoid going out on a boat on any day bad weather threatens and, certainly, always heed the National Weather Service's recommendations for small craft. When your child is ready for a little more bouncing, go boating on a day when the wind's up and the water is slightly choppy, but there are no storm warnings.

SEQUENCE OF EXPERIENCES WITH BOATING

1. Sit in a boat tied to the dock.
2. Crank the engine at the dock or put a sail up and down.
3. Back the boat in and out of a slip.
4. Ride in a boat around the dock.
5. Leave the dock area but remain in sight of it.
6. Proceed farther from the home dock.
7. Boat from one marina to the next.
8. Cruise into open water.
9. Gradually increase the boat's speed.
10. Go boating when it is a little windy but the water is not choppy.
11. Go boating when it is windy and the water is choppy.

Books

Four Brave Sailors. Mirra Ginsburg. New York: Greenwillow, 1987. The four sailors are fearless mice, brave and true. Very little children will be caught up in the colorful voyage.

Harbor. Donald Crews. New York: Greenwillow, 1982. Color illustrations of a busy harbor and the various boats and ships that are found in port.

The Little Sailboat. Lois Lenski. New York: Walck, 1934. A small book
   with a simple story and pictures that is useful for the youngest child.
Little Toot. Hardie Gramatky. New York: Putnam, 1939. Little Toot the
   tugboat loved to play, and he thought work was for other boats. One
   day, Little Toot finds himself face-to-face with a terrible storm and an
   ocean liner in distress.

FEAR OF BRIDGES

A fear of bridges doesn't seem unreasonable. In fact, many adults fear bridges and go to great lengths to avoid them. We once knew an executive who backed down a busy bridge in the middle of rush hour. It was very hard for him to explain what he was doing when the policeman stopped him.

A fear of bridges is not as rare as you might think. The Chesapeake Bay Bridge Authority assigns officers to chauffeur people who cannot drive themselves over the bridge. Many people have panic attacks during the crossing; others are able to complete the trip if they are passengers and cover their eyes so that they cannot see.

It's often impossible to reach a destination by interstate highway without going over or under a bridge. However, since children do not drive, it is rare for them to develop a severe fear of bridges. Some youngsters, though, are so frightened of heights that standing on a bridge or walking across one is very difficult. Brent really didn't know he feared bridges until he encountered a suspended walkway during a school field trip. His fear was so intense that a parent volunteered to retrace their steps and meet the class at the end of the tour.

IMAGINATION

Begin to build a positive view of bridges by reading books and using your child's imagination.

1. Read books that include bridges in the story line. Immediately, the story of "The Three Billy Goats Gruff" probably comes to mind. Unfortunately, this story is not very helpful in easing a child's fear, since a mean old troll controlls passage over the bridge. Look for stories where bridges are incidental to the plot. Discuss how easily the characters crossed the bridge and how much fun they had on the other side.

2. View movies or films about bridges. Many times bridges are used as a plot device in a story. Often, though, in those situations someone is either jumping off of it or a catastrophe is about to occur. Avoid those stories! Look for films with settings like San Francisco and New York City that might include images of hundred of cars driving across bridges with no problems. Count the cars passing and talk about how safe everyone is.

3. Use positive images to bolster your child's self-confidence. When your child is feeling relaxed, lead her through an imaginary scene in which she sees herself setting out on a trip. She drives along the road enjoying the beautiful scenery. Portray her as passing over bridges without concern, looking at the rivers, streams, and the countryside below. When she stops for lunch, describe how she walks along a grassy park by the road and crosses a small bridge to reach the spot where she decides to picnic. Always describe positive scenes in which your child confidently walks and drives across the bridges she finds.

INFORMATION

To a child, a bridge is a magical span suspended across two points. It sways in the breeze and manages to stay put for no apparent reason. Your child will not become an engineer during these sessions. Yet understanding the amount of planning that is involved in building a bridge will help her feel more confident.

1. Gather information about bridges. Bridges are structures that have been used for centuries to help people cross obstacles. Using an encyclopedia or other elementary references, help your child understand that most modern bridges have a concrete, steel, or wooden framework and a concrete or asphalt roadway. Illustrate with pictures how most bridges have at least two supports that are set firmly in the ground. Depending on the length of a bridge, many of them have additional supports or piers between the end supports, called abutments. The distance between two supports is called a span. Most short bridges are supported by abutments and are designated as single-span bridges.

2. Identify kinds of bridges. Your child might be more comfortable crossing bridges if he recognizes how they are built. Using the reference texts or documentaries and videos look at pictures of a number of kinds of bridges. Identify those that are girder bridges, like the ones most often found on highways; truss bridges, which most often cross deeper ravines; arch spans, which are the oldest type of bridge; drawbridges, which open to allow traffic to pass underneath the bridge; or suspension bridges, which are very impressive (and often quite frightening) because of their long main span and graceful appearance.

3. Collect data about the bridges in your area. The department of transportation for your local government should be able to provide statistics about the major bridges in your area. Identify for your child how many cars safely pass each day and year over the bridges that frighten her the most. Discuss the kind of bridge each one is and how deep the abutments are planted in the ground.

4. Create a series of positive statements your child can use to reassure himself. Based on the information about bridges your child collects, develop a series of positive statements your child can use to counteract each frightening thought he has.

POSITIVE SELF-STATEMENTS ABOUT BRIDGES

1. This bridge was designed by talented engineers to make it very strong.
2. Thousands of cars and people safely cross this bridge daily.
3. This is a _____ ; it is very strong.
4. This bridge is inspected often; it is very safe.
5. _____

OBSERVATION

After pinpointing the types of bridges that frighten your child, select one on which to focus your attention.

1. Identify the kind of bridge. Study the structure without going over it. What kind of bridge is it? Where are the abutments and piers? What is the bridge made of? As you study the bridge, ask your child to give you feedback on his fear ratings. Should he become very anxious, remain at a distance from the structure until his fear subsides. Study other bridges in the area from a comfortable distance.

2. Position yourselves at the entrance of a bridge so that you can watch the traffic crossing it. Be sure not to block traffic or put yourself in any danger. Observe the cars and trucks passing over the bridge. Speculate about where you think the people might be going. Look for families in the cars. How do the passengers look? Where does your child think they might be headed? Count the number of cars that pass over the bridge in ten minutes. Multiply that number by six and then by twenty-four to estimate how many cars cross the bridge in a day.

3. Have your child observe family members crossing a bridge. Maintain a safe position at the entrance to the bridge. Depending on the size of the bridge and your child's fear, have an adult and a child, if possible, cross over a bridge as you and your child observe. Tell your child to pretend he is also crossing the bridge. Discuss what the individuals are doing and how they look when they pass by. Take your child's fear measurement to gauge whether the observations should continue.

EXPOSURE

Plan a series of experiences that will permit your child to gradually meet his fear and overcome it.

1. Identify a series of bridges of various kinds. Using these bridges as the sites for the practice sessions, rank the bridges in order from the least feared by your child to most feared. Depending on what characteristics concern your child, you might arrange the bridges in order of lowest to highest or shortest to longest. The bridges might also be grouped according to whether they traverse land or water.

2. Plan a series of experiences for each bridge. As you work your way through the practice sessions, have your child give you frequent fear ratings. If your child's anxiety level increases to five or greater, repeat that experience until his fear subsides. Remind your child to use positive self-talk and other coping strategies to lower his anxiety.

If possible, begin with a bridge on which you can safely drive or walk closer to the center of the bridge so that your child cannot easily look over the edge of the bridge. Distract your child during the crossing with conversation or by listening to music. If your child's fear ratings are low enough, follow this experience with practice sessions during which your child walks on the sidewalk or is driven in the normal transit lane so that he can look over the side of the bridge.

When walking across a bridge, begin by walking with your child, holding hands if that is comforting. As she becomes less anxious, walk next to each other and then walk single file across the bridge. Stop and deliberately look over the side, throw a pebble into the water below, and then continue across the bridge. Repeat the experiences until your child is comfortable.

3. Repeat experiences with other bridges until your child is comfortable with a variety of bridges. A sequence of experiences to desensitize your child to a fear of bridges is listed below.

SEQUENCE OF EXPERIENCES WITH BRIDGES

1. Stand on the end of a low, short bridge over land.
2. Holding someone's hand, walk down the center of a low, short bridge.
3. Walk next to someone down the center of a low, short bridge.
4. Walk alone down the center of a low, short bridge (as a parent supervises).
5. Walk closer to the railing of a low, short bridge.
6. Stop at the railing of a low, short bridge and peer over the side.
7. Repeat the sequence on a series of longer bridges.
8. Repeat the sequence on higher bridges.
9. Repeat the sequence on bridges that span water.
10. Repeat the sequence riding as a passenger in a car.
11. Repeat the sequence riding over bridges with other passengers in the car.
12. Drive yourself over a bridge.

Books

The Get Along Gang and the Big Bully. Margo Lundell. New York: Scholastic, 1984. The Gang is trying to help Rocco the bully. They can do anything if they stick together, including crossing a bridge.

9

MEDICAL FEARS

FEAR OF GERMS AND OTHER CONTAMINANTS

You probably never thought you'd have to worry that your child was washing too much. Adults usually complain about children getting dirty and not washing well enough. There are, however, children who wash too often or who are afraid of coming into contact with things they believe will contaminate them.

Children sometimes worry about hygiene and cleanliness—especially if they've been scolded for messing up their "Sunday best." Children who are newly toilet trained frequently feel the need to check out every bathroom when they are away from home. Although the child is simply making sure he knows where it is, he can be disturbed by what he finds. Old, poorly cleaned public bathrooms leave a lasting impression that is not good. When you tell your child not to touch a toilet seat, that confirms his suspicion.

School bathrooms are often a problem, too. When many children use the same facility, it is hard to maintain standards. Many students refuse to use the bathrooms at school, and that's not easy to do.

It is not just bathrooms that bother children. A child may be concerned with cleanliness in all types of situations. If you are extremely neat or fastidious about cleanliness, it reinforces the tendency. Ten-year-old Karen washed her hands at least thirty times every day. When we met Karen, her hands were red and chapped from constant washing. It was not mere coincidence that her mother was obsessed with keeping the bathrooms clean. Brad took his mother's concern about passing germs to an extreme; he insisted on holding every doorknob with a tissue or washing his hands after touching it. The children at school teased him, so he tried to avoid using the school bathroom when others were around. Eventually he could not touch the toilet handle to flush it.

A relentless need to be clean doesn't always run in families. The concern isn't as rare as you might assume, nor is it likely to disappear on its own. More and more children are being diagnosed with an obsessive-compulsive disorder (OCD). People with OCD have an irrational fear that they will be contaminated by germs, chemicals, or contact with other substances. This fear often leads people to wash their hands too frequently and compulsively and to avoid touching whatever they fear. Moreover, people who suffer from this disorder can spend endless hours checking doors, windows, locks, and appliances they fear they have left on. For more information about this disorder, you might be interested in reading *The Boy Who Couldn't Stop Washing* by Judith Rappaport (New York: NAL/Dutton, 1989).

The desensitization steps that follow will help decrease your child's concerns about contaminants. If, however, you find the problems persist or worsen, seek professional help for your child.

IMAGINATION

A child who is worried about germs or other contaminants usually has a very vivid imagination. She may visualize grime that you can't see and be more sensitive to the look and smell of dirt and chemicals than other children. The series of steps that follow will use your child's imagination in a positive way.

1. Read books that have "dirty" pictures. This is one time that "dirty books" are good. Select books with illustrations of things that worry your child, such as toilets and toilet training, bathrooms, garbage trucks, pigpens, zoo cages, hospitals, factories, or whatever your child considers contaminated.

Begin by looking at the illustrations and having your child point out what bothers him. Ask your child to rate his fear. After dealing with the illustrations your child might be ready to tackle the story. For older children more graphic descriptions in the stories may trigger your child's worries about being contaminated. For example, a story about a plumber fixing an overflowing toilet could engender fears about plumbing problems at your house. A number of books on these subjects are listed at the end of this section. Remind your child to use relaxation techniques and other coping skills to counter any anxiety he feels as he reads these books.

2. Look at photos of things that bother your child. Encyclopedias, home-repair manuals, magazines, and old textbooks are potential sources. From bathrooms to hospitals and sewers, and from bug sprays and cleansers to farms and zoos, you will be surprised by how many pictures you will be able to locate.

Begin with the photographs that you believe will trouble your child least. As you look at the pictures together, have him rate his level of anxiety from time to time. Remind your child to use his coping skills so that the fear ratings decrease or remain at a comfortable level. When your child gets used to a picture, you may leave it posted in his room or another appropriate place in the house to reinforce the familiarity.

3. Lead your child through scenes related to his fears of contamination. When your child is in a relaxed state, guide him through imaginary scenes in which he successfully manages his fears. For example, if your child is afraid of using bathrooms other than his own, have him imagine himself using a favorite relative's bathroom with little anxiety. In the next experience he might imagine himself successfully using the bathroom at a friend's house. On another occasion, it might be the rest room at a favorite restaurant. Describe places your child knows well so that he can envision the settings clearly. Continue this process until your child can imagine the most difficult settings with less anxiety. For one young boy, the location that was the most difficult was the public rest room at the football stadium. That might make sense to you, too. Over time the child was also able to picture this image with less anxiety.

INFORMATION

If your child fears germs and contamination more than his peers, it might be because he is misinformed or has very little factual knowledge about the subject. Teaching him the facts about transmission of diseases can reduce his concern.

1. Learn about germs. Most children hear the word "germ" and automatically think about bad diseases. Use the information in the encyclopedia and science books to teach your child about the value of good bacteria. For example, discuss how the bacteria in your child's stomach aid digestion. In fact, when your child gets an upset stomach, sometimes it's because there are not enough bacteria in the stomach.

Many germs have a limited life span outside the body. Try and get the facts that will help counter your child's beliefs about germs. Request information from your local health center or the Center for Communicable Diseases in Atlanta, Georgia. One boy we worked with who washed his hands frequently learned that the germs he was afraid of needed moisture to live. He drew a picture of the germs swimming happily in a pool. He then drew another picture of them dying of thirst in the desert. Once he understood the importance of this, he decided not to wash so often. He realized that washing his hands thirty times a day left them red and chapped but not necessarily healthy.

Children need to understand that most of the diseases they can catch through the air or by touch are not serious, life-threatening ailments. For most people, the common cold is uncomfortable but not dangerous. Reassure your child that washing his hands before he eats or touches food and after using the bathroom are effective ways to prevent most contagious illnesses.

Explore what types of diseases your child thinks he might get using soiled bathrooms and correct any misconceptions he might have. Using a dirty bathroom is not pleasant, but it is likely to be less dangerous than your child assumes. Reassure him that covering the toilet seat with paper is an effective technique to protect him.

2. Learn about chemicals. Many individuals with contamination fears are as frightened of chemicals and cleansers as they are of germs. If your child is afraid of coming into contact with everyday chemicals, he needs to understand how they work. First, remind your child that you use only chemicals that are safe for home use and that hazardous chemicals are always kept in a safe place. Most cleansers and other substances commonly used around the house are composed primarily of water and other inert ingredients. Read the labels with your child. Refer to the encyclopedia and other texts about any chemicals your child is concerned about. Provide facts about the dilution and evaporation of most liquid products. Your child may assume that once you wipe something with a cleanser, the chemical stays forever. Explain to your child that even when you spray to rid your house of insects, the chemicals quickly dissipate so that they lose their effect within a few days. If your child has questions about the chemicals you use around your home, call the Environmental Protection Agency, the poison center in your city or your county extension service so that you can provide correct information. Always store any potentially dangerous substances safely away from your children.

3. Help your child create a series of statements she can use to counter any anxious thoughts she has. Your child may practice positive self-talk more often if you write the sentences on index cards she can carry with her.

POSITIVE SELF-TALK ABOUT GERMS

1. Germs cannot live very long in the air.
2. When I wash my hands well one time, that is a good job.
3. After I put paper on the toilet seat, it is okay to use.
4. I do not need to wash my hands more often.
5. _____

OBSERVATION

Observing others dealing with germs and contaminants is sometimes difficult and at other times very easy. After all, most of the things that are likely to frighten your child are around him all the time, so he must deal successfully with many things everyday.

1. Have your child watch you. Clean the bathroom, take out the garbage, wash the car, and do any other chore that frightens your child. If you happen to be a cleanliness freak, tone down your inclinations around your child. As you go about your work, explain what you are doing. For example, tell your child why you use toilet bowl cleaner and show him how to use it. Show him how you dust the furniture. Avoid doing the same task repeatedly.

2. Teach your child how to wash her hands. Show your child how you wash your hands. This should be a simple cleansing instead of a prep job for surgery. Talk to your child about when and how often you wash. If your child spends inordinate amounts of time washing, have her time how long it takes you to do a good job of hand washing. Next, time your child. Those steps provide a reasonable frequency and time frame for a washing regime.

3. Visit bathrooms. Have the same-sex parent or a close adult friend take your child to various bathrooms. Begin with those that are not "perfect" but are certainly acceptable and work down from there. Of course, depending on the age and sex of your child, you will determine how much he can observe. The purpose of these expeditions is observation only; do not force your child to use the facility.

Demonstrate how you deal with less-than-ideal bathrooms. Wipe the toilet seat or use toilet paper to create a clean seat when no sanitary seat covers are available. Have the child report her fear measure to indicate how much anxiety is caused by each step and progress accordingly.

4. Have your child watch siblings and peers. Have your child observe in an appropriate manner siblings and others his own age handling situations that your child views as contaminating. This might include watching a sibling empty a trash can, use a household cleanser, or use the toilet (if they are young enough or of the same sex). Have your child report back to you what he observes and rate how much anxiety these situations cause.

Throughout the exercises have your child rate his anxiety level and report to you his observations. Encourage your child to note positive observations. Your child might notice whether his friends were able to use the urinal without touching it, that the bathroom was pretty clean, or that there were plenty of paper towels for drying hands. When making your comments, do not compare or pressure your child to duplicate what he sees. If your child does relate that he modeled his actions on what he saw, praise and reinforce him, but don't push.

EXPOSURE

The observations your child has made have readied her for direct exposure. Although she has watched you and taken part in some experiences, direct exposure by completing the feared actions is important to overcoming this fear. One other aspect of the treatment is significant. It will not be enough for your child to accomplish certain feats, such as cleaning a table or using a bathroom. She must also block the ritualistic need to wash her hands, clean surfaces, and perform other compulsive actions. The combination of contact with the fear and avoidance of decontamination motions is the key to overcoming this fear. Select the appropriate experiences from those that follow.

1. Use bathrooms. If using restrooms other than your own is what troubles your youngster, develop a list of feared or avoided bathrooms. Start with the one that is least threatening and work your way through the list. Enter the bathroom with your child and take a fear measurement. Remind your child to use the coping skills described in Chapter 2 to manage his anxiety. Approach those parts of the bathroom that bother him. A boy may begin by standing near the urinal. If his fear ratings are comfortable, have him move toward the toilet, and so forth. A girl would start by walking toward the toilet, then standing near it, and finally sitting on the commode, although you might place extra layers of paper toilet-seat covers to make the experience more comfortable. It may take several tries for your child to use a particular bathroom, so praise and reward your child appropriately for all attempts. After your child uses the toilet, supervise one good wash; don't allow "extra" washing. Gradually work your way through the list of restrooms.

When your child is ready to attempt to use the school bathrooms, make arrangements to do the practice sessions when classmates are not around—before and after school or before and after evening meetings. Once that is accomplished, have your child report to you his daytime experiences.

2. Use sprays and other household products. Children who are afraid of chemicals must come into contact with them to get over the fear. Make a list of chemicals solutions, from the least to the most frightening. Again, read the ingredients of the items you work with and correct any misconceptions your child might have. Instruct your child on the safe use of the products. Then, beginning with the first item on the list, design a series of experiences for your child to come into direct contact with the contaminant in a safe and supervised manner. This may include simply touching the kitchen counter after you have cleaned it, holding the bottle, pouring some into a dish, and finally wiping the table herself. Putting detergent in the washing machine or dishwasher or helping wash the car are also important experiences. After each experience, prevent your child from ritualistically washing her hands more than once. Ask your child to give you fear measures not only right after the exposure but also over the next hour, so she can feel the fear fade. Continue on to more difficult steps. According to your child's age, help her use window cleaners and bug sprays correctly. Show your child how you wash after using such substances but prevent overwashing.

3. Get dirty. If your child is a cleanliness freak and doesn't like to play in the dirt, arrange some experiences to overcome this problem. Dress your child in play clothes that both you and he won't worry about getting filthy. You might begin by digging in the garden, planting seeds, or making mud pies. No child should grow up without these experiences. Have your child help you oil a squeaky door. Getting greasy can cause some children great anguish, so go slowly and be sure to get fear ratings. Praise your child for each step of progress. After you finish any of these experiences, supervise your child's cleanup so that he doesn't overclean or wash repeatedly over the next few hours. Repeat feared experiences using your child's fear rating as a guide to how fast to move. Always supervise hand washing afterward to prevent ritualistic cleansing.

SEQUENCE OF EXPERIENCES WITH GERMS AND CONTAMINANTS

1. Touch a doorknob without washing hands.
2. Wash hands one time before eating a meal.
3. Wash hands one time after using the toilet.
4. Hold bottle of cleaning liquid or other "contaminant."
5. Clean kitchen counter then wash hands one time.
6. Use a toilet at a family member's or friend's home and wash hands one time.
7. Walk into school bathroom.
8. Use school bathroom and wash hands one time.
9. Walk in public bathroom.
10. Place toilet paper or paper seat cover on toilet seat.
11. Use public restroom.

Books

Germs Make Me Sick. Melvin Berger. New York: Harper & Row, 1985. An informative book about germs and what they do. Helpful hints are given for ways to avoid them.

The Human Body. Joan Western and Ronald Wilson. Mahwah, N.J.: Troll Assoc., 1991. This book is all about understanding the body and its parts for the older child.

Marvelous Me. Anne Townsend. San Diego: Lion Publishing 1984. This book will help you discover the secret inner workings of the human body. It includes information about germs and how the body counteracts them.

The Visual Dictionary of the Human Body. London: Dorling Kindersley. 1991. This book is a very graphic display of the body for the older child.

What's Inside My Body? New York: Dorling Kindersley, 1991. This book helps young children understand the inner workings of the human body.

What's a Virus Anyway? David Fassler and Kelly McQueen. Burlington, Vt.: Waterfront Books, 1990. A kids' book about AIDS presented in a childlike style that says what the disease is and what it isn't.

Why Does My Nose Run? Joanne Settel and Nancy Baggett. New York: Ivy Books, 1985. This book presents information about the human body and how it works. It includes information about germs.

FEAR OF SHOTS AND BLOOD

It's time for six-month-old Sharon to have her next set of shots. Mom braces herself for the loud wails and screams that she knows are coming. She comforts her daughter and it is all forgotten in a few minutes. At this age a baby reacts to the momentary pain and not the sight of the shot.

It is a different story for Aubrey, age seven. She's always reacted strongly to getting a shot. At four years old, Aubrey had to be held down to draw blood. When she was five, she began to have weekly allergy injections. From that time on, the mere sight of a needle sent her into hysterics. She would plead first with her mother and then with the nurse. Eventually, her mother found that it was best to leave the room. The weekly shots became so terrifying for Aubrey and her mother that the family sought professional help at our clinic to overcome the problem.

Frank is twelve years old and has always hated the sight of blood. It is not just needles and syringes that bother him. If he scrapes his leg or cuts his finger and sees blood, he gets nauseated and feels a little faint. It doesn't have to be his blood either. Watching medical scenes on television or reading a first aid book brings the same response. Worried that when he takes biology in high school he will embarrass himself in front of his friends, Frank asked his mom to find someone to help him.

If your child's reaction to shots and blood doesn't lessen with age, you cannot assume the fear will disappear. Many adults avoid going to the doctor or dentist because of a fear of injections or other medical procedures. Quite a few adults faint at the sight of blood. To ease your child's fears and minimize future problems, use the program that follows.

IMAGINATION

*A child who is afraid of blood and needles doesn't spend much
time looking at these things. More than likely her eyes are
squeezed shut when a needle is around. So there's a good
chance that the hypodermic has taken on super-sized proportions
in the child's imagination—by now, the needle is a foot long and
blood flows like a river. You can help your child use her
imagination in positive ways to counter her fears.*

1. Read books. There are a number of books for young children that describe getting shots and dealing with other medical procedures. In the books listed at the end of this section, the main characters successfully contend with various medical procedures. These images will stimulate your child's own private scenario of similar events. Always read any book you select before using it with your child. Emphasize the fact that the main characters of these stories were apprehensive at first but overcame their fears. Take your child's fear measure as you read the stories, repeating such experiences until she feels comfortable.

2. Play doctor. Young children love playing this game with each other. With your involvement the game will take on more meaning. Purchase a toy doctor's kit that includes pretend shots and bandages. First let your child pretend to give you shots and take blood samples. Next, reverse roles. Have your child rate her fear as she gives you a shot and then gets one from you. Your child's fear level is your guide to how long to continue a particular experience. Keep it fun.

When your child seems ready for the next step, it's going to get a little messy. Use ketchup to simulate blood. Smear some ketchup on a "wound" on your arm. Let your child put a gauze bandage over the spot and talk about how it looks as it stains the bandage. Ask your child how she feels during this task. If her anxiety remains low, reverse roles. Tell your child to pretend that the ketchup on her arm is real blood. Have her rate her anxiety level as you bandage her wound. Play this game over days or weeks until your child is comfortable with the red bandages.

3. Simulate an experience. After you explain why you need it, obtain a new, unopened syringe from your physician. Remember that all needles must be dealt with hygienically and disposed of safely. Never let your child play with such needles or other sharp objects without your supervision. If you can't get a real needle, use a sewing needle but this will not be as realistic.

Begin by explaining to your child that *at no time* will anyone receive a shot with this syringe. Show your child the syringe. Ask for her fear rating. Repeat the exercise until she can look at the syringe and remain calm. If simply looking at a needle creates too much fear, back off and repeat the experience on other days until your child can comfortably look at a needle. Don't be too surprised if you must place additional distance between your child and the needle. There have been a number of children at the clinic who at first could look at a syringe only when it was in its original wrapping and placed across the room.

Next, from whatever distance your child can tolerate, tell her to watch you as you pretend to "inject" someone's arm but really inject an orange. When your child's fear rating permits, have her carefully hold the syringe. Again, when she is ready, have her poke the needle into the skin of an orange. If you are using a real syringe, push the plunger, too. You can also fill the syringe with water and inject this into the orange. Finally, when her fear rating indicates she is ready, take turns pretending to give a doll a shot. Reiterate the fact that syringes are not toys and they must be handled carefully. Once you are finished with the syringe, break the needle off and throw it away.

4. Play with the empty plunger. Syringes without needles make good water pistols for your child to squirt in the tub or for you to squirt at each other.

INFORMATION

*Your child probably knows very little about shots or blood other
than the fact that she doesn't like them. She may have
misconceptions that make her fear worse. One child we worked
with thought he had very little blood in his body and if any spilled
out he would die. Many children think that all shots go into the
veins rather than the muscles. Giving your child correct information
can ease her fears.*

1. Read about blood. Use an encyclopedia or books appropriate to your child's age to gather information about the human body. Using a diagram of the circulatory system, show your child the heart and how the network of veins and arteries transport blood to every part of the body. Explain how important this network is and how much blood there is in the body. Fill several pitchers or use a one-gallon milk carton to show your child how much blood there is in the body.

Looking at her own arms, point out a path of veins in her arms. Explain to your child that the veins look blue because the blood inside the body is blue until it touches the air. Read together about how blood clots when it touches the air so that it will not continue to pour through a small cut or needle puncture. Talk about the protective work of scabs. As you approach various topics, take fear readings so that you can gauge how slowly you need to move through the material.

2. Keep in mind not all needles are created equal. To most children, all medically related needles are the same. If you can locate a medical text that shows the various sizes of needles, it will be very helpful. For most procedures, the needle is quite small. As an alternative, with your physician's assistance, take snapshots of different-sized hypodermic needles.

Sometimes children see a needle and syringe as one and the same.

Point out that the needle itself is really only a small part of the implement. Show your child where the medicine is placed and how the plunger slowly pushes it out. Explain also that the needle is made very thin so it won't hurt as much.

3. Help your child create several sentences to counter any negative thoughts he has about shots and blood. Remind your child to use positive self-talk whenever he becomes anxious.

POSITIVE SELF-TALK ABOUT SHOTS AND BLOOD

1. I have four quarts of blood and I will not lose it through this scratch.
2. This is a very tiny needle; it will hurt for just a second.
3. The medicine will make me well more quickly through a shot.
4. My brother had a shot like this and it didn't hurt much.
5. _____

OBSERVATION

One of the best ways to help your child overcome a fear of shots or blood is to arrange a series of observational experiences. If your child gets to watch you, other family members, and other people getting injections and taking blood tests, this should make it easier when her times comes along.

1. Have your child watch you. The next time you get a routine shot or have a blood test, take your child along with you. In advance, explain to the nurse or doctor what you are trying to accomplish so your child will not be embarrassed. Usually medical personnel are extremely supportive of such efforts—less frightened patients are easier to work with. If your child tends to pass out at the sight of blood, postpone this experience until after she is more comfortable with the sight of blood.

Have your child sit at a comfortable distance as the nurse draws your blood, pricks your finger, or gives you a shot. At first your child may only be able to watch from across the room. Take frequent fear measures and praise your child's progress. Talk your child through the procedure, relating what is happening at each step of the way: "The nurse is cleaning my arm with alcohol. It feels cool and doesn't hurt. Now she is sticking the needle in the muscle of my arm. It hurts a little but now it is over. See how fast it went."

If you can, take a camera so you, a medical assistant, or your child can take pictures of the procedures. These pictures will bridge the gap between experiences. If your child reacts strongly to watching you, he might fare better watching the procedure through the lens of camera. Afterward, have your child keep the pictures in his room at home and view them as often as he can. Take ratings of how much fear each picture produces and praise your child for using his relaxation techniques and other coping skills to counter the anxiety.

2. Have your child watch siblings and other kids. Get the assistance of older siblings or other children who you know react well with shots or blood. It's most helpful if you can work with a child who is the same age as your youngster. This will provide an opportunity for your child to model on someone who is not frightened. Avoid making any comparisons as your child observes these scenes.

During the episode, encourage the child who is not afraid to talk positively about what is happening. It is great if you find a child who was once afraid of shots and got over the fear.

3. Watch videos together. There are a number of instructional videos that teach first aid procedures. Some show how to stop a wound from bleeding; others depict various medical procedures and operations. It is important to preview any film before showing it to your child and then show only those portions of the footage that will help your child. As your child watches the film, have him rate his fear. According to the feedback from your child, start and stop the video until he is comfortable watching a section. Repeat the scenes that increase his fear until he is able to view them with less anxiety. Your child may feel more comfortable if he governs the remote control. Repeatedly view the video until it no longer causes anxiety.

4. Have your child watch blood collection. If your child passes out at the sight of blood, she will need extended exposure sessions. Ask the local Red Cross about the location of blood drives in your community. Discuss with the person in charge what you are trying to accomplish. We have found the sponsors and personnel at blood drives to be very helpful. However, they don't want your child to scare away donors, so be sensitive in designing your experiences.

As you work through the experience, take your child's fear ratings to determine how long to stay at the blood drive and how many experiences to undertake. Remain with a level of experience until your child's anxiety subsides. Don't expect your child to become comfortable in one session.

Begin by visiting the blood drive site before the donors arrive. Ask the nurses to explain the procedures for giving blood and how the blood is collected. This will not be as difficult for your child as it might sound, since there won't be any open needles or blood. Once your child understands the process, have her sit in a seat located away from donors. You may stay for only a few minutes the first time. Take ratings and praise your child for using her coping techniques. If your child begins to feel faint, have her put her head between her knees or lie completely flat until the sensations ease.

Before moving any closer to the donor area, arrange for your child to view a bag of collected blood. Once she masters this feat, she is ready to move closer to the donor area. You may be able to stay at a location for only a few minutes the first time. Repeat this experience as frequently as possible. Fortunately, most localities have blood drives every few weeks. Gradually your child will progress to the point where she is sitting right next to a donor.

When your child is comfortable viewing a stranger having blood drawn, it is time for her to observe someone she knows. This would be a good time for you or a friend to give blood, but there must be another supportive person with your child when you do. Instruct the donor to talk to your child during the experience. It's likely to be difficult for your child to believe that a needle that stays in you for a number of minutes and drains a bag of blood can be bearable. Seeing you and other donors give blood is very important to overcoming this fear. Your child's ability to see all that blood without passing out builds great confidence that will make it easier when she cuts or scratches herself.

Like most fears, overcoming a fear of shots and blood is not accomplished in one session. In a few sessions, though, your child is likely to make a lot of progress. One youngster became so fascinated by blood and needles that eventually his interest led him to the medical field. Obviously he didn't mind going back to his doctor for a routine finger prick.

EXPOSURE

By now your child has had a great deal of indirect exposure to needles and/or blood. Her anxiety level should be low enough to permit her to approach her fear more directly. At this point, with your doctor's help, arrange a series of experiences that will help your child overcome her fear. These experiences should not occur when your child is ill. Be preventive; don't wait until your child needs a shot or must have a blood test. A sequence of suggested experiences are listed at the end of this section.

1. Get a finger pricked. The place to start is with a simple finger prick test that the doctor does to get a blood count. Nowadays, this is done with a pin-like device. Before your child experiences the test, have the nurse explain the procedure and the information gained. Get your finger pricked first. Be honest; tell your child that it hurts a bit but it's over in an instant. Assure your child that he will not be tricked; the nurse or doctor will tell her when the procedure is to be done.

Have the nurse prep the finger and instruct her to explain why. Next, have her run the pin back and forth across your child's finger without pricking your child. Remind your child to use the coping skills. Take a fear rating. If your child is not ready for the procedure, ask the doctor if you can continue this process yourself for awhile. To give your child a sense of control let him guide your hand or run the pin back and forth against his own skin. When his fear rating subsides, your child will be ready for a simple prick by the nurse or doctor. The first time your child's finger is pricked, it isn't necessary to draw off the blood for a count. Your goal is for your child to have the prick and sense that the experience is not as bad as he anticipated. Praise your child for this accomplishment and return another day for an accurate test result.

2. Manage a shot. Once your child has mastered the pin prick, it is time for an injection. Of course, you don't give a child a shot simply to help her overcome a fear. There are, however, a number of inoculations that your child will need over the years. Talk to your doctor about these so you can plan in advance. It is likely that you will achieve this stage of the desensitization process and wait awhile. If this occurs, repeat previous experiences periodically so that your child remains comfortable with them.

Before getting any shot, have the doctor or nurse explain again which part of the arm or buttocks the shot is injected into so that she will know it is not going into a vein. Have your child distract herself by talking to you, counting backwards, looking at something else in the room, or repeating positive self-statements such as "This will only hurt for a second"; "The medication will keep me safe and healthy"; "I won't be able to feel the shot in a few minutes." Have your child rate her fear as she readies for the injection so that she becomes aware of what a long way she has come. Reinforce your child for going through the experience even if the first time is not a calm one. Help your child focus on how quickly it is over. Explain that any residual irritation or pain is caused by the medicine and not the needle. With future shots your child will get more used to the procedure, but she'll never like them. Who does?

3. Have blood drawn. The ultimate experience for your child may be having a test tube or more of blood drawn. By this time your child will have witnessed this done to you and others. Still, she may be apprehensive about the procedure. Have the nurse or doctor explain what they are doing and why and estimate how long the procedure will take. If your child can watch the clock, knowing it will only take a few minutes, the procedure will be more palatable. Again, help your child distract herself from the procedure the first few times. Later, as her anxiety decreases, she might want to watch. After a series of experiences you should see your child's anxiety drop.

SEQUENCE OF EXPERIENCES WITH NEEDLES AND SHOTS

1. Watch blood being drawn from across a room.
2. View a bag of donated blood.
3. Stand near a donor.
4. Watch a donor giving blood.
5. Look at various sizes of needles.
6. Watch a finger being pricked.
7. Observe a shot being filled.
8. Be prepped for an injection.
9. Get an injection.
10. Have blood drawn from an arm.

Books

Big Book About the Human Body. Joe Kaufman. New York: Western Publishing, 1987. An excellent book about the human body.

Blood and Guts. Linda Allison. Boston: Little, Brown, 1976. A working guide to your own insides. Cartoons are used to illustrate the text.

The Emergency Room. Harlow Rockwell. New York: Macmillan, 1985. An elementary and straightforward introduction to a place many families visit at least once.

Going to the Doctor. Fred Rogers. New York: G. P. Putnam's Sons, 1986. Realistic illustrations show a visit to the doctor. In one scene a child is shown receiving an actual shot with an explanation of why we get shots.

The Human Body. Gilda Berger. New York: Doubleday, 1989. A clearly written, easy-to-understand text on the inner workings of the human body.

The Human Body. Jonathan Miller. New York: Viking, 1983. Discover what happens inside the body. An older child can operate the realistic scale models in this book to further understand the body.

A Trip to the Doctor. Margot Linn. New York: Harper & Row, 1988. A funny book that asks questions about a visit to the doctor with three possible answers to choose from.

A Visit to Sesame Street Hospital. Deborah Hautzig. New York: Random House, 1985. Grover prepares for surgery.

The Visual Dictionary of the Human Body. New York: Dorling Kindersley, 1991. More technical text with realistic illustrations.

FEAR OF DOCTORS AND HOSPITALS

It's not surprising that some children are afraid of doctors. It is amazing that many children who have had the most medical procedures are not the ones that are frightened of doctors and hospitals. Janelle used to get so scared about visiting the doctor that she tried to hide her illness. When she would get an earache, she would wait until the pain was intense or her fever made the condition obvious. Even before a routine physical examination, Janelle would cry so much that she would sometimes throw up when she arrived at the doctor's office.

Few of us enjoy going to the doctor. Taking off your clothes, weighing, being probed and pricked are awkward and uncomfortable experiences. Naturally enough, the experiences that most children have with doctors and hospitals occur when a child is feeling lousy. Rather than being seen as an agent of health, the doctor is associated with shots, medicine, and throat cultures.

When your child is very ill, she senses your concern and that, too, raises her anxiety. Introducing your child to doctors and nurses when she is well will relieve some fears; explaining the procedures will help alleviate others.

IMAGINATION

Introducing your child to the doctor and the hospital before she must visit them is a good way to begin a positive association. If your child is more frightened by particular procedures than she is of individuals, read the section "Fear of Shots and Blood."

1. Read books about going to the doctor and the hospital. Mister Rogers has been there, and so have the Berenstain Bears and Curious George. A number of books that are helpful are listed at the end of this section. As you read together, use your child's favorite characters as role models and teachers. They will acquaint your child with medical personnel and the types of things she will see in those settings. Review any books before reading them to your child. Although the characters might be initially apprehensive about visiting the doctor, use only the stories that show the characters getting over their concerns.

2. Watch movies and television shows in which the doctors and nurses are positive, friendly people. Although you must screen these carefully to avoid scenes that include procedures that might frighten your child, there are many films that use medical personnel as the heroes. Realistic rescue shows depict the heroic measures medical people take to save lives. Medical dramas also show the human side of these people. Take your child's fear ratings as you watch various shows. If the ratings are high continue these types of experiences until she becomes more comfortable simply watching kind doctors and nurses delivering medical care.

3. Play doctor. Children have played it for years. Get out the toy medical bag and play with your child. Pretend you are sick and let your child check you over, giving you medicine and a shot. Take turns looking down each other's throats and pretending to take a temperature.

4. Go on an imaginary trip to the doctor's office. At a time when your child is relaxed and well, lead her through a trip to the doctor's office or hospital. Describe the drive to his building and searching for his office. See yourselves signing in at the desk and waiting in the waiting room until your child is called. Guide your child through typical experiences she might encounter at a well-child checkup. Always describe your child as happy and successfully handling the experiences. Use the sequence of experiences at the end of this section to expand your imaginary scenes. Repeat such trips until your child's rating indicates she is comfortable imagining herself at the doctor's office.

INFORMATION

Most of us have learned whatever we know about medical procedures through experience. You know how frightening it is for you when someone is diagnosed with an illness you have never heard of or when you must have a test you've not had before. It's natural to be apprehensive about the unknown. Familiarizing your child with the human body and how it works, and with how doctors and nurses help us take care of ourselves, will alleviate many fears.

1. Gather information. Hospitals have gone to great expense to transform themselves into friendly places for children. Inquire about the types of literature and materials local children's hospitals have for their young patients. The encyclopedia and other reference texts written for children are also helpful.

For most people, hospitals are huge, faceless institutions. Familiarizing your child with the kinds of people who work there and why people are put in the hospital is an important part of desensitization.

2. Help your child to understand more about the human body and how it works. Not only is it interesting for your child to learn how the common cold is transmitted, but the information may encourage your child to take steps to stay healthy. In addition, describe what a doctor is likely to do during a checkup. Explain why the doctor measures your child's height, weight, and temperature, as well as other parts of a physical examination.

3. Make medical procedures less mysterious. Teach your child how to weigh herself and read a thermometer. Let your child practice these procedures on her teddy bear, her dolls, and other toys. Let her take your temperature. As these medical procedures become less mysterious, your child will feel more comfortable.

4. Create a series of positive statements your child can use to counter the anxiety she feels. Using the facts you have gathered, have your child write several sentences about the positive things that doctors and nurses do.

POSITIVE SELF-TALK ABOUT DOCTORS AND HOSPITALS

1. Doctors make people feel better.
2. The doctors and nurses in the hospital want to help people get well.
3. When the nurse takes my temperature it does not hurt.
4. My parents will be with me the whole time.
5. _____

OBSERVATION

At a time when your child is not ill, reintroduce her to the doctor's office and hospital. On each occasion reassure your child that she is not the patient.

1. Take your child with you when you have a doctor's appointment. Either at a time when you know the examination will not put you in a compromising position or on a preplanned trip, have your child watch as you are weighed and have your blood pressure taken. Talk about what the nurse is doing and introduce your child to your doctor. Have your child report her fear measurements as you are examined and undergo various procedures.

2. Let your child accompany you when a sibling or friend visits the doctor. Select a cooperative child who doesn't mind going to the doctor. Again, have your child watch the various procedures that typically occur during a checkup. Have your child describe how her friend responds to the proceedings.

3. Visit a hospital. Before you have a need to visit a hospital and especially in advance of any planned surgery, take a tour of the facility. Many hospitals are set up to take children throughout the hospital, visiting the children's ward, the maternity ward to see new babies, and an operating area. In addition, explain to the tour guide your purpose for the trip. Your child's fear rating may warrant another visit in a particular area until she is more comfortable. The staff also will be delighted to answer your child's questions and often gives young visitors paper surgical garb and other mementos of the trip.

4. Visit someone in the hospital. When the opportunity arises to visit a friend who is mending or one who has had a baby, take your child with you to the hospital. Seeing a new baby or someone who is getting better and being able to ask questions about the equipment in the room is very helpful.

EXPOSURE

Now it is your child's turn to visit the doctor. Arrange a series of experiences that will acquaint your child with the doctor and medical procedures when she is well. Explain to the medical staff

*your purpose and discuss what will occur during the visit
so there will be no surprises.*

1. Plan a series of experiences to help your child become more comfortable in medical surroundings. Begin by accompanying your child to the doctor's office to make an appointment for a well-child checkup. This will provide an opportunity for your child to become comfortable in the waiting room without any chance of being called in herself. Remain in the waiting area talking about the children she sees and how nice the nurses seem until your child's fear ratings are at five or less.

Speak to your doctor in advance of the appointment about your goal. Ask him to pause between treatment procedures and to explain to your child what he is doing. If possible, arrange for any treatments and medical procedures to be given in the order of difficulty they present to your child. For example, your child might be weighed and her temperature taken; then, after a few minutes, the doctor talks to her, then examines her, and finally, her finger is pricked. If your child's fear ratings remain very high for particular procedures, you might work on those separately—for example, you might return to the doctor's office on another occasion to have her finger pricked. (See the section "Fear of Shots and Blood.")

Arrive early at the doctor's office on the day of your appointment. Remind your child to use her coping skills to counter any anxiety she feels. While you're waiting for the doctor, read a favorite book to your child or play a game to pass the time. The sequence of medical experiences listed at the end of this section will help you plan your child's exposure. Always follow your child's lead, repeating a particular experience until her fear rating indicates she is comfortable with the procedure.

2. Plan your child's hospital stay. There is nothing good about having to go to the hospital and you cannot check in just to desensitize your child.

Explain your child's fears about the hospital to the nursing staff on his floor. Ask your physician to explain in advance the procedures that will occur each day so that you can prepare your child. Lead your child through the relaxation exercises daily and remind him to practice belly breathing and other coping techniques when you see him becoming anxious.

Make your child's hospital room as comfortable and cozy as possible, bringing a favorite stuffed animal, your child's pillow, and a few appropriate toys to help him pass the time.

SEQUENCE OF EXPERIENCES WITH DOCTORS

1. Visit a doctor's office.
2. Make an appointment for a well-child check-up.
3. Sit in the waiting room.
4. Sit in an examining room.
5. Visit the nurse's station.
6. Take weight and height measures.
7. Talk to the doctor.
8. Experience a "painless" examination, such as checking reflexes, ears, and eyes.
9. Experience rest of examination—throat exam, finger prick, and so forth.

Books

Come to the Doctor, Harry. Mary Chalmers. New York: Harper & Row, 1981. This small book about Harry the Cat might help some children overcome the fears they may have about visiting the doctor.

Curious George Goes to the Hospital, Margaret and H.A. Rey. Boston: Houghton Mifflin, 1966. George swallows a piece of a jigsaw puzzle and must go to the hospital.

The Emergency Room. Harlow Rockwell. New York: Macmillan, 1985. Elementary and straightforward book about the emergency room.

The Hospital Book. James Howe. New York: Crown, 1981. A realistic photo essay of what a hospital stay is all about.

Some Busy Hospital. Seymour Reit, New York: Western Publishing, 1985. This big book gives kids a look at the many workers and jobs they do in a busy hospital.

A Trip to the Doctor. Margot Linn. New York: Harper & Row, 1988. A funny book that asks questions about a visit to the doctor with three possible answers to choose from.

A Visit to the Sesame Street Hospital. Deborah Hautzig. New York: Random House, 1985. Excellent book about Grover's preparation for a tonsillectomy.

FEAR OF THE DENTIST

This may be one childhood fear that you can relate to in a big way. If you grew up before the era of fluoridated water and "painless dentistry," you could have some dental fears of your own. It's estimated that as many as forty-five million Americans fear going to the dentist. Many adults with such fears delay dental visits or make appointments only to cancel them at the last minute. Even if you haven't had any traumatic dental experiences, few people are crazy about going to the dentist for treatment.

Contemporary dentists are more skilled in dealing with dental fears. Pedodonists, dentists who specialize in the treatment of children, are especially well equipped to handle children's fears. Others at least have taken special courses in dental school on the subject.

Many dental offices are designed to decrease a patient's fear. Research has shown that seeing other children being treated lowers many children's anxiety, so many offices are designed with open spaces accommodating several dental chairs. Offices may be equipped with built-in distractors, including stereo headsets and pictures on the ceiling.

Another way to prevent dental fear is to introduce a child to the dentist before there are any problems. Melanie began visiting the dentist when she was two years old. She loved to play with the toys that she found in her dental seat and delighted in making the chair go up and down. She had her teeth cleaned every six months and never showed any fear of going to the dentist. Her mom was amazed that Melanie's attitude didn't change after she had her first cavity. Early checkups help create a positive association with the dentist. However, even in the age of fluoride, kids get cavities. When it comes time for treatment, your child may be one who panics. Although novocaine can block pain, some children are more afraid of the injection than the drilling. Sometimes dentists suggest the use of nitrous oxide, or laughing gas, but for some children going to the dentist never becomes a laughing matter. Kyle avoided going to the dentist. He was petrified of the procedures and the metal instruments he saw on the dentist's tray. His cousin had told him all about what dentists do and he was panicked. Occasionally, a dentist will recommend delaying treatment until a child is better able to tolerate it. Unfortunately, when decay is involved you can't wait for the child to just grow out of this fear.

If your child has dental fears that make going to the dentist a problem for everyone concerned, there are ways to desensitize your child. The goal is to have a child who practices good dental hygiene and, as a teen and young adult, gets regular checkups and doesn't postpone needed treatment.

IMAGINATION
Most of what children know about the dentist is hearsay.
Introduce—or reintroduce—your child to the dentist through books.

1. Read books about going to the dentist. If your child has not been to the dentist before, start him off right. If he has had a bad experience, then begin the desensitization process by reading about some well known characters going to the dentist. The Berenstain Bears have been there, and so has Mister Rogers. Use the books listed at the end of this section and others to introduce your child to the dentist. Select stories in which a child learns that the dentist doesn't hurt and many times actually eases pain. Be sure that whatever story you read to your child has pleasant pictures, a friendly dentist, and a happy ending.

2. Play dentist. Just like playing doctor, pretend that you are at the dentist. Purchase a small plastic mirror and a rubber-tipped probe at the drug store. Have your child lean back in a chair and open her mouth. Then examine her teeth, poking around only a bit—make sure you don't hurt. Take fear readings. If your child gets anxious or gags, stop and prompt her to practice her relaxation techniques. When you have examined all of her teeth, switch roles. If siblings get in on the act, emphasize that they must come to you before playing dentist on their own. Any time instruments are placed in the mouth like this, you should supervise.

3. Imagine positive dental scenes. Lead your child through a series of imagined trips to the dentist. Take fear readings at each step and pace your progress accordingly. Have your child relax between each scene and always portray your child coping positively with each step.

Start with a visit to the dentist for a checkup. Have your child imagine herself climbing up into the chair. The dental assistant might let her play in the chair by manipulating it to go up and down. Describe the friendly dentist looking into her mouth, giving her a good report, and praising her for having very clean teeth. The next imagined trip could be about a teeth cleaning. Again, she has a good checkup and the cleaning is easy. Gradually work your way through other procedures, including any treatment your child might need. If your child needs a baby tooth extracted, have her imagine the procedure occurring just like in *The Berenstain Bears Visit the Dentist*. If she needs a cavity filled, describe the dentist putting sweet-tasting anesthetic cream on her gum before giving an injection, so the shot does not hurt. Make the scenes realistic but positive.

INFORMATION

The main thing children know about teeth is that they sometimes come out. And when teeth fall out, most children think only about putting them under the pillow for the tooth fairy. Few kids pause to examine a tooth or wonder about the shape of different teeth. Since children don't visit the dentist from birth on, most children

*don't know too much about the dentist's office. Educating your
child in the care of his teeth and what a dentist does are
important steps in overcoming dental fears.*

1. Ask your dentist for any information he can share. The
American Dental Association publishes many pamphlets that will
educate you and your child about the teeth. Your dentist may also
have models of the teeth he will let you borrow.

2. Get the facts. Look for information about the purpose and
placement of teeth in the body, when they erupt, and what causes
cavities and how to prevent them. Some of the books listed at the
end of this section include discussion of dental treatments, the use
of X rays, how novocaine works to prevent pain, and why the dentist
drills. All of this is done in the most positive of terms from a child's
point of view.

**3. Create a series of positive statements to counteract each
fearful thought your child has about going to the dentist.**
Write the statements on 3″ × 5″ index cards, so that your child will
have the positive statements at her fingertips when she needs them.

POSITIVE SELF-TALK ABOUT THE DENTIST

1. The dentist will help teach me how to care for my
teeth so they will be strong and pretty.
2. It does not hurt when the dentist looks into my
mouth.
3. The novocaine shot only hurts a little; it makes all
the pain go away.
4. The dentist takes care of my teeth so I will have
them for a long time.
5. _____

OBSERVATION

Simply observing others and acclimating to the sights, sounds, and smells of the dental office can lessen your child's fears. Be careful, however, not to expose your child to any potentially frightening procedures or terrified patients.

1. Visit a dental office. If your dentist's office is designed so that patients can observe each other during treatment, arrange to have your child watch on a number of occasions. If your dentist doesn't have such a setup, you will have to use a little more ingenuity. Your child could accompany you and other family members when cleanings or other procedures are scheduled.

2. Vary the experiences. Begin by having your child observe simple procedures such as teeth cleanings exams. Later experiences might include drilling and any specific procedures that frighten your child. As your child observes the procedures, take frequent fear readings. If watching creates too much anxiety, let your child leave the room, relax, and then return. Your child may be more comfortable at first watching from the corner of the examining room or from the doorway. As her anxiety decreases, suggest that she edge closer to the patient area.

It is helpful if the dentist explains what he is doing, and if the patient shares the fact that the procedure is painless. Encourage your child to relate more about what aspects of the treatment bother her—the sound of the drill, the tilt of the chair, or the smell of the chemicals. Accept her comments and get ratings of how much these factors bother her.

EXPOSURE

Your child is armed with correct information about the dentist and the art of dentistry. She understands the purpose of the teeth and how to take care of them. She has also observed a number of dental procedures. It is time to plan a series of experiences that will help your child become much more comfortable with dental procedures. The sequence of dental experiences outlined at the end of this section will help you plan a hierarchy of practice sessions designed to overcome your child's particular fears.

1. Take care of any related fears. Before you begin, deal with any other fears your child might have that contribute to her fear of dentists. If your child is afraid of needles or is claustrophobic, for example, treat these fears first. They are directly related to your child's feelings about dental experiences.

2. Talk to your dentist about planning a series of visits for your child. Begin with visits to meet the dentist, tour the office, discuss dental hygiene, and have the dentist look into your child's mouth. Using her fear ratings as a guide, progress to teeth cleanings and other needed dental procedures. At each stage be sure you and the dentist take fear readings to guide the pace of the experiences.

3. Remind your child to practice her coping skills during treatment. Define a signal your child can use to alert the dentist or hygienist when something hurts or she needs a pause in the treatment. Research shows that this one technique helps children feel more in control and less fearful. As she sits in the chair, have your child practice her relaxation skills, including belly breathing. She may even want to bring a tape recorder so that she can listen to her favorite music or a relaxation scene you have prerecorded.

4. Get help for particularly frightened children. Sometimes a child must have a difficult procedure at an early age or is very fearful. Discuss with your dentist the possibility of using nitrous oxide or some other agent to ease treatment. This would be preferable to forcing a panicky child to sit in the chair. Sometimes children ask for laughing gas; your dentist can judge when it is appropriate.

Keep in mind that your goal is to help your child have a series of positive dental experiences so that she does not avoid treatment later. Plan checkups and cleanings in between more serious procedures so that your child's fear will not grow back and her teeth will stay healthy.

SEQUENCE OF EXPERIENCES WITH THE DENTIST

1. Visit a dentist's office.
2. Sit in a dental chair.
3. Have the dentist look in mouth.
4. Have the teeth cleaned.
5. Have a minor, painless procedure done.
6. Get a shot of novocaine.
7. Have other procedures done.

Books

Alligator's Toothache. Diane DeGroat. New York: Crown, 1977. Poor Alligator has a toothache but is scared of going to the dentist. So the dentist comes to Alligator to help him.

The Bear's Toothache. David McPhail. New York: Little, Brown, 1972. Someone who frequently suffers from a painful toothache will see the humor in this story.

The Berenstain Bears Visit the Dentist. Stan and Jan Berenstain. New York: Random House, 1981. The Bears visit the dentist. This book has wonderful illustrations of what it's like to go to a dentist's office.

Dr. De Soto. William Steig. New York: Farrar, Straus and Giroux, 1982. The kind-hearted dentist, Dr. DeSoto, and his able assistant, Mrs. DeSoto (both mice), never treat cats or other dangerous animals, except in the case when the fox needs help. A funny story about a large fox going to the dentist.

Going to the Dentist. Fred Rogers. New York: G. P. Putnam's Sons, 1989. This book shows realistic illustrations of what it is like to visit the dentist and explains the entire experience in a sensitive and helpful way.

Going to the Dentist. Marianne Borgardt. New York: Simon and Schuster, 1991. A pop-up book about going to the dentist. Excellent illustrations will show your child all about the procedures and how we can care for our teeth.

Little Rabbit's Loose Tooth. Lucy Bate. New York: Crown, 1975. This book sensitively presents one of life's inevitable crises faced by children when their first tooth is loose.

My Dentist. Harlow Rockwell. New York: Macmillan, 1985. This book is all about the dentist.

Norman Fools the Tooth Fairy. Carol Carrick. New York: Scholastic, 1992. A charming story about Norman, who loses his first tooth and waits for the tooth fairy. A motivational chart at the end of the book shows how to brush your teeth with Norman. It also reinforces the idea that Norman visits the dentist to help him care for his teeth.

10

SOCIAL FEARS

FEAR OF MEETING NEW CHILDREN

Many young children pass through a stage when they are afraid of strangers (see the section "Fear of Strangers"). Sometimes, though, children are afraid to meet other children. This hesitancy may grow out of the child's shyness or his general discomfort in a new situation. Three-year-old Brandon was comfortable with adults but he wanted nothing to do with other boys and girls. He stuck like glue to his teacher at the day-care center. He wouldn't speak to any other children. When his mother invited other children to play at his house, he would play with his toys as though the child wasn't there. At six, Tracy had a few good friends at school and said she wasn't interested in meeting anyone else. She was quiet at home and enjoyed playing alone. When she went somewhere new, she rarely spoke to anyone, either adult or child, and would look down at the floor to avoid making eye contact. Although many researchers think shyness is an inherited trait, they have also found that a child can be taught to be more outgoing. You can help your child overcome this fear so he is able to feel confident when he meets other children and adults.

IMAGINATION
Open the doors to meeting new people by showing your child how other children meet each other.

1. Read books about making friends. Choose books that concentrate on characters making new friends and ones that show the characters learning how to speak for themselves. You'll find many books in which some characters are shy or timid and others outgoing. Talk about which characters your child identifies with.

2. View movies and shows that feature kids who are in situations where they have to meet new people. Many children's shows focus on situations where children have to meet new people or do things for the first time. Talk about the characters in each situation and how they manage their concerns. Notice how these individuals interact with each other and how they overcome their shyness. Focus on the good things that happen in the stories when the children meet new people or learn to speak up.

3. Pretend that you are strangers. Take on a pretend personality. Choose new names and pretend that you are strangers meeting for the first time. Introduce yourself to your child and have her do the same. Take turns asking each other questions and making small talk over a snack. Like an actor in a play, taking on a new personality will help your child interact freely. As you both assume roles, you become a model for the social skills your child needs to meet new people and make new friends.

4. Lead your child through an imaginary afternoon when she makes a new friend. When your child is relaxed, you might begin with an imaginary excursion to the park or anywhere else that she is likely to come in contact with children she hasn't met before. Begin by having her imagine herself playing alone in the sandbox as you relax on a park bench. There are a number of children in the park and one comes to play in the sand. Describe how the child initiates a conversation with your child and she answers. Prompt your child to see herself interacting with the child as they pour the sand and make roads through it. Prompt your child to imagine herself having a good time and agreeing to climb on the jungle gym when her new friend suggests it. At various points during these scenes ask your child how anxious she feels. During the following sessions, continue to lead your child through imaginary situations until she can comfortably see herself successfully interacting with other children.

INFORMATION

Social skills are not inherited. Your child needs information about how to interact with other children.

1. Let your child in on the secret. Everyone gets a little anxious in new situations. Talk to him about the times you have felt shy and reluctant to go somewhere that you didn't know many people. Share how you handled the situation and how much easier it was than you expected.

2. Rehearse making introductions. Some people make small talk easily. Others don't. Be your child's drama coach and give him a head start by scripting and rehearsing what he can say in typical situations. Afterward he will feel more comfortable taking off on his own. Two common situations and suggested scripts are presented:

Introducing Oneself *There are many situations when a child will need to introduce herself.*
"Hi. I'm ——. What's your name? I'm here because . . ."
"Hello. I don't know very many people here. . . . My name is ——. I know ——. Who do you know here?"

Starting a Conversation *Many children who are shy in new situations just don't know what to say. Help your child get started by practicing some conversation starters:*
"Hi! That looks interesting. What are you doing?"
"Hello. You have on a pretty dress."
"Hello. Have you been here before?"
"Hi. Can I play too?"
"Hello. Do you want to hear a riddle?"

3. Help your child give himself a pep talk. When your child gets nervous in a new situation, it's helpful to have a few sentences he can use to counter anxious feelings. Create a list of positive statements he can use, and encourage him to practice saying them to himself whenever he feels frightened entering a new situation.

POSITIVE SELF-TALK ABOUT MEETING NEW PEOPLE

1. These people are very nice. They would like to meet me.
2. A lot of children are probably feeling the same way I am.
3. Once I introduce myself, I'll have a friend.
4. That child doesn't know anyone either and would like to meet me.
5. _____

OBSERVATION

Your child has a number of models to watch. Seeing you and other people your child knows well handle new situations is very instructive.

1. Watch you talking to people. When it is appropriate, take your child along to situations where you are unlikely to know everyone. She will have opportunities to watch you introduce yourself and make conversation. When you go to the mall and see someone you know, take the opportunity to greet the person and introduce your child. In each situation, ask your child to rate her anxiety level as you introduce her to a friend of yours. Continue such outings until she feels comfortable making simple greetings.

2. Observe friends and siblings in new situations. Your child is not the only one who feels this way. Suggest she ask friends how they feel when they go places they don't know anyone. What do they do and how do they handle the situation? Have your child observe friends in groups: What do they say to each other? How does another child make her way into a group? At the end of each day talk to your child about what she has observed.

3. Observe new situations. Feeling uncomfortable and frightened stems from not knowing the "lay of the land." Whenever your child will be joining a new group, attending a new class, or entering a new situation, talk to someone who has been there previously and visit the location. For example, if your child is attending a new school, visit it before the first day of school. Talk to her teacher, get the names of some classmates, and try to arrange an introduction before school starts.

EXPOSURE

*Repeatedly through the years your child will be involved in
situations that you cannot prepare for in advance. Give your child
a head start by planning a series of situations where he can try his
new skills. At each step take a fear rating to gauge how many
similar experiences you should arrange. At the end of the section
is a list of sample situations that would provide opportunities for
your child to meet other children.*

1. Invite a new friend to play. Many times adults have friends
with children of similar ages. Perhaps you know someone your child
has not seen in a long time. Invite him to play. Before the child
arrives, talk to your child about what he is feeling. Also help him
plan some activities he might suggest when his new friend arrives.
Until the friendship takes off, keep initial visits short and stay
around to offer suggestions when the children need a new idea about
what to do.

2. Go to the park. Pick a beautiful day when there will be a lot
of children in the park. As you walk around the area, suggest that
your child play near the other children and then talk to one child
who is playing on the playground. Perhaps he spies a child swinging
or climbing on the jungle gym. Take your child's fear rating before
he walks over to the other child so that over the next weeks and
months you both will be aware that he is becoming more comfortable meeting new people. If the other child is not particularly
friendly, assure your child that that's okay and praise him for talking
to the other child.

3. Enroll in a group. The most natural way for your child to
meet new children is to enroll in a class. Through the years your
child will begin school and a variety of classes. Depending on your
child's age, there are also a variety of activities available where your

child can meet children with similar abilities and interests. From gym tots to dancing and soccer, t-ball, karate, music, art, and computer classes, each of these provides ready-made conversation starters your child can use: What do you think we will do here? Have you met the teacher? Have you ever done this before? Praise your child when you see him initiating a conversation or responding to a question or comment from another child.

4. Attend a party. Invitations for birthday parties arrive all the time during the elementary years. If your child has been reluctant to attend previously because he knew there might be a lot of guests he didn't know, here's another opportunity to overcome his fear. Remind your child to use his positive coping exercises to counter any anxious feelings he might have. Use the suggestions in the section "Fear of Parties" for additional ideas.

EXAMPLES OF EXPERIENCES MEETING NEW PEOPLE

1. Meet a new friend.
2. Attend a birthday party with a lot of friends.
3. Attend a small play group that includes a few children.
4. Attend a new activity or class.
5. Meet a new neighbor.

Books

In the Year of the Boar and Jackie Robinson. Bette Bao Lord. New York: Harper & Row, 1984. This book recounts the experiences of a child who leaves her homeland in China to begin a new life with her parents in Brooklyn in 1947. Making friends and finding a place as a member of the group makes this a memorable story for kids who know what it's like to be the "new kid."

Just Imagine with Barney. Mary Shrode Allen: The Lyons Group, 1992. Barney helps a little girl imagine the positive experiences she will have with new friends when she moves.

Ramona Quimby, Age 8. Beverly Cleary. New York: Morrow, 1981. Independent Ramona runs into a lot of problems trying to cope with a new school, meeting new kids, her parents' busy schedule, and a misunderstanding with her teacher. Cleary paints a real world kids can readily relate to.

Stay Away from Simon! Carol Carrick. New York: Clarion, 1985. Many people in the neighborhood are afraid of Simon, a retarded boy, who turns out to be a hero to Lucy and her brother.

Very Shy. Barbara Shook Hazen. New York: Human Sciences Press, 1983. It's a comfort to Nancy to discover that she's not the only one who feels self-conscious.

FEAR OF PARTIES

Most children begin counting the days until their birthday party long before the big day arrives. However, some children actually dread the idea, and attending someone else's party sends them into a panic.

Billy had always been a little shy, but he seemed to enjoy going to preschool and had made a number of new friends. However, when he started to get invitations to their birthday parties he panicked. Even when his mom promised to stay for the entire party, he clung to her and wouldn't join in the fun and games. As time went on, he balked at attending any parties and said he didn't want a birthday party for himself.

A fear of parties usually stems from some event that occurred during a party—perhaps there was a larger-than-life character like a clown or Batman, or an overwhelming amount of noise or activity. Your child might be uneasy in new situations or feel uncertain when there are a lot of people around. You don't want to label a child as "shy," but if your child tends to be this way then it can make going to social gatherings uncomfortable. No matter what the reason, a fear of parties or social gatherings interferes with a child's friendships and opportunities to have a lot of fun.

IMAGINATION

*Parties are supposed to be fun. Reintroduce your child to parties
in a very safe way—visit them through her imagination.*

1. Read books that involve parties. Parties are a favorite topic
for many children's books. You'll easily find your child's favorite
book characters celebrating a birthday or attending a party with a
friend. As you read the story, talk about what the characters are
doing and how they look. Do they appear to be having fun? As you
read any of the books listed at the end of this section or others you
find, have your child imagine that she is a character in the story. Ask
your child what she would bring as a gift and how it feels to be a
guest at a party. Emphasize that when you are invited to a party, it
means that someone really likes you and wants you to be there.

**2. Watch movies and television shows that have party
scenes.** Select party scenes that suggest that the people at the party
are having a good time. As you watch the films, have your child
imagine she is going to the party. What would she wear? What
would be her favorite part of the party? Be sure to preview the films
you use to make certain there are no unpleasant occurrences that
would add to your child's concerns.

3. Pretend to have a party. Stage a party with your child's
stuffed animals, favorite dolls, or just you. Make invitations, plan
the refreshments, and get ready to have a good time. Keep it simple
or set the table with colorful plates and napkins, party favors and
anything that might suggest the idea of a real party.

4. Lead your child through an imaginary party. After practicing the relaxation techniques introduced in Chapter 2, lead your
child through a party scene. With your child lying down with her
eyes closed, begin describing the day of a party. Picture your child
getting ready for the party and how she is looking forward to it.

Describe how your child rings the doorbell and wishes the host a happy birthday. Describe the guests, the entertainment, and the refreshments, always being sure to portray your child as relaxed, calm, and having a great time. Include in the party scenes elements that you know disturb your child. Have your child report her fear ratings at points in the imaginary journey. Continue the imaginary exercises on various occasions until your child can comfortably imagine herself at a party.

INFORMATION

One element that makes parties scary is not knowing how to act. Teaching your child about party manners and answering your child's questions about parties will help him feel more comfortable.

1. Gather the facts. Help your child learn all about parties by collecting information about them. Talk about the reasons people give parties and what people do at parties. When you visit the skating rink, pizza parlor, bowling alley, or other places where children frequently have parties, point out that it is a party location and discuss what the guests might do.

Look at invitations. Identify the kinds of information given on an invitation. Discuss how you know what appropriate dress is or anticipate what you might do at the party.

2. Teach your child party manners. Practice saying hello and wishing the party child a happy birthday. If your child is the host, role-play welcoming guests and what you say when you open a gift. From saying hello and making eye contact to knowing which fork to use and how to say thank you for a great time, basic social skills can help put your child at ease. Finally, when in doubt, teach your child how to ask an adult or watch other guests at a party to know what to do.

3. Find out about make-believe characters. If your child is afraid of clowns and larger than life cartoon characters, read the section "Fantasy Characters."

4. Gather information about the actual party to help put your child at ease. If your child is going to a party, gather information about it. Find the answers to your child's concerns, such as will a clown be present, how long will the party last, where will you be during the party, or, perhaps, who will take your child to the bathroom?

5. Use this information to help your child create positive statements to help him put himself at ease. Your child's negative thoughts increase his fear. Have your child practice countering each negative thought with a positive one.

POSITIVE SELF-TALK ABOUT PARTIES

1. My good friend invited me to this party and he wants me here.
2. My mother will be back soon.
3. In a little while we will have cake and ice cream and I love cake and ice cream.
4. The party character is only a person in a costume.
5. If I have a question, I can ask the party mom.
6. _____

OBSERVATION

Your child needs several opportunities to observe children at parties when she is not a guest herself.

1. Watch a party. Ask your favorite birthday party haunts—such as the local pizza parlor that caters to children, the skating rink, fast-food restaurants, and miniature golf centers—about when parties are being held at the facility. Go for a snack and observe the festivities. Discuss with your child what the guests are doing, how they look, and how much fun they seem to be having.

2. Have a party at your house. If there are other siblings, give a party for one of them. That way your child can observe the activities firsthand. Before the guests arrive, discuss what they will be doing. Give your child specific things to look for during the event, such as how people walk around and talk to others, if anyone sits alone, whether people look happy, and what they do when they have a question.

EXPOSURE

Now that your child is more accustomed to parties, it is time to attend one. Don't expect her to stay the whole time; that's something to look forward to.

1. Reintroduce your child to parties. Using the sequence of possible experiences listed at the end of this section, gradually reintroduce your child to parties. At each step have your child report fear measurements to gauge how often you will need to repeat similar activities. Together list a series of kinds of parties or group situations that have frightened your child. List them in order of least to most feared. Arrange a series of parties or take advantage of the invitations that come for her to acclimate your child as a party guest. The first parties you arrange may include just one or two close friends, and then perhaps a few more children for a planned activity. When your child is comfortable with small-group activities at her own home, suggest she attend other parties.

2. Break the party into sections. With your child's help, divide the time for a party into sections. For example, a birthday party might include the time before the guests arrive, entertainment, refreshments, opening presents, and when the guests are leaving. Arrange these party activities beginning with the one that would be easiest for your child to the most difficult. When the first invitation arrives, explain to the host what you are working on and arrange for your child to attend the part of the party she identifies. One child might find it easiest to go to the party before the guests arrive; another might want to go just to see the presents opened.

Over a succession of parties, expose your child to each part of the party until she is comfortably able to remain at a party the entire time.

SEQUENCE OF EXPERIENCES WITH PARTIES

1. Go to a party before the guests arrive.
2. Greet the host.
3. Meet other guests.
4. Attend during the entertainment.
5. Have refreshments at a party.
6. Watch the presents being opened.
7. Say good-bye.

Books

A Birthday for Frances. Russell Hoban. New York: Harper & Row, 1968. Frances is jealous of her little sister's birthday.

The Half-Birthday Party. Charlotte Pomerantz. Boston: Houghton Mifflin, 1984. An appealing story about a party Daniel gives for his sister's half-year birthday.

The Happy Birthday Book. Peter Seymour. New York: Macmillan, 1992. It's a birthday party and you're invited. Colorful illustrations show children having a wonderful time. Traditional birthday routines are highlighted. This is an ideal book for showing your child what will happen at a party.

Happy Birthday Max. Hanne Turk. Boston: Neugebauer Press, 1984. A story about an imaginative mouse named Max. Here he stages an elaborate birthday picnic for himself alone on a hill.

Happy Birthday, Moon. Frank Asch. New York: Simon and Schuster, 1982. A colorful story that will be very appealing to young children.

Mary Wore Her Red Dress and Henry Wore His Green Sneakers. Merle Peek. New York: Clarion, 1985. Katie's animal friends wear different-colored clothing to her birthday party.

FEAR OF BEING TEASED

The old saying "Sticks and stones may break my bones but words will never hurt me" is not exactly true. You can probably remember many times from your own childhood when being teased and embarrassed hurt much worse than any cut or bruise you ever had.

Bart was small for his age. There always seemed to be some bully calling him names such as "shrimp" or "peewee". What made things worse was that Bart would get upset and then the other kids would join in the teasing and call him a crybaby. Reputations like that are hard to live down and begin to carry over from one year to the next.

Children can be very mean to each other—especially when it's easy to draw a reaction or get another child's "goat." Getting angry or crying attracts attention. Sometimes it appears that some children have a sign inscribed on their backs that says, "Tease Me." Getting help from an adult might temporarily suppress teasing, but often it makes matters worse.

Once a child has been the brunt of a lot of teasing, it is natural to want to escape the tormentors. The child learns to fear situations that might be embarrassing or where he might be the focus of negative attention. The problem is there will always be another teaser around the bend. While the behavior is sometimes called "making fun," there's nothing fun about it for the person who is continually teased. To help your child deal with teasing you must teach him not only how to respond overtly but also how to react differently internally. When your child learns to react less, his teasers will lose interest and your child will be less frightened and fearful of situations that put him in the teasing arena.

IMAGINATION

A child who has been teased a lot might be able to imagine himself not being teased, but it is harder to see himself reacting effectively or not at all to teasing. It's too emotional for him at this point. And if he knew another way to handle it, he would. Begin to desensitize your child to teasing by introducing him to characters who learn how to handle it.

1. Read books about characters that are teased. Many books have characters that are vulnerable to being teased, left out, or made fun of. Whether you choose a book at the library or even create one yourself with the help of your child, share stories with him about others who were able to overcome teasing. As you read the books, talk about why the character is teased and how she could respond to her tormentors to change the situation. Have your child pretend he is one of the characters in a book that you have read. He won't have to invent his behavior; he can respond like the character in the book.

2. View movies and shows. Many contemporary shows on television deal with children making fun of others. Today's TV kids are real people. They come in all shapes and sizes and frequently deal with real-life situations. Use these shows to initiate discussions with your child about how the characters react and what else they might have done in the situation. Suggest that your child imagine himself as one of the characters in a show. How does that make him feel? What would she have done?

3. Lead your child through typical experiences when he imagines himself effectively handling teasing. Make a list of the things kids say to tease him. Identify the epithets, labels, and phrases tormentors use to heckle your child. Have your child rank them in order of the phrases that hurt him the most to the ones that bother him the least.

At a time when your child has practiced the relaxation exercises presented in Chapter 2, have your child imagine himself reacting effectively to children teasing him. Begin by describing a situation when it would be likely for the children to tease your child. Use the least bothersome phrases on his list. Describe what your child is doing, where they are, and what his friends are doing. Depict them teasing him and how he feels. Next, describe him not responding at all to the taunts. The children may tease him some more, but describe how they finally leave him alone because their words didn't get a response. Get readings of your child's anxiety level as you proceed with the imaginary experience. Repeat each imaginary experience until your child feels no reaction to the teasing described.

Continue imagining various episodes, using phrases on your child's feared list, until he can imagine an intimidating situation without reacting or feeling anxious.

INFORMATION

Gather information that will help your child react less to teasing. Sometimes all it takes is helping your child understand that the names she is being called have no meaning or validity. Here are some informative ways to help her overcome her persistent fear of being teased.

1. Use famous success stories to help your child realize that everyone has something they could be teased about. Research and share with your child famous people who overcame the odds. From athletes who were too small to make the team but succeeded anyway to famous scientists who were called dumb and failed in school, there are endless success stories of individuals who must have been teased by peers but "made it" anyway. Your child will probably be surprised to learn about many idols and superstars around the country who faced tremendous odds as they pursued their dreams. From Pete Maravich ("Pistol Pete") who, despite what he was told, never stopped perfecting his game, and Johnny Unitas, who was considered too small to be a quarterback, to Albert Einstein, who was called retarded because of his big head, and Thomas Edison, who was labeled uneducable, there are many famous individuals who rose to stardom and made significant contributions despite what others said.

2. Teach your child a new response. Of course, the simplest response to teasing is no response at all. That is likely to be hard for your child. In addition to ignoring, teach your child to surprise her teasers with a quick retort. Using the list of tormenting phrases developed for the imaginary experiences, begin by having your child categorize the remarks. Sometimes the phrases children use to irritate a peer are silly: "Your mother wears combat boots." Laughing about some of these together will cause the comments to lose their effectiveness so she might not need to reply.

Another approach, though, is a quick answer that does not enrage the teaser. For example, "That's silly—no mom wears combat boots around the house," leaves the teaser speechless.

Identify a variety of verbal responses your child can utilize to counter an opponent. Include successful retorts that other children use. The response might be hilarity: "That's ridiculous; of course my mother has hair in her nose. Don't you?" A serious approach might put the teaser off guard—for instance, "What is your goal in teasing me?"

3. Help your child create several sentences he can say to himself when others tease him. Have him practice repeating each sentence to himself. This technique will help your child appear calm and unruffled.

OBSERVATION

Other children also get teased; they simply don't react the same way as your child does. Helping your child understand that his reaction to teasing is sometimes what keeps it going.

POSITIVE SELF TALK ABOUT TEASING

1. They are just trying to get me to react and I am not going to.

2. What he's saying is silly.

3. If I don't react, they will stop teasing me.

4. Other famous people were teased and they succeeded; I can, too.

5. _____

1. Watch the family interact. Sometimes family members can be more ruthless than anyone else. Although everyone should be supportive of your child, observing how you as well as other family members react to gentle teasing from loved ones will be constructive. If you have older children, bring up the subject of teasing at the dinner table. Avoid comparisons, yet encourage older siblings to share some of their experiences with teasing and how they handle it.

2. Instruct your child to be a detective. Send your child to school with the task of observing others being teased and how they respond. At home discuss what he observed and how the children being teased reacted. What kinds of things were said? Did the comments seem to be as hurtful as what is said to him? How did the children appear to feel? Which children are also picked on? Why does he think they are singled out?

3. Suggest your child talk to good friends. Good friends are helpful and truthful. Encourage your child to talk to several good friends about how they handle teasing and why they think your child is teased. Enlist their help in how your child might avoid being teased.

EXPOSURE

Build a series of experiences that harden your child to teasing. At each level of experience have your child report her anxiety level so that you both can sense improvement and you can gauge the amount of practice your child needs to change her reactions. Add to the list of experiences that follow this article with other experiences appropriate to your child's situation and fear.

1. Use role-playing to desensitize your child to the comments of peers. Using the list of teasing phrases you created for the imaginary scenes, devise a series of role-playing situations. Begin with the comments that your child is least likely to respond to and build to more difficult taunts. First, let your child tease you and show how you shrug off the words or reply with a quick retort. You might also indicate how you whisper positive comments to yourself to retain your resolve not to react. Next, change roles so your child can practice a nonchalant attitude. Replay each situation until your child's response to the words is neutralized and his anxiety ratings indicate he is comfortable. When the words no longer draw a visceral response, your child will be well on his way to ignoring his peers.

2. Elicit the help of a friend or sibling. Up until now you have assumed the offender role. Begin working your way through the list again with a friend or confederate as the teaser. In addition, have the friends create new situations that might develop as they play. When your child's fear ratings indicate she is not anxious, she will be another step along to controlling her reactions to teasing.

3. Tease your child unexpectedly. Tell your child that you will be teasing her when she least expects it so that she can rehearse and get a little toughening under her belt. Praise your child whenever she uses the practiced responses.

4. Have your child report episodes of teasing and his responses. Like feathers in his cap, have your child relate the occurrences when a peer teases him and he responds in a new way. Keep a record of these successes; they will soon dwindle to fewer teasing episodes as your child gains new confidence and overcomes his fear of teasing.

SEQUENCE OF EXPERIENCES WITH TEASING

1. Role-play planned teasing with parent.
2. Role-play planned teasing with a friend or sibling.
3. Have a parent use the list of comments to tease the child unexpectedly—but only at home.
4. Have a sibling use the practiced teases unexpectedly—but only at home.
5. Experience gentle teasing from parent in public.
6. Experience unexpected teasing with new comments from parent.

Books

Crow Boy. Taro Yashima. New York: Viking, 1955. A touching story about a boy who is "different" but discovers, as do his classmates, that everyone has something special to offer and be appreciated for.

Libby's New Glasses. Tricia Tusa. New York: Holiday, 1984. Embarrassed by having to wear glasses, Libby runs away from home and meets an ostrich who has buried his head in the sand to hide his own spectacles. They learn to see the light together, clearly through their glasses.

Little Men in Sports. Larry Fox. New York: Norton, 1968. The lives of Bobby Riggs, Phil Rizzutto, Mario Andretti, and others who became sports heroes in spite of their size. This book may be especially meaningful to a youngster who is small for his age.

Watch Out for the Chicken Feet in Your Soup. Tomie de Paola. New York: Simon and Schuster, 1974. When he brings his friend along for a visit, Joey is embarrassed by his old-fashioned, foreign-style grandma. It's Grandma's special qualities that amuse Joey's friend the most.

Wingman. Manus Pinkwater. New York: Dodd Mead, 1975. Donald Chen is the only Chinese-American kid, and classmates are making his life miserable by teasing him. Through his fantasy life reading comic books, he is able to cope with prejudice and to use his creativity in school.

11

SCHOOL FEARS

FEAR OF TESTS

Anyone who has ever taken a test can relate to the symptoms. Prior to the test you fear you won't remember anything that you studied, your heart beats rapidly, and you have a few butterflies in your stomach. When you are given your exam, you feel slightly queasy when you see a few questions on the first page that you cannot answer.

Most students get beyond those feelings. In a little while, they catch their breath, settle down, and do the best they can. There are, however, children and adults whose fears about tests hamper and inhibit their performance. Adam was in sixth grade when his problems were recognized. He studied hard, knew the answers during class discussions, but always did poorly on essay tests. When a test was passed out, his mouth would begin to feel dry. He'd look at the questions and panic. He couldn't remember what he had studied and would spend a good portion of the exam period worried that he would fail the test.

When a student's test anxiety reaches the point that it interferes with performance, it can affect the teachers's perception of her ability, her own self-concept and eventually her acceptance to college and professional schools. If your child gets anxious before tests, just saying "Calm down," and "Do your best" won't help. Learning how to study and the tricks to taking particular kinds of test will help, but your child may also need some help coping with the anxiety she feels in the test situation.

IMAGINATION

Helping your child see herself succeeding on a test—even if it is only in her imagination—is a major step in overcoming her fear.

1. Read books about school experiences. You probably won't find a story just about tests, but many books will include situations in which school-age characters are involved in school activities, including taking tests. If you cannot find a book appropriate for your child, make it an opportunity to involve your child and let her dictate her own. Write down the story as your child tells it, then read the story aloud. If your child has difficulty creating a positive story, suggest she tell the story from the character's point of view.

2. View television shows where the characters take tests. Most children's shows eventually get around to including a test in the story line. While they are not predictable, when they do come up use the show to ignite discussion about the plot and how the actors coped with the situation.

3. Play school. Get out old books, pads, pencils, and other school materials. If your child feels comfortable, invite a sibling or good friend to round out the class. Take turns being the teacher. Pretend it is test time. Continue such pretend activities until your child's fear ratings are in a comfortable range.

4. Have your child imagine himself taking a test. When your child is in a relaxed state, lead him through an imaginary test. Have your child imagine that his teacher announces a test in his best subject. Picture your child bringing home his books and studying for the exam. Describe how he feels prepared and has little difficulty falling asleep the night before the test. In the morning, he gets up, has breakfast, and looks over his notes before going to school. Continue by relating how he walks in the classroom and sits at his desk awaiting the exam. Always picture him feeling confident and relaxed in the situation. He starts the test, hits a question he doesn't know, and proceeds to the next. The imaginary situation can conclude with time being called and your child turning in his paper. You might resume with him talking to friends about the test, waiting to get the results, and going over his exam after it is returned. Always end your account with your child imagining himself earning a good grade. Repeat such scenes until your child feels little anxiety as he imagines himself coping successfully in a test situation.

INFORMATION
Most children assume that no one else—especially adults—gets nervous about tests. Tell her the truth and then teach her some facts about tests that will help your child feel more confident.

1. Explain the symptoms of fear. Use the second chapter of this book to explain to your child the sensations she experiences when a test is placed before her. Let her know that everyone gets nervous and she can control some of those feelings by using belly breathing and the other techniques you have taught her. Talk about your feelings about tests and the difference between anticipatory anxiety that one naturally feels before an experience and fear during a test.

2. Identify various kinds of tests and practice test-taking skills. If your child is young, he hasn't had a lot of experience with tests. Older students may need more instruction on study strategies and test-taking skills. Discuss how the kind of test that will be given affects the way your child should study. For example, with a multiple-choice test he needs only to be able to recognize the answer, while with a short-answer or essay exam, the student must supply the information. Ask your child's teacher to provide old sample tests and some information about test-taking skills and how to study. In addition, you might go to the book store or a teacher's supply store and choose age-appropriate skill-building books that will show a variety of tests. Help your child recognize the kinds of questions that are used in tests. Distinguish short-answer, multiple-choice, fill-in-the-blank, true-false, essay tests or others that are appropriate to your child's age. Practice taking the tests.

3. Teach your child how to study. Certainly, having effective study habits helps any student feel more confident. Sometimes children who have anxiety about tests need to overstudy to feel prepared. Young students do not have a lot of experience studying. Talk to your child about how to study for a test. Show your child how chapters in a text are organized. Demonstrate how chapter headings can be used to formulate study questions. He may not know that vocabulary words are italicized or presented in isolation. Help him define a study schedule so that he does not get in the habit of cramming for tests.

4. Help your child create a series of positive statements to counteract test-taking fears. Using the information your child has learned, develop a positive statement to combat each negative thought. Have your child write these on an index card and get permission from his teacher to bring the card to the test. Instruct him to set it on his desk and repeat the phrases when he begins to feel anxious.

POSITIVE SELF-TALK ABOUT TESTS

1. I know the material very well.
2. If I slow down I will remember the answers.
3. My mind is not blank.
4. This test is only one part of my grade.
5. I studied this material. If I take a deep breath, I will remember.
6. _____

OBSERVATION

Your child's fear stems from his concerns about performance. Watching other students take tests—seeing them scratch their heads, look around the room, and continue the task—helps your child realize that most people have some concerns about performance.

1. Have your child talk with other students about how they study for and feel about tests. Ask an older sibling or cousin to discuss with your child how he studies for a test. How does he know what to study? What kinds of feelings does he have before an exam? What does he do during the test? How does he correct negative thoughts that he has during a test?

2. Arrange for your child to watch a test session. Talk with your child's teacher or principal about observing another class as it takes a test. You will want to help your child make specific arrangements so no one gets the idea he is cheating. After the sessions, ask your child what the students were doing. How many got started answering questions immediately? Did anyone finish the test early? Did he see anyone looking worried or confident?

EXPOSURE

It's time to take a test, but your child will work her way through it gradually so that she is able to show how much she knows. Make sure your child is able to use the relaxation techniques taught in Chapter 2. Practice using the mini-relaxation skills to cue relaxed feelings in various situations. Have your child smile to herself, take a deep belly breath, and slowly exhale as she hears the word "relax" in her mind. Practice this technique with your child until she uses it automatically when she begins to feel tense.

1. Make a plan. Get the facts about the test. When will it be? What material does it cover? What kind of test will it be—short-answer, fill-in-the-blank, multiple-choice, essay? Help your child develop a study plan for the test and mark it on a calendar. Divide the material in sections that can be reviewed easily. Have your child write study questions based on the concepts or section headings in the chapter to be studied. Praise your child for keeping to the study plan.

2. Arrange for your child to sit in the classroom where the exam will be given. Explain to your child's teacher or the test administrator the difficulty your child is having. Get permission for your child to sit in the empty examination room several days before the test. As you sit in the classroom, lead your child through the exam using the sequence of experiences at the end of this article. Again remind your child to practice using positive self-talk and his relaxation skills to counter his anxiety.

3. Give your child a mock test. After your child has studied, create a study exam based on the material and the type of test the teacher gives. Next, choose a quiet location to administer the test. Have your child report his fear level as you hand out the exam and he answers the questions. Remind your child to use his coping skills to counter any anxiety he feels. Correct your child's test together, reviewing the material that was difficult for him.

4. Ask the teacher to administer a practice test. Most teachers will be happy to administer a practice test or a series of quizzes based on the material the class is studying. This will provide an opportunity for your child to practice his test-taking skills in a setting nearly identical to the actual one.

5. Help your child practice taking timed tests. Some children are particularly frightened by the clock. Help your child plan his approach to a timed exam. He might first answer all the questions he knows, then return to complete the rest. A second approach would be to allot time for each portion of the test. This might work best for an essay exam.

Continue the sequence of taking timed mock tests and practice tests until your child's anxiety lessens. If your child feels comfortable taking tests but is ruffled by the time factor, ask the teacher about the possibility of your child's taking an untimed exam until she feels more confident.

6. Have your child prepare for test day. In addition to helping her study for the exam, encourage your child to get a good night's sleep the evening prior to the test. Make sure there is enough time between the last study session and bedtime for a winding-down period. Your child might watch a videotape or a favorite television show, read, or take a long bath. Practice the relaxation exercises with your child before bedtime and then guide her through a positive scene in which she sees herself confidently taking the exam and doing well. In the morning make sure your child gets up early enough to eat a good breakfast. If you have time, lead your child through a positive scene in which your child sees herself getting a little nervous before the exam. She uses the mini-relaxation exercise and goes into the test feeling confident.

Remind your child to practice her coping skills before and during the test.

SEQUENCE OF EXPERIENCES WITH TESTS

1. Imagine taking a test.
2. Take mock tests of various types.
3. Take a practice test of specific material.
4. Take timed tests of various kinds.
5. Sit in the room where the test will be given and imagine taking the test.
6. Take an untimed test.

Books

How to Get Better Test Scores [*Grades 3–4; grades 5–6; grades 7–8*]. Edited by Jeri Hayes. New York: Random House, 1991. An excellent series of books to teach a student how to answer various kinds of questions. Although the books focus on standardized tests, the strategies taught will be helpful in many situations.

FEAR OF PUBLIC SPEAKING

His dad says he's shy; his mother says he just doesn't like to talk around strangers. Mario has been a quiet child since he started talking. Now, as a second grader, he haltingly reads aloud in reading group, although his teacher says he's a very competent reader. When he's called on to answer a question he freezes, and he never shares his opinion in class discussion.

Marla is a social butterfly with lots of kids around her. She's so concerned about what her friends think of her that she gets very nervous when she must stand up in front of her class. The butterflies in her stomach have gotten so strong she's afraid she will throw up. One time, much to her dismay, she had to leave the room during a presentation and she is sure everyone snickered behind her back.

Most of us experience some anxiety when we speak before a group. It's commonly thought that a little stage fright helps one "break a leg" during a performance. If you have an embarrassing experience or are shy, without a lot of opportunities to speak publicly, your fear can grow so that eventually simply announcing your name to a group is torture.

Studies show that a fear of public speaking is the number-one fear among adults; as many as forty to sixty million American adults are frightened to speak to groups or avoid it altogether. A number of organizations solely dedicated to helping individuals who are fearful of speaking in public have been formed over the years.

Every day talented men and women turn down nominations to be committee chairpersons and officers, promotions for managerial positions, and other career opportunities to avoid having to speak to groups. Helping your child overcome this fear will help her achieve in school, in life, and, most important, feel better about herself.

IMAGINATION

If your child is afraid to speak aloud, ask a question in class, talk at a family gathering, or give a report, it is evident that a fear of speaking in public is affecting his ability to socially interact with others.

1. Read books. In addition to reading books with stories about characters who are afraid to speak publicly, read aloud to your child from his favorite selections. Turn to old standbys that your child can easily read himself. Take turns reading aloud and acting out the dialogue in the stories. On other occasions have your child read into a tape recorder and then listen to himself.

2. View movies and shows. Anyone on television has a big job and must speak in front of many people in order to accomplish it. View favorite television shows with your child and talk about how he thinks the character is feeling during the episode. Watch live broadcasts like the morning news, local children's shows, and interview programs. Local programming is a valuable tool because the hosts are often very casual. Talk about what happens when something doesn't work as it should. How do the actors and personalities handle those situations?

3. Plan imaginative parties and build socialization skills. For a younger child, give a pretend party and have your child welcome her little stuffed guests. Play games where each person tells a story. Tell jokes to each other. Pretend your child is a movie star making an acceptance speech for an award. Create a variety of opportunities for your child to get up in front of her stuffed pals.

4. Lead your child through an imaginary speaking experience. Most people who are frightened to speak publicly cannot imagine themselves easily speaking to a group. After your child is relaxed, begin to describe a presentation your child gives to her class about a favorite hobby, a trip, or anything she truly enjoys. Picture your child preparing for the presentation, gathering notes, writing her speech, and practicing it. Portray your child feeling some butterflies before she speaks and even feeling a little trembly as she steps before the class. Describe how she counters these feelings by using her mini-relaxation exercise and begins speaking. Relate to your child the responsiveness of her audience and the compliments she receives from her teacher.

Repeat the imaginary experiences until your child's fear ratings indicate she can positively imagine herself asking questions and speaking before a group.

INFORMATION

Many children don't realize they are afraid to speak—they simply don't do it. Understanding that everyone has a little fear of speaking publicly is very helpful.

1. Gather some facts. Request information from the local chapter of Toastmasters International or other public-speaking groups. Explain to your child that one out of every four adults has the same feelings she does. Talk about famous actors who are frightened before appearing on stage.

2. Arrange a conference with your child's teacher. When a child is reluctant to share comments or ask a question in class, it is helpful to talk with the teacher. Many students consider asking a question a show of ignorance rather than a step toward learning. Hearing directly from her teacher that asking questions and taking part in discussions are important can clarify your child's misconceptions.

3. Explain the feelings. Your child needs to recognize and understand the physiological reactions that create butterflies in her stomach and make her feel anxious before speaking. Present the information in Chapter 2 to explain the dry mouth, sweaty palms, trembly feelings, and other sensations she experiences. Always emphasize that these are real feelings that rarely "show" on the outside.

4. Use the facts that your child gathers to create several positive statements she can use to counter any anxious feelings she might have about speaking publicly. Have her practice saying these to herself whenever she begins to feel nervous or frightened.

POSITIVE SELF-TALK ABOUT PUBLIC SPEAKING

1. Even if my knees knock, no one else sees them.
2. I have practiced my presentation and I am well prepared.
3. My teacher wants me to ask questions and share my opinions.
4. I feel more nervous than I look.
5. _____

OBSERVATION
Most people think that everyone can see how nervous they are when they speak publicly. The trembling hands, shaky voice, quivering lips, and sweaty palms are most noticeable to the speaker and rarely recognized by the audience. Even when someone is nervous, the audience commiserates. A major step to overcoming this fear is recognizing how the experience feels.

1. Have your child observe speakers at small meetings.
Suggest that your child observe the scoutmaster, his teachers, religious leader, and others who regularly speak to groups. Do they

seem nervous? Do they stumble over words and make mistakes? Does anyone think any less of them? Talk to the speakers about how their feelings change when they have to make a prepared presentation versus the extemporaneous kind of speaking most group leaders do. Ask them what they worry about. These people are likely to be very willing to share their feelings with your youngster when you explain your purpose. Your child is likely to be very surprised to hear that each of these people is nervous at various times. They might have been nervous during the presentation your child observed and will share the kinds of sensations they experienced.

2. Have your child talk to classmates. Before the next oral report, have your child ask a few good friends if they get scared before speaking. As your child watches a friend present a report, ask him to note whether he sees any obvious nervous characteristics. Even if he does, as an audience member, how does it make him feel about the speaker?

During class discussions, have your child note who asks questions and shares opinions. Are there other children who are typically quiet in class?

3. Listen to speeches with your child. Professional speakers go into training for their speeches. They work long hours to get the words and mannerisms right—and it still takes a lot of practice. Listen to audiotapes of famous speakers and watch them on videotape or in person. Have your child look for the mistakes they make. The point is, a few mistakes go completely unnoticed and detract little from a speaker's presentation.

4. Let your child watch you make a speech. If you do have opportunities to speak publicly, share with your child how you prepare for a presentation, as well as your feelings during a presentation. Arrange for your child to watch you firsthand and videotape the speech to watch together. Ask your child how he thought you felt. Share those points in the speech when you might have felt uncomfortable or been nervous. Does it show on the video tape?

EXPOSURE

Those of us who do public speaking know the only way you ever become comfortable with it is to do it often. Over the next weeks and months, provide a series of experiences and many opportunities for your child to become comfortable with speaking aloud to others. Stay with a particular experience until your child's fear ratings indicate that her anxiety is reduced and she is ready for a new level of experience. A complete sequence of practice activities is found at the conclusion of this section.

1. Have your child ask and answer questions at the family table. Some children are so inhibited that asking a question or sharing a comment at the dinner table isn't easy. Make it a practice that each person at the dinner table shares something about his day at the evening meal. In this way, your child is not singled out, but has a ready-made opportunity to speak. Encourage everyone to ask questions about world events, what is happening in the household, and what you will be doing during the weekend.

2. Have your child plan a question or two. When your family is attending a family gathering, encourage your child to talk with relatives about what she is doing. Have her plan one question she will ask a relative whom she hasn't seen in a long time. In addition, invite a favorite aunt, grandparent, or other relative to ask your child a general question, such as "How are things going?" Praise your child for whatever response she makes. Your child's fear rating after each of these encounters will provide feedback on how many more planned "impromptu" encounters you need to provide.

3. Help your child practice a short speech for family members. Have your child make a short speech for you on a topic he can easily speak about, such as his favorite foods, presents he would like to receive for his birthday, or a summary of the last movie he saw.

When his fear rating indicates he is comfortable giving this short presentation to you, add another family member to the audience. Continue with a series of speaking experiences, alternating short extemporaneous presentations and slightly longer planned presentations, such as reports about what he learned in school or book reports. Keep the audience friendly and small as your child becomes more comfortable talking before this kind of group.

4. Arrange for the teacher to ask your child questions in class that might be answered with a yes or no. Have your child keep a tally of the number of questions she asks or answers in class and reward your child's cooperation. Initially the teacher might call on your child once during the day and build from there. After your child is comfortable with this level of response, arrange for the teacher to ask your child questions that require a brief response. The teacher might make these requests in reading group or other small-group activities before requiring participation during whole-class sessions.

5. Read aloud. Reading aloud is a lost art, but one your family can easily develop. In addition to reading to your child before bedtime, have family members take turns reading the classics. Or select a book of childhood poems and alternate reading them aloud. You might also have your child dictate a story in his own words, illustrate it, and then read it back to you.

School provides many opportunities for your child to read aloud. Again, plan with your child's teacher several opportunities for your child to read aloud in class. Reading aloud during reading group or finding a passage that answers a question the teacher poses are natural opportunities in every classroom. Have your child keep a tally of the number of times he reads aloud each day and praise his participation.

6. Have your child present a planned report. It will be easiest if your child prepares her report and reads it to the class. Arrange many opportunities for your child to practice her report before she must present it to the class. Every opportunity to present the report—to you, to other family members—helps relieve anxiety for the public presentation. Reading the report into a tape recorder and listening to herself will also be helpful. If you have a video recorder, film your child's presentation. Explain to your child that many people don't like listening to or seeing themselves and that, in fact, we sound very different to ourselves than we do to others.

Have your child continue these practice sessions until her fear ratings are at five or less. Remind your child to use her relaxation skills and positive coping strategies to counter the anxious feelings she might experience.

When the opportunity arises, tape-record or videotape your child's presentation to a group. Compare the feelings she reports having experienced during the presentation with what you observe on the tape. What was her fear rating before the presentation? How does she sound or appear? Your child is likely to be quite relieved to know that most of these sensations are not visible to the audience.

7. Help your child work toward a large-group presentation. Continue the planning and practice sessions each time your child must make a presentation. Over time your child will come to understand that being prepared and practicing public speaking are the keys to overcoming her fear.

Books

The Berenstain Bears Get Stage Fright. Stan and Jan Berestain. New York: Random House, 1986. Sister Bear gets stage fright and overcomes it.

SEQUENCE OF EXPERIENCES WITH PUBLIC SPEAKING

1. Answer yes and no questions.
2. Answer short-answer questions.
3. Practice short talk to both parents.
4. Practice longer talk to parents.
5. Practice short talk to parents and siblings.
6. Practice longer talks to family.
7. Arrange with teacher to answer yes and no questions in class.
8. Arrange to answer longer questions in reading group.
9. Answer longer questions during whole-class discussions.
10. Read aloud to small group.
11. Read aloud in front of class.
12. Give short report to small group.
13. Give longer report to whole class.
14. Say a few lines in auditorium assembly.
15. Appear in a class play before whole school.

FEAR OF FAILURE

All of us remember what it felt like waiting for a teacher to return an exam. Did we pass or fail? How did we do in comparison to the rest of the class? Fear of failure runs deeper than concern over test grades. Many children are afraid to volunteer information in class or answer a question for fear of being wrong. An inability to take risks thwarts a child's ability to get information, to demonstrate what he knows, and to succeed in a variety of ways. Sometimes a child is unable to finish assignments within a given time limit because he is so afraid of making a mistake in print.

Fear of failure lives outside the classroom, too. Who isn't afraid of looking foolish? But does it keep you from trying something? For some children, it does. Other children worry that their error might affect others, so that they won't try out for sports, audition for the school play, or take part in group activities.

Everyone makes mistakes. Accepting the fact that no one is perfect is as important for your child as it is for you. Todd couldn't stand it when he made mistakes. When he was very young, he would get angry and quit a game if he made a mistake. After Todd made a foul in a basketball game, a teammate called him a "loser." After a while Todd was afraid to make a move on the court and eventually dropped off the team.

Assess your attitude to make sure you haven't set goals that are too high for your child to reach. In addition, consider your response when your child has made mistakes in the past. Every poor grade, every missed catch, and every misstep should be viewed as a natural part of life and an opportunity to learn. Avoid phrases like "Do your best." Although you mean well when you use it, children hear the phrase as "Nothing less than your best is acceptable."

IMAGINATION

Anticipating an error is worse than making one. Gently introduce the idea that everyone makes mistakes—and can learn from them. No one is "goof proof."

1. Read books about winning, losing, and making mistakes. Read books about normal children who, like the rest of us, don't always succeed—they make mistakes, lose games, and don't have all the answers. Read biographies of sports figures who share their triumphs and their failures. How did they handle the mistakes? Discuss how your child feels when he sees a friend make a mistake. A list of books with appropriate situations is found at the end of this article. But don't just stick to those; there are many others that you can add to your list.

2. Watch movies, TV shows and sports events. Laugh and the world laughs with you. Having a sense of humor helps a lot. Watch bloopers—the outtakes of various commercials, sports events, and television shows. Help your child to understand that what looks so perfect (and easy) is often the result of many trials and errors.

All sporting events offer opportunities to see someone make an error—they even count them in baseball. Spend time talking about the mistakes the participants make and how they handle them.

3. Take turns pretending to make mistakes. As you work on this fear, play a game in which the goal is to catch each other's mistakes. Purposely make mistakes as you write your shopping list, add change, or dial phone numbers. Encourage your child also to make mistakes on purpose. Take your child's fear rating when she makes a mistake. Continue the game as long as making mistakes on purpose causes her anxiety to soar.

4. Lead your child through an imaginary exploration of his greatest fears. Talk to your child about what kinds of mistakes he fears most. Is he frightened he will fail a test? Is he scared that he will make a mistake giving an oral report or drop a ball in the big game? Make a list of your child's feared mistakes in order of severity. Next, one by one lead your child through an imaginary experience in which he successfully handles whatever mistakes he makes. For example, after your child is relaxed, begin describing a situation in which he is giving an oral report at school. In the middle of the report, his mind goes blank, and he can't think of what happens next. He looks through his papers and they are out of order; he stands in front of the class shuffling papers, saying, "I forgot what I was going to say." As he looks at his classmates, who have encouraging smiles on their faces, his teacher says, "That's okay; take your time." Continue to describe how he successfully continues his presentation, ending with a rousing round of applause from his classmates.

At various sessions, guide your child through other embarrassing scenes until he can see himself getting through them successfully.

INFORMATION

Many children who are perfectionists have the misconception that everyone else does better than they do. Your child might think you were a perfect student or that you never make mistakes now. Help your child see the error of her thinking.

1. Share some failures. Unless you were a perfect student, pull out some old report cards and dispel the notion that you were an A + + student. Most of us can do that quite easily. Tell your horror stories and embarrassing moments both in the classroom and on the playing field.

2. Bring the story up to date. Why do pencils have erasers? Why are word processors so popular? They both make it easy to undo the mistakes everyone makes daily. Mistakes are correctable, and that's why there are hundreds of products in all shapes and sizes to assist your child—and everybody else. Talk about ways that people undo and appropriately cover their mistakes.

3. Create a series of statements your child can say to himself to counter his fear of making a mistake. Write them on index cards so your child will have his list at hand whenever he feels anxious.

POSITIVE SELF-TALK ABOUT FAILURE

1. Everyone makes mistakes.
2. No one is perfect.
3. If I make a mistake, I can correct it.
4. My friends and teachers understand that everyone makes a mistake.
5. _____

OBSERVATION

Your child needs to see other people making mistakes, not just hear about them.

1. Make your mistakes obvious. Be a good model. When you do make a mistake, talk it through out loud: "I forgot Aunt Martha's birthday; I will have to call her." "My bankbook won't balance; I must have added wrong somewhere." Share with your child that the word mistake suggests that even though you "miss" the first time, you should "take" another try to correct it.

2. Have your child relate what siblings and friends do when they make a mistake. Suggest that your child observe others or keep a simple log of the mistakes that peers and siblings make. Be sure your child shares his reasons with classmates before getting started. The important part of the observation is recognizing how others handle the mistakes they do make.

EXPOSURE

Many children who are frightened of making mistakes have unrealistic goals. The first step toward correcting this situation is to help your child set realistic goals for himself. If your views have promoted these attitudes, it is time for you to reassess your point of view.

Plan a series of experiences in which your child makes mistakes in public on purpose so that when he makes mistakes by accident he will be able to handle them.

1. Discuss his fears with his teacher, coach, piano teacher, and anyone else who can help. Agree not to react negatively when your child makes a mistake. Suggest that each adult acknowledge the mistake and ask your child how he feels about it. Finally, provide the opportunity for him to correct the mistake or start again.

2. Plan for your child to make a mistake. Some children have such a strong fear that they must be talked into making a mistake. Create a list of situations in which your child will make an error. Use the list that follows this article to provide a variety of opportunities for your child to learn it is not the end of the world if she makes a mistake. Your child might agree to set the table incorrectly. When she does this, take her fear rating. Have her leave the misplaced forks and knives until mealtime and admit to the rest of the family she made a mistake. After everyone applauds her error, permit her to correct the place settings. Next, suggest that your child purposely make a mistake on her homework, dial a wrong number, or misspell a word. Whenever your child purposely makes an error, have her take her fear rating before correcting it.

3. Have your child keep a diary of her own errors. Have your child keep a record of the number of questions she answers in class and the number of errors she makes. Mind you, we're not trying to create lousy students, just ones who will risk asking questions and be willing to share ideas and information without fear of being wrong.

EXAMPLES OF EXPERIENCES
WITH FAILURE

1. Dial a wrong number.
2. Make a mistake on homework.
3. Tell a joke wrong.
4. Answer a question incorrectly.
5. Miss a catch during a game.
6. Swing and miss the baseball.
7. Set the table incorrectly.
8. Sing a song with the wrong lyrics.

Books

The Berenstain Bears' Trouble at School. Stan and Jan Berenstain. New York: Random House, 1986. Brother Bear concentrates on the wrong things and starts failing in school. He gets a second chance and learns that it's never too late to correct a mistake.

The Beast in Ms. Rooney's Room. Patricia Reilly Giff. New York: Dell, 1984. This small chapter book features Richard "Beast" Best, who was left back in second grade because he had a slow start in reading. With time and assistance, Richard grows up some and actually enjoys reading.

Leo the Late Bloomer. Robert Kraus. New York: Simon and Schuster, 1971. A reassuring story of a small tiger who couldn't read, write, or do many things other small tigers could do, until "in his own good time" he blossomed.

The Little Engine That Could. Watty Piper. New York: Platt & Munk, 1930.

This is the saga of the little engine that didn't believe in failure but thought that it could help deliver toys and foods to the children living over the mountain. Children love this story, if for no other reason than its refrain: "I think I can, I think I can."

Petunia. Roger Duvoisin. New York: Knopf, 1950. Silly Goose Petunia thinks that just owning a book makes her wise, until she learns it's what's inside the book that really counts, and so she learns to read.

SCHOOL PHOBIA

Many children are a little jittery on the first day of school. What will the teacher be like? Who will be in my class? and Will the work be too hard? are questions that run through every student's mind. Even when they don't get the teacher they want, most children quickly acclimate to the new situation, and the majority trudge cooperatively, if not happily, to school each day. Occasionally a child will develop a real aversion to going to school. It might begin with a simple complaint on Sunday night that he doesn't want to go to school. He might not sleep well on school nights, or complain of stomachaches and headaches. Eventually every morning becomes a struggle to get the child out the door and onto the school bus. When the battle persists, there's a problem. It may come and go, but if the pattern repeats itself week after week, the chances increase that the child is school phobic.

Children have difficulty expressing their fears about school. A child might have a learning problem that makes school work very frustrating. He might not want to admit it to his teacher or you. Sean felt he couldn't do the work. Everyone else seemed to have the answers, but not him. Instead of asking for help, he avoided the situation by complaining about the teacher, the work, and his classmates. Other times he said nothing but simply resisted going to school. He had headaches and was nauseous. He dawdled in the mornings and picked fights with everyone.

A very sensitive child—especially a young child—might be frightened by an intimidating teacher. Though the child might never have done anything wrong, he could be traumatized by observing how the teacher disciplines other students.

Sometimes a child's anxiety has nothing to do with the school, the teacher, or the work, and everything to do with his classmates. A very shy or sensitive child might be lonely, afraid to speak out, or frightened of the class bully. Tanisha was seven years old when her problems came to the forefront. She refused to go to school. She was sick every morning and fought getting in the car. She would not say what was bothering her and there were no immediately discernible reasons. Finally, an older child in the school car pool mentioned to Tanisha's dad that there were a group of boys who were taking younger children's lunch money on the playground. Tanisha's problem is a classic example of being tyrannized by an older and bigger child.

There are many reasons why a child might unconsciously fear separating from a parent and refuse to go to school. Fear of a parent dying is very common and often arises when children are around the age of seven and again when they become preteens. If a parent is ill, injured, or going through a very difficult emotional period, separation fears intensify. Marital problems also cause a child's fears to surface. He might worry that his parents will argue if he is not around to prevent it. If one parent is depressed or dependent emotionally on the child for support, this, too, makes it difficult for a child to go to school.

Once a fear of school begins, it can persist long after the initial cause is resolved. After a bout with the flu, old fears can reappear so that the child mimics illness to avoid school.

It takes a concentrated effort to overcome school phobia. The following suggestions offer many opportunities to overcome this fear. If the problem persists, seek professional help.

IMAGINATION

Your child's imagination works against him when he envisions the problems he is going to have at school. Helping your child imagine school as a positive place is an important step to overcoming his fear.

1. Read books. Books broaden a child's view by exposing him to new experiences and new solutions. The books listed at the end of this section are but a few of the ones you can find to help your child feel more comfortable about going to a new class. For the older child, realistic novels show children dealing with the same issues and problems that your child might face: being teased, trouble with friends, family problems, and academic difficulties. How the characters overcome their problems can be very enlightening. Use the plots as a starting point for discussion.

2. Play school. Playing school is a favorite pastime of many young children; it gives your child an opportunity to be in control of the situation. You can steer the play into areas of concern and play out old scenes with new endings. In the process, you may get a new handle on what is bothering your child.

3. Lead your child through imaginary school experiences. Use positive images to build new views about leaving home and being at school. When your child is relaxed, have her imagine getting up in the morning and getting dressed for school. Describe a pleasant household with everyone getting up, having breakfast and leaving for school. Focus on positive experiences at school. If there are academic or social concerns, have her imagine coping well with each of the problems. If she is worried about something happening to herself or you while you are apart, alternate scenes of you at home or work with scenes of her at school. Always end your fantasy trip with a positive outcome and a happy reunion. Continue the imaginary trips until your child can imagine herself at school without becoming too anxious.

INFORMATION

Most children who develop school phobia have either realistic concerns or misconceptions about what is going on in the family or at school. Providing accurate information is an important aspect of overcoming fears.

1. Explain the problems at home. Parents frequently assume they can hide problems from their children. Unfortunately, children have a sixth sense about these things. Without your input, your child might magnify the problems that do exist.

Sometimes children overreact to the normal arguments that spouses occasionally have. Your child might be aware that friend's parents are getting divorced and fear that your fights mean that you will get divorced. Correct such misconceptions and attempt to tone down the arguments. If you and your spouse are having marital, financial, or other problems, explain it at the child's level of under-standing—tell him that just as brothers and sisters sometimes argue, so do parents.

If, in fact, you and your spouse are on the verge of a separation, you will not be able to hide it from your child. Avoid placing your child in the middle of an adult conflict. Instead, reassure your child that you love him and answer his questions as honestly as possible. In these matters, children have very specific concerns: Where will I live? How will I get to see each parent and how often? If you are getting counseling, explain that you are working on these issues so there will be fewer fights and strained silences.

2. Discuss the problems at school. When a child is afraid of something at school, you must search for the reason. Your child might have incomplete or incorrect information about teachers, the school building, other students, or the work they will be doing. Every year many children panic about being placed in the class of a particular teacher who they heard was strict or hard. Many students attribute a teacher's actions to simple meanness rather than instructional style. Correct any misconceptions your child might have by arranging for your child to meet the teacher and talk to other students who have a better perspective. "Mrs. Jones is the meanest teacher I ever had" from a fourth grader may become "Mrs. Jones taught me more than any other teacher I ever had; if it weren't for her I wouldn't be doing so well in seventh grade" when the same child reaches middle school.

School buildings look like labyrinths to young children. Learning how to get to his classroom seems like a big deal; other floors and hallways are unknown territories with lots of big kids. Take your child on a tour of the school; introduce him to the school secretary, the counselor, the librarian, and the principal. Knowing a few friendly faces throughout the school will make the place less intimidating. One young boy became friends with the school custodian. This special friend was always there with a friendly smile when the child needed one.

When a child has fears about bullies and gangs, turn to the school for the facts about the situation. If his fears are unfounded, correct the misconception. However, if there is some basis for concern, work out solutions for the problem. Arrangements were made, for example, so that recess periods for one child and the bully that frightened him never coincided. Take practical steps to make your child feel safe.

3. Help your child to create a series of positive statements he can use to counter any anxiety he feels. It is important for your youngster to have positive thoughts about school. Based on the information you have discussed, write a positive statement that contradicts the negatives thoughts that have filled his mind.

POSITIVE SELF-TALK ABOUT SCHOOL

1. My teacher is here to help me.
2. I have friends at school.
3. I know my way around school.
4. If anyone bothers me, I can tell the teacher.
5. _____

OBSERVATION

If your child is at the point where he is having trouble going to school or staying there, the observation step is especially important. With the cooperation of school officials, make arrangements for your child to be an observer.

1. Reassure your child that you will not trick him into staying at school. Drive your child to school, park, and watch the students arrive or exit at the end of the school day. Look for children your child's age. What are they doing? How do they appear? Are they having fun with friends? As you sit in the school parking lot, take a fear rating. Repeat the expeditions until your child is comfortable sitting outside the school.

2. Arrange for friends to share school experiences with your child. To keep up with the work and the classroom gossip, keep in touch with classmates. Ask classmates who like school to share their daily experiences with your child.

3. Have your child observe before and after school. Your child has many logical reasons for going to school. First and foremost, he needs to keep up with the work load. Arrange for your child to visit his teacher before or after school to get assignments. This provides an opportunity for your child to observe the classroom, the school, and the teachers or other students who might be around. It also provides one-on-one time with the teacher that can benefit your child in a number of ways. He will receive extra help with his work, and he will get to know the teacher better.

EXPOSURE

Observing school experiences is not the same thing as being a full participant. Whatever the original causes, you will have to ease your child back into the school setting in order to change his experience to a more positive one. A list of possible experiences follows this section.

1. Attend school with your child. Many children with school phobia have extended periods of time when they will not attend school. If your child has been absent from school for a long time, begin by going with him to school for a few minutes at the beginning or end of the school day. Remind your child to use his positive coping skills to reduce anxiety. Take your child's fear rating to indicate whether attending with you produces fear.

2. Move slowly out of sight. When your child is comfortable with you in the classroom, wean yourself from the immediate area, but remain elsewhere in the building. Once your child is comfortable remaining alone for a short period of time in the classroom, extend his stay, assuring him you will remain in a designated area in the building. In this manner, work toward your child staying alone in the classroom for longer time periods. Use your child's fear measurements to guide how quickly you escalate the periods of time your child is alone in the classroom.

3. Have your child enter school without you. The school psychologist, counselor, teacher, and principal all realize how difficult this is for your child. Often they will help your child become independent from you by becoming in-school liaisons for your child. The first step would be to have one of these individuals meet your child at the entrance to the building and escort him to the classroom.

4. Increase the length of time your child is able to remain at school. Once your child attends school for certain periods of the school day, work toward lengthening the time he remains at school. Some children find they can tolerate one part of the school day but become very anxious during another. Rather than leaving school for the difficult period, make arrangements for your child to spend time in another classroom or in the infirmary, and then return to his normal schedule. Always keep in mind that the ultimate goal is for your child to attend full days at school regularly. Prompt your child to use his relaxation techniques, positive self-statements, and other coping techniques to counter anxiety. If you do not see progress or the problem recurs, seek professional help. Many agoraphobics experienced school phobia as children.

SEQUENCE OF EXPERIENCES WITH SCHOOL

1. Visit before or after school to get schoolwork.

2. Visit during school to get work and talk to school personnel.

3. Attend school with parent for small period of time at beginning or end of day.

4. Stay at the beginning or end of day for a small amount of time without parent.

5. Stay longer at school with parent in other part of building.

6. Stay longer at school with parent gone.

7. Stay more of the day. Go to counselor or infirmary if feeling ill or anxious.

8. Stay more of the day in the classroom. If anxious, stay and work through anxiety in classroom.

9. Stay all day in school in classroom when anxious.

10. Stay at school with low or no anxiety.

Books

The Cat Ate My Gymsuit. Paula Danziger. New York: Delacorte, 1974. Entering junior high school is one of the traumas of this age-group. In this story, an understanding teacher helps a young girl over her feelings of insecurity about her new school.

A Child Goes to School: A Storybook for Parents and Children Together. Sara Bonnet Stein. New York: Doubleday, 1978. An informal, helpful introduction, in stories and photographs about going to school.

First Grade Jitters. Robert Quackenbush. New York: Lippincott, 1982. A small boy rabbit worries about going to first grade. He's concerned that his teacher will say "Oogley boogley" and expect him to understand things he doesn't know yet.

Ramona Quimby, Age 8. Beverly Clearly. New York: Morrow, 1981. Independent Ramona runs into lots of problems trying to cope with a new school, her parents' busy schedule, and a misunderstanding with her teacher. Her family is depending on her to be brave.

Steffie and Me. Phyllis Hoffman. New York: Harper & Row, 1970. A story about the friendship of two girls. This story appeals to children who have preschool experience, as they can visualize the schoolroom where much of the story takes place.

Timothy Goes to School. Rosemary Wells. New York: Dial, 1981. How comforting it is when Timothy finally finds a friend after what seems to him an unhappy start.

Will I Have a Friend? Miriam Cohen. New York: Macmillan, 1967. Anxiety about the first day of school ends up in happiness.

12

SPATIAL FEARS

CLAUSTROPHOBIA

First you begin to feel hot; the air around you becomes warm, close, and stale. You feel like you cannot get enough air into your lungs. The walls around you close in.

Approximately two out of every hundred adults are claustrophobic, but the feelings often began in childhood. When Kayla was six years old, she was caught in an elevator in her pediatrician's building for more than an hour. Thirty years later, Kayla still won't ride in elevators, and until she confronts her fear, that situation is not likely to change.

A teenager recently commented to us that both she and her mother always climb the stairs in buildings and at the mall. No elevators for them—they might get stuck in one!

Besides avoiding elevators, many people who are claustrophobic also fear crowds. Consider what it must be like to be a child in the middle of a crowd of adults. It's a sea of legs. If you look straight up you might be able to see the ceiling, but beyond that, forget it. It's a similar situation to an adult being in a small car situated behind a tractor-trailer rig and between two large trucks in a traffic jam. You can't see in any direction; you don't know when you will be able to move or why you are stuck; and you experience a loss of control.

In a crowd, there is the added element of heat caused by packed bodies. After being caught in a large crowd, a person remembers the warm, smothering feelings and begins to avoid places where people congregate—crowded pews at church, packed movie theaters, busy malls, small stores, parades, concerts, and even the back seats of cars. You can see that severe claustrophobia can lead to a person's isolating himself from humanity.

If your child shows signs of claustrophobia, help him get over it now. If you have this fear, use these procedures to help you overcome it first or have someone else work with your child.

IMAGINATION

The problem is that your child is already using his imagination too well. He imagines himself smothering and being pushed by a crowd. Help your child change those pictures.

1. Read books in which the characters experience crowds.
Select books where the characters go caving, attend the circus, view parades, and go other places where there might be crowds or they might feel closed in. Preview any book before sharing it with your

child. Avoid stories with dangerous situations or disastrous outcomes. As your read the stories, talk about how the people in the
crowds feel and what they do when they feel crowded.

2. View movies and shows. Any movie that shows street
scenes of masses of moving people is useful. Scenes of people walking on crowded sidewalks, army platoons marching, parades, and
crowds at football and baseball games will do. Talk and game shows
where the audience is shown offer another view. Don't forget movies
like 20,000 Leagues Under the Sea and other films that include sub-
marine shots. Have your child place himself in the crowd as you
watch. What's his fear rating? Continue these nonthreatening experiences until your child is comfortable simply viewing these settings
on screen.

3. Play make-believe. Make a list of situations that frighten
your child, then simulate each one as well as you can. Pull some
chairs together and pretend you are attending a movie in a crowded
theater. Stand in the corner of the room and pretend you have
stepped into an elevator. Crowd your child a little so she is pressed
closer into the wall. For each experience, use your child's fear measurement to gauge how many times you repeat the experience before
continuing to another one.

4. Lead your child through imaginary experiences. When
your child is feeling relaxed after completing the exercises outlined
in Chapter 2, begin to guide her through an imaginary elevator ride.
Take frequent fear ratings to determine how detailed and how long
to make the narrative. Describe how you get on an empty elevator
together. The elevator stops on the first floor and a couple of people
get on; it stops on the second floor and a few more people get on.
Your child feels the sleeve of the person next to her. She is pushed
to the back of the space as people continue to enter the elevator.
Continue your description as long as your child is able to imagine
herself in such a scene without too much anxiety. If your child's fear
rating is above five, end the scene and help your child relax. Continue having her imagine short elevator rides until you can build to
longer, more crowded trips.

On other occasions, have your child imagine herself enjoying a
movie in a crowded theater, making her way through bustling side-

walks, and experiencing other feared situations. Always describe your child as comfortably managing each experience.

INFORMATION

Helping your child understand the physical feelings that accompany claustrophobia as well as gaining the facts about elevators will help dispel some of the fears he has.

1. Explain the physical sensations that accompany claustrophobia. Your child needs to understand why he feels like he is smothering. Human bodies produce heat. Having a number of bodies in a small space actually increases the temperature of the surroundings. That's good news if you are caught in a snowstorm, but it makes things a little warm in a crowd. Use the information in Chapter 2 to explain to your child the other sensations he experiences.

2. Gather facts about elevators, auditoriums, and crowds. There are more than two million elevators in the world. Approximately four hundred million passengers safely ride in them daily. That's a lot of elevators carrying a lot of people.

Elevators in the United States must operate according to strict safety codes. Passenger elevators must have steel doors that can withstand fire. In fact, most elevators have two sets of doors, one set in the walls of each floor and the other attached to the moving elevator. A special safety device causes the doors to reopen if something is caught in them, and the doors to an elevator must be completely closed before the elevator will move. If an elevator moves too quickly, there are devices in the elevator shaft that grab and slow it. All automatic elevators have alarm bells and a phone or intercom system to connect passengers to the outside world. Elevators also must have another means of access for maintenance or emergencies, such as a door in the ceiling. If you work in a building with elevators, arrange with the maintenance staff for your child to inspect a stopped elevator. Ask the maintenance personnel to explain the built-in safety devices and the posted information that indicates how many people the elevator may safely carry and the last time it was officially inspected.

Large public buildings must also adhere to safety codes. Contact the ombudsman or official in your local government who is charged with the responsibility of handling complaints and providing information or the department official responsible for building codes. Request information about safety codes required in public buildings. Many buildings have emergency generators that supply light during power outages.

3. Create a series of positive statements your child can say to himself when he is frightened. Based on the information you have collected, help your child write several sentences to counteract negative thoughts. Remind him to practice saying them as he works through the desensitization experience.

POSITIVE SELF-TALK FOR CLAUSTROPHOBIA

1. Millions of people safely ride elevators every day.
2. I have plenty of air.
3. Nothing will happen to me, and I can call for help if I need to.
4. If I use my belly breathing I will feel better.
5. _____

OBSERVATION

Provide experiences that permit your child to watch adults, family members, and children participating in the experiences that frighten him. Many people would never consider walking the stairs when an elevator is available. Many children and adults adore

the smell of the popcorn and the excitement of being in a crowd.
For them, watching a film or a sporting event on the little screen is
no match for the "real thing." Observing others is an important
part of your child's work to overcome his fear.

1. Find an observation point that will permit your child to watch many people getting on and off elevators. Select a bank of elevators that have floor indicators above the doors. As your child observes, discuss what people do as they wait for the elevators. Do they look nervous or concerned? How do they look when they get off? If they're in a rush, do you think it is because they are frightened of the elevator or are they hurrying to an appointment?

2. Have your child watch family members ride in an elevator. Arrange for another adult to stay with your child as you ride the elevator from floor to floor. Measure your child's fear level and continue the experience until she can observe your ride without feeling anxious.

Repeat the experience, with siblings or friends riding an elevator. Have the child (always accompanied by an adult) ride to the first floor and return, then two floors and return, and so forth until your child's fear level as a spectator decreases.

3. Observe crowds with your child. Arrange to sit in the foyer of a movie theater as filmgoers enter. Before the movie starts, escort your child down the aisle as she looks at the rows of people. Repeat such experiences at church, theaters, and other places where audiences gather until your child can easily observe the crowd. Discuss how the people in the crowd look. Point out the things your child might notice that tell you that individuals in the audience are having a good time.

EXPOSURE

To desensitize your child to claustrophobia, you will help him participate in a sequence of experiences. Depending on how his particular fear manifests itself, you might have to provide a number of practice sessions for elevators, crowds, or other types of experiences. Use the suggestions that follow as well as the sequences of experiences listed at the end of this section as your child works to overcome his fear.

1. Provide a series of experiences with elevators. It will work best if you can ride the elevator at a time of day when few people will need it. As you hold the "open" button and block the door with your body, have your child step on and off an open elevator. Use your child's fear ratings as a guide to how much practice is needed at this level before proceeding to a new experience. Repeatedly remind your child to use his positive coping skills and belly breathing to counter anxious feelings. Next, walk onto the elevator with your child, press the button for the floor that you are on, so that the elevator doors will close and then open. At the next stage walk onto the elevator, allow the doors to close but do not push a button. The doors will not open until you push the "open door" button or press the button for a floor. Once your child's fear rating indicates he is comfortable, ride with your child up one floor while another adult remains in the lobby. When your child is comfortable with that experience, continue with both adults riding with the child. Proceed one more floor at a time, until your child is able to ride to the top floor of a building and back with little anxiety. If your child is old enough to ride alone, proceed by having him repeat the same sequence of experiences alone.

At the next level of experience, initiate rides with other passengers. Add siblings or friends, one at a time, to the entourage. Later, get on an elevator with a few strangers, working your way through each situation until your child's fear rating indicates he is able to ride on a crowded elevator.

2. Provide a series of experiences to help your child overcome a fear of crowded auditoriums. Begin by entering the space with your child and sitting together on the end seats of the back row. Remain sitting at the back of the auditorium or theater until your child's anxiety ratings indicate he is comfortable. Remind him to breathe slowly from the diaphragm and to use positive self-talk to counter negative thoughts and feelings. Next, move over one seat at a time until your child is able to sit with people on either side of him in the center of the row. When your child's fear ratings are steadily below five, begin moving up one row at a time toward the front of the auditorium. At each row, sit in seats on the aisle and then in middle of the row with as many stopping points in between as needed to help your child become comfortable.

3. Provide experiences to help your child feel more comfortable in crowds. Begin by walking with your child down the sidewalk of an uncrowded street in the business district or a mall area that is typically frequented by many people. Next, walk down the same street as it gets more crowded. At first, walk on the edge of the crowd. According to your child's fear ratings, move toward the center of the crowd as your child becomes more comfortable. Over the next weeks and months continue with experiences at malls and arenas as they become crowded during sales or when people enter or leave sporting events.

SEQUENCE OF EXPERIENCES WITH ELEVATORS

1. With a parent or adult, get on and off elevator, leaving door open.
2. With a parent, get on empty elevator and permit door to close for a few seconds.
3. With a parent, stand in closed elevator for an increasing period of time.
4. With adult staying on the main level, ride with another adult up one floor and back down.
5. With both adults, ride up one floor and back.
6. Continue the experiences, adding one floor each time.
7. Repeat the rides one floor at a time, adding siblings and friends until the elevator is crowded.
8. Ride one floor on an elevator where there are already one or two strangers.
9. Get on crowded elevator and ride to gradually more floors.
10. For older youngster or teenager: Ride elevator alone as adult waits in lobby.

SEQUENCE OF EXPERIENCES WITH AUDITORIUMS

1. Sit in the aisle seat in the back row of empty auditorium.
2. Sit in the back row, moving one seat in at a time until able to sit in center seat.
3. Move one row up, sitting in aisle seat and working toward center, continuing until child is able to sit in center seat of front row of empty auditorium.
4. Sit in center seat of empty auditorium with friends on either side.
5. In an empty theatre, move up one row, sitting on aisle and center seats with friends on either side.
6. Repeat series of experiences with friends seated nearby in a normally crowded theater.
7. Repeat series of experiences with strangers seated nearby.

SEQUENCE OF EXPERIENCES WITH CROWDS

1. Walk down a street when it's not crowded.
2. Walk down a street along with others.
3. Walk down a street along the outside of a crowd.
4. Walk down a street, moving toward the center of the crowd.
5. Walk inside a covered mall when there are few shoppers.
6. Walk inside a covered mall when there are increasing numbers of shoppers.
7. Leave a crowded event before most people do.
8. Leave a crowded event with most of the crowd.

FEAR OF HEIGHTS

Four-year-old Jonathan had been going up and down stairs for a long time when suddenly one day he became terrified while coming downstairs for dinner. He clung to the banister and wouldn't move until his dad carried him downstairs. Now he will not go up or down steps without holding on to someone.

Seven-year-old Samantha has never been fond of heights. On the playground she won't climb up the steps to the slide. She only likes to swing gently and doesn't want anyone to push her higher. Her younger brother taunts her as he flies through the air and jumps from his swing.

Jamal is a good swimmer and loves the pool except when his friends try to get him to go off the high dive. At thirteen, he has tried to hide his fear for years, but it is getting harder to come up with excuses. He once got as far as the top step but couldn't go any further. He backed down in utter humiliation.

Three children, three different stories; and these are only a few of the many we have heard. A fear of heights might embarrass a child but more important, it's likely to prevent him from participating in many childhood activities. Often these children try to avoid heights. That's not easy. On a school field trip, one eight-year-old discovered he couldn't walk across a balcony at the state capitol. A parent had to walk him across the building by another route.

Ignoring this fear will not make it go away. In fact, a fear of heights is one of the most common adult fears, affecting approximately 165 out of every 1,000 people. Many adults won't drive over bridges, fly, or even take a hotel room on an upper floor because of it. Many more won't climb ladders or look out high windows. If your child has a strong fear of heights that has persisted longer than the fears of his friends, he will need some help to get over it. If you have the same feelings, you must get over your fear before you can help your child. The steps below will aid both of you. Enlist the assistance of another family member or a good friend.

IMAGINATION

Your imagination is a hindrance when it runs wild. Help your child to imagine himself successfully dealing with heights.

1. Read books. Look at the illustrations and read stories that include characters who successfully deal with activities that involve height. With a younger child, read books about children enjoying various activities that take place off the ground, such as swinging, going down slides, climbing trees, going on amusement rides, hiking up mountains, and riding on airplanes. Stories about trips in hot-air balloons and high-wire acts are perfect, too. For older children, look for more mature stories about amusement rides, mountain climbing, flying, and other elevated pursuits. Remember you are not pushing the notion that your child will do all of these activities; you simply want to introduce characters having fun "above the ground."

2. Watch movies that have "lofty" scenes. From *Around the World in 80 Days* to *Those Magnificent Men in Their Flying Machines* and the opening scenes of *The Sound of Music*, watch films in which the characters contend with heights without any problems. Watching circus acts and shows like *Circus of the Stars*, in which actors learn new high-flying skills, will stimulate your child's imagination. Take fear ratings as you watch these shows. If your child gets too scared at any point, stop the film. Back up and repeat the scenes until your child's anxiety returns to a manageable level, then continue the movie. On another occasion, have your child watch the film and pretend she is the main character. Stimulating her imagination like this might increase her anxiety, but continue until her fear decreases.

3. Pretend you are in various situations. Acting out various situations you've seen in movies or read about can be very effective with a young child who has a good imagination. For example, pretend that you are walking on a high wire strung across the floor. Carefully balance your way across the span. Take an imaginary trip in a hot-air balloon. Talk about the people and places you can see on your trip. Pretend to pick a leaf off the top of a tree. Play airplane with your child; let him be the pilot and you the copilot. Make each session fun and don't indicate that you think that pretending alone will overcome the problem.

4. Lead your child through a planned sequence of imaginary steps. When your child is feeling relaxed, begin to describe an imaginary scene in which your child successfully copes with some of his fears. Add many details to make the scene realistic. As you move through the scenes take frequent fear measures to guide how fast you progress.

Start with imaginary situations that you anticipate to be easier for your child, such as standing on the first step of the ladder on a slide. Gradually picture your child climbing one step at a time to the top of the slide. When your child's fear ratings indicate she is comfortable, continue the story with her sliding down the slide and into your arms. Follow a similar sequence with diving boards, swings, stairs, balconies or whatever setting frightens your child. Be sure to end each session with a successful experience.

INFORMATION

It will be helpful for your child to understand his fear as it relates to the body.

1. Learn about how the body balances. A fear of heights is inborn. Studies have shown that infants as young as six to fourteen months will not crawl across a clear glass section of floor. This fear kept our forbears from going over cliffs, off mountains, and into ravines.

It is important that your child understand why he feels the way he does when he approaches heights. When you near the edge of an overlook, you become aware of your body reacting to keep itself in balance. As you lean forward, your inner ear sends a signal that causes you to rock back. This natural act of balancing is often misinterpreted as feeling like you are going to fall forward. Use children's encyclopedias and other resource books that gather information about the body's sense of balance.

2. Demonstrate the body's sense of balance. After reading about balance with your child, demonstrate the concept. Stand up and close your eyes. Although you are not standing on the edge of anything, you will naturally sway back and forth. Accentuate the motion by standing on one foot. Next, have your child close his eyes and feel the sway. Discuss with your child how this feels.

3. Explain the architecture of the structures your child fears. Some children who are afraid of heights fear that the structures they are standing on may collapse. Feeling vibrations on bridges or balconies, observing the sway or rattling of elevators, or seeing bolts on swings and slides can cause distress. Explain to your child how the architects and engineers design these constructions so that they are safe. Depending on your child's age, talk about safety procedures and the amount of education people must have to design these structures. Assure your child that the engineers who design bridges and balconies build in steel reinforcements to handle any swaying or vibrations. Explain how the expansion joints on bridges and in buildings are put there to deal with the expansion and contraction of the materials when there are changes in temperature. Show him how lock-washers work to keep bolts from coming undone. Discuss how swings, slides, and other pieces of playground equipment are anchored in the ground and reinforced with concrete below ground level.

4. Help your child create a number of positive statements he can say to himself when he feels anxious about heights. As you work through the various practice situations, remind your child to repeat these statements to block negative thoughts.

POSITIVE SELF-TALK ABOUT HEIGHTS

1. I will not fall over the edge.
2. What I am feeling is natural.
3. The _____ is built according to strict safety standards.
4. I can look out this window; I will not fall out of it.
5. _____

OBSERVATION

It will be difficult for your child to relate to children who are daredevils and hang upside down from trees. To help your child overcome his fear of heights, help him observe you and then other children deal with typical situations. Watching someone else go higher is bound to increase your child's anxiety. Have your child rate his fear frequently and prompt him to use the mini-relaxation exercises and other coping skills to remain calm.

1. Have your child watch you climb a ladder one step at a time. Ask your child to rate how much fear it causes him as you progress to each step. Continue accordingly. Climb a set of stairs. Stand close to the banister while your child watches from a safe distance. Work your way up to higher floors. You may find yourself swinging, going down slides, and going off diving boards to help your child overcome this fear. In each situation talk about how watching you makes your child feel.

2. Observe other children together. Go to the playground, pool, or other places where your child can watch children dealing with heights. Focus on children who are close to your child's age. Have your child describe what he sees. Without making any comparisons, point out how much fun children seem to be having. Ask your child to rate his anxiety as he watches his peers. Repeat these observation excursions until your child is comfortable watching other children do things that frighten him.

3. Have your child imagine himself playing with the children. When your child is comfortable watching other children, have him imagine what it would feel like to be up where they are. As he imagines himself in various situations, remind your child to use his relaxation skills to control his anxiety level. As your child gets more comfortable, move closer and closer to the playground and children. You may even talk to some of the children as they hang above you, sit on the jungle gym, or get ready to dive off the diving board. If your child decides on his own to try to climb or swing, let him do so at his own pace, but don't prompt the action yet.

EXPOSURE

Now that your child has learned about heights, imagined himself going higher, and observed others, it is time for him to move up in real life. To accomplish this, you must attack heights one step at a time. Depending on your child's age and which heights he has been avoiding, use the following exercises to overcome his fear.

1. Pace your child through a series of experiences to overcome a fear of climbing ladders. Use a sturdy, self-standing ladder. It doesn't have to be a tall one. Any ladder that raises your child's fear is fine, as long as it isn't so tall that you truly have to worry about your child's safety. Although you will be standing near the ladder as a safety precaution, don't communicate this message to your child. Position the ladder on a carpet or some other soft surface—just in case.

Begin by having your child climb the bottom rung. Take a fear reading. If this height doesn't create anxiety, instruct your child to climb the ladder one step at a time until he reaches a point where he experiences a moderate fear rating (around five, or "half-full"). Praise your child for using his relaxation and other coping skills to stay at this height until his fear drops. If you need to, place your hand on your child until he feels more stable. Once his level goes down, have your child climb one more step up the ladder.

Repeat the same process. Between trials, let your child climb down the ladder to rest. Being able to climb up and down the ladder at will is an important accomplishment. It will give your child a sense of control and help the desensitization process. Continue with this practice over a few weeks until your child can reach a reasonable height for his age. Remember to praise him for each step of progress.

Between sessions or opportunities to climb, your child's fear might creep back up. Reassure him and simply work your way back to where he was in the previous session. There is always another day and another practice session. If he continues to practice he will get where he wants.

2. Help your child overcome a fear of playing on various pieces of playground equipment. The playground provides many natural ways to practice overcoming heights. You may start on the swing if that is what bothers your child. Agree on how high she wants to be pushed and stay at that level at first. If your child's fear reading is not too high, ask your child if she is ready to swing a bit higher. Stay at each new height until her level once again drops. Continue on in this fashion until you reach a height that is reasonable for a child her age.

Slides also offer good opportunities to deal with heights. Find the smallest slide that your child is comfortable with. Use the procedure described with ladders to help your child reach the top of the slide. Initially, to help your child feel more comfortable, you may follow him up the ladder and slide down with him. Be sure to take fear readings and praise your child for using coping skills. As your child progresses, he should be able to climb the ladder and slide down by himself. Eventually he will be able to tackle taller slides. Repeat the steps, accompanying your child on the slide the first few times until he is ready to conquer it alone.

3. Help your child overcome a fear of stairs and ramps. Stairways and ramps seem pretty scary to a child who has a fear of heights. At first, position yourself between the railing and the child. Slowly walk up the ramp or stairway one flight at a time. At each level, work on your child's being able to get closer and closer to the edge. At first he may only be able to peer over the side for a second. That's okay. Reinforce him for staying at that spot and then looking over the edge for a few seconds longer. Take frequent fear measures and as your child's levels drop, work your way to new heights. One boy who was terrified to go up the ramp at the baseball stadium went from clinging to the inside wall and his father's hand as he walked the ramp to walking in the middle of the path and holding his dad's hand to walking by himself near the outside railing and looking over on the edge. It took attendance at several baseball games to master this skill, but this young fan felt as if he was doing better than the home team.

4. Help your child overcome a fear of inside heights. Many modern hotels and buildings have inside balconies. These afford an excellent way to practice dealing with heights. Begin at the lowest floor that your child can tolerate with moderate anxiety as he stands back from the rail. Start by helping your child move closer to the railing. At first she may need to hang on to you. With each step, praise her for getting closer to the railing and staying there until her fear drops. When your child feels comfortable standing near the railing of the balcony as she holds your hand, it is time to prompt her to let go of you, if only for a few seconds. Praise your child for standing by herself near the railing for longer periods of time. Once your child feels little fear standing by herself near the railing, it is time to move up a floor. Repeat the same sequence on each floor until your child is able to stand near the railing of the highest floor in the building.

5. Provide a series of experiences to help your child feel comfortable on amusement park rides. Not everyone likes riding roller coasters and parachute drops. However, if your child is too afraid to go on even the tamest amusement rides because of his fear of heights, you may want to help him approach some rides. Select a ride that is designed for younger riders. If your child is older and would be embarrassed by being seen going on one of these, take along a younger sibling or cousin to act as a shill. Before going on any ride, let your child observe others for as long as it takes for his anxiety ratings to decrease to a comfortable level. Discuss what aspect of the ride might bother him. When he is ready, let him pick where he wants to sit (inside seat or outside, front or back). If your child becomes anxious and you must pass up your place in line, make an excuse to the attendant that puts the blame on you, not your child. One teenage boy accompanied his parents and his younger brother on a small roller coaster. None of the onlookers saw anything strange and after numerous trips on this, the teenager rode the hanging airplanes with the family. No one knew he was working on his fear of heights, not even his little brother. After a few trips to the amusement park, he was able to ride the cable car system from one end of the park to the other and a few other rides with decreasing anxiety. Although he didn't get up the nerve to try the "scream machine," the young man felt very comfortable that he wouldn't be embarrassed if he went to the amusement park with friends.

It's a mistake to push your child to try a ride he is not ready for, but exposure to some rides can help him feel more comfortable overall.

SEQUENCE OF EXPERIENCES WITH LADDERS

1. Stand at base of ladder.
2. Stand on first rung of ladder with parent's hand for support.
3. Stand alone on first rung of ladder.
4. Repeat sequence for each rung of ladder.
5. Slide down small slide with parent.
6. Slide down small slide alone.
7. Repeat sequence with bigger slides.

SEQUENCE OF EXPERIENCES WITH RAMPS OR STAIRWAYS

1. Stand next to inner wall of the bottom landing of a flight of stairs or ramp, holding parent's hand.
2. Stand next to inner wall of the bottom landing of stairs alone.
3. Move closer to railing, holding parent's hand.
4. Stand at railing alone.
5. Quickly look over railing.
6. Stand at railing and look over side for longer period of time.
7. Move to next floor and repeat sequence.
8. Work through sequence for each floor of stairs.
9. Practice walking up and down stairs or ramp.

Books

At the Circus. Better Homes and Gardens. Des Moines: Meredith Corp., 1991. Max shows the reader different parts of the circus, including the high wire.

The Big Balloon Ride. Eleanor Coerr. New York: Harper & Row, 1981. Ariel, a stowaway, experiences her first balloon race with the best lady balloonist in America—her mother.

Jack and the Beanstalk. Tony Ross. New York: Delacorte, 1980. The story of Jack, who visits the giant by way of a very tall beanstalk.

Spot Goes to the Circus. Eric Hill. New York: Putnam, 1986. Spot investigates the circus and is in awe of the huge animals and flying trapeze artists.

13

FEAR OF FEAR

Eleven-year-old Ann has always been a nervous child and a fearful one. She was afraid to swing or climb a slide; she hid from the family dog, and has always been wary of new faces. Leaving her at preschool was a struggle; day after day she clutched her mother's hand so she could not leave. In fact, Ann is the type of child who might be described as being afraid of her own shadow.

Sometimes now when Ann is away from home or separated from her parents, she begins to feel strange. Her heart races; she feels faint; she complains that she has a lump in her throat; and she feels like she can't catch her breath. Her parents have taken her to doctors on many occasions, but extensive tests have revealed no medical cause for her symptoms. Great-aunt Mary says, "It's nerves."

Without a logical explanation, Ann's fears have escalated. Not knowing when the feelings might recur, she's afraid of having another "attack" at any moment. As a result, she is reluctant to go places without her parents. They are ready to take her to a therapist.

The symptoms Ann is describing are a classic panic attack. It used to be thought that only adults had panic attacks, but we now realize there are many children like Ann. Some suffer in silence, trying to hide their feelings from everyone. Others become hysterical and demand more and more attention. Fear reactions of this degree rarely go away on their own.

After experiencing a few panic attacks, a child becomes afraid of fear itself. Whenever she begins to feel anxious, she worries she's about to have another full-scale attack. She doesn't understand what is happening, and her parents usually don't, either. Without help, the fear of fear spreads. A child may develop school phobia (see Chapter 11) that comes and goes over the years. Many adults who suffer from panic attacks or who have agoraphobia (fear of leaving home or going into public places) were school phobic or had panic experiences during childhood.

If your child is showing signs of panic, address the problem now. The suggestions in this section may help with this process, but if your child's problems are strong or don't lessen as you work through these exercises, seek the advice of a therapist who specializes in working with children with such problems.

IMAGINATION

With a fear of fear, a child's panic can be ignited by a thought. Help your child use his imagination to counter past experiences and understand the feelings he is experiencing.

1. Read books. Identify the various kinds of situations in which your child has felt panicky previously. Select books that depict children who are happy in those settings. As you read the stories, have your child pretend she is the main character in the stories. Read similar stories until your child indicates she is comfortable imagining herself in those situations.

2. Use the child's imagination to his advantage. Your child may seem to panic even though there is no immediate danger, but a past experience may be the cue. He might remember a previous occasion when he panicked, experienced scary feelings, struggled through, or fled a situation. Getting ready for school or a visit from a friend might call to mind an experience when he had the same feeling. Quickly his mind launches into a series of images that send him into a panic.

To counter images of himself panicking, have your child imagine himself in positive scenes, successfully coping with any fears he might have until the scary sensations subside. List a series of situations that frighten your child. After using the relaxation techniques described in Chapter 2, lead your child through an imaginary scene from his list. Describe the scene in detail, having your child imagine himself relaxed and calm as he participates in the experience. Picture him as having a good time in the setting. Have your child report his fear ratings as you work through various scenes, repeating each episode until his fear ratings indicate he can comfortably imagine the positive outcomes you suggest.

3. Focus on the physical sensations. Focus on the physical sensations that bother your child. Using the same techniques described in Chapter 2, have your child imagine the sensations he experiences as positive feelings by trying to associate them with more pleasant experiences. If your child is troubled by his rapid heartbeat, have him imagine running a race or doing any exercise he enjoys and feeling his heart pumping strongly but safely. If he is afraid of feeling lightheaded or dizzy, have him imagine himself spinning on an amusement park ride or turning around as he dances or plays Pin the Tail on the Donkey. You might be able to associate the jittery feelings he experiences in his stomach with the beautiful butterflies he sees outside in the spring.

4. Identify typical situations in which everyone feels nervous. Your child is having difficulty identifying those situations in which the feelings she is experiencing are normal and natural. Identify common situations in which most children feel nervous—playing in a piano recital, giving an oral report, or acting in a play. Have your child imagine herself awaiting the cue for her entrance in the school play. Describe the feeling of butterflies in her stomach. When she finishes her lines, the feelings subside and she receives a round of applause. In a similar manner, describe your child successfully taking part in various situations even though she experiences the feelings that worry her.

INFORMATION

Your child does not understand what is happening to him.
Providing the information to explain the physical symptoms he
experiences is crucial to beating the fear of fear.

1. Explain fear to your child. He doesn't know why he panics or what it does to his body. He only knows that he is very scared and doesn't like the way he feels. Use the information in Chapter 2 to explain the fear response to your child. Adapt the contents to your child's age. For very young children, simply label the emotion and the feelings: "You get scared. You feel kind of shaky." As a child gets older, you can use more precise explanations: "When you get scared, your body feels like it wants to run. When you get ready to run fast, you start to breathe more quickly, your heart beats faster, and your muscles tighten like a rocket ship getting ready to take off. Your body prepares you to take off in a similar way when you get scared." It is the perfect time to reiterate the importance of belly breathing and the relaxation exercises to counter anxiety. Using relaxation skills is the most important thing you can encourage your child to do to counter panic.

Preteens and teenagers have an understanding of the human body that permits a more detailed explanation of the relationship between the fight-or-flight response and the nervous system. Read and discuss Chapter 2 together.

2. Explain your child's pattern of avoidance. Your child, like other children and adults who experience panic attacks, associates his panic attack with the place that he happens to be when it occurs. With the mistaken assumption that the place caused the panic, it is logical that he prefers to avoid those locations and similar ones. This is the way that fear spreads.

Explaining the association and avoidance process to your child is an important step in breaking the cycle of fear. By avoiding a location, he simply increases his fear of that place. The connection is not real, but the fear is. *If,* instead of avoiding a location, he goes there again and again, your child will become more comfortable.

3. Make a list of positive statements your child can use to counter anxiety. What your child says to himself adds to his fear. Based on his new understanding, help him create several positive statements to counter anxiety.

POSITIVE SELF-TALK ABOUT PANIC

1. I am not sick; I'm just scared.
2. Everyone gets anxious sometimes.
3. If I continue what I'm doing, the feelings will go away.
4. If I practice my belly breathing and relax, I will feel better.
5. _____

OBSERVATION

Everyone gets anxious sometimes. Before performances, presentations, and speeches, most people experience butterflies in the stomach, sweaty palms, and a lump in the throat.

1. Share the experiences of friends and family members. Encourage your child to talk to family members and friends about their experiences. He will be very surprised to discover how many people have had similar experiences. When he attends plays or recitals of friends, have him ask how they felt before and during the performance. It will be helpful to know that they were experiencing butterflies, knocking knees, and other symptoms that didn't show. Have your child watch for signs of anxiety in family members and friends.

2. Learn about the experiences of others. It will be hard to observe anyone having a panic attack. Occasionally a television show or movie will incorporate a scene when the actor experiences acute fear. However, your child must know that he is not alone and that numerous people have experienced panic attacks and gotten over them. Willard Scott, weather forecaster on the *Today* show, Carly Simon, singer and songwriter, and other television personalities appear at ease on the screen but have worked hard to overcome their fears of performing in public. Sharing the experiences of known personalities can be very helpful. Watch the president and other public figures as they appear on TV. Your child might be surprised to see that even these professionals get nervous.

EXPOSURE

Panic can control your child's life if he lets it. The key to taking away the power of panic is for your child to continue to enter the situations he fears and to experience the feelings of panic without fleeing the situation.

1. Prove to your child that the sensations are not harmful. Many people who experience a panic attack are afraid they are going to die. Panic attacks are one of the major causes of emergency room visits by adults. After having ruled out any medical causes with your child's physician, it is important for your child to be convinced his symptoms will not hurt him. Talk to your doctor about the types of exercises that are suggested and proceed only with his approval. If your child is frightened by his rapidly beating heart, walk stairs, jog, jump rope or do other kinds of aerobic exercise with your child. Before and after exercising, take pulse readings for each of you so that your child can see the change in heart rate and realize that it is not a sign of danger. Similarly, blow up balloons, inflatable toys, and pool rafts with your child so that he can experience a lightheaded feeling and learn that he will not faint. Eating salty crackers will prove to him that he can still speak with a dry mouth. Of course, don't allow your child to stuff his mouth so full that he chokes.

2. Plan a series of experiences to expose your child to the feared situation. Once your child is assured that the feelings that accompany panic will not hurt her, she will be more willing to enter situations she has avoided. Make a list of feared places, ranking them in order of least to most feared. If your child is avoiding public places such as theaters, crowds, or malls, then these are the places you must go. Go to the location that your child indicates is least worrisome. Stay in that location for as long as your child is able—it's likely to only be a few minutes the first time. Use your child's fear ratings to guide your experience, repeating each experience until your child's level of discomfort decreases. Remind your child to use her belly breathing and other relaxation skills to counter the anxiety she feels. In addition, use the appropriate sections of this book for specific suggestions on dealing with separation and other fears that may contribute to her panic. It will take numerous practice sessions for your child's feelings of panic and anxiety to subside. Stick with it; over time your child will be able to enter each situation without feeling the sensations that paralyzed her before.

14

FEAR OF DEATH

In the book *On Children and Death*, Elisabeth Kübler-Ross states that those who learn to know death, rather than fear it and fight it, become our teachers about life. She's talking about children who are dying. No parent wants his or her child to have such an intimate knowledge of death. It frightens us more than any words can ever convey. Perhaps that is why we have such a difficult time talking to our children about death. If we shield them from it, we think we can protect them.

Children are not born with a fear of death. The only two fears we are born with are a fear of falling and a fear of noises. Those are life-preserving fears that protect one from harm. Within a year after birth, though, your child will probably show signs of another fear: the fear of separating from you. Although, at that age, your child cannot verbalize his fears, the idea that you might not be around forever is also in its infancy.

As far as a very young child is concerned, parents were there when the youngster arrived on the scene and will continue to be around forever. Time is a nebulous concept with unclear distinctions between past, present, and future. It is a rude and life-changing discovery when your child learns you might not be with him forever. Or perhaps your child has had an experience that brings this thought to mind. It might be prompted by the sight of an animal lying in the street or the death of a pet. The tragic loss of a family member or friend may provoke a most serious and personal awareness of death.

A six-year-old was riding to school with her father. At first, Dad thought she was just trying to practice her addition. "Daddy, when I am ten, how old will you be?" He answered, "Forty," and she asked, "When I am forty, how old will you be?" He answered, "Seventy." She countered, "When I'm seventy, how old will you be?" Her father tried to explain that he would be one hundred, a very old age. His daughter pushed again asking, "And when I'm 100, you'll be one hundred thirty?" Are these simple questions or inquiries into issues of mortality? Around the age of four or five, most children begin to get an inkling that people do not live forever. Six- and seven-year-olds alternate between wanting to deny the prospect that anyone they love might die and having a million questions about what happens to you when you die. Nine-year-olds have an emerging understanding that they, too, are vulnerable to death.

A child's questions about death can be endless or fleeting. It is hard to explain why a grandparent who dies cannot come back for your child's birthday party, that dead people don't need to eat, and where people go when they die. A child's questions may be poignant, frustrating, elementary, and profound. Sometimes the questions might seem repetitive, but each one is important to the child. Underlying all the questions is a struggle to understand what most people can't comprehend. And as a result a child can become more fearful.

There are ways to help your child cope with a fear of death. You will note we did not say *overcome* a fear of death. Death is an issue each one of us must deal with repeatedly over the years of our life.

Most parents prefer to avoid the subject. It's unlikely your child will allow that to happen. He might develop tangential fears, like fear of the dark, separation, illness, injury, or perhaps going to sleep. Address each of those individually using the appropriate sections of the book. If a family member or friend is very ill or if your child is coping with a serious illness then you will have to confront this issue soon. At the end of this section several books are listed that provide valuable help as you cope with the emotions of life-threatening illness.

If you believe your child is frightened of death, take your time and don't push. Elaborate discussions and abstract conceptualizations will fly right over his head. You cannot desensitize your child to death as with the other fears in this book. This time it is your words, your presence, and the interactions between you and your child that will provide the most comfort as he develops the faith to overcome his fear. Consider these suggestions as you help your child become comfortable with the concept of death.

- Explain death at your child's level of development. Young children are not ready for abstract discussions of the meaning of life or questions of immortality. Be honest with your child and you will be off to a good start. Be sensitive to his attention or lack of it. You are likely to provide more information than your child is ready to handle. Follow your child's lead and respond to his questions.

  The first time your child asks about death, he is likely to want to know what happened to the bird lying still on the sidewalk or a pet that died. Your garden offers an ongoing example of the cycle of life to which your child can relate. The evolution of flowers from buds to wilted petals and shrunken blossoms provides a clear illustration of the finality of death. Your personal faith and religious beliefs offer the basis for a comfortable explanation.

- Reassure your child. A young child might not accept the finality of death. Many young children believe death is reversible. In their favorite cartoons, the characters fall off mountains, are run over by trucks, are flattened like pancakes, and still pop back into action. However, once your child understands that death is the end of life, he may also become frightened by the notion that you will not be around someday. Assure him that you plan to be with him more years than he can count.

- Consider both the spiritual and physical aspects of death. There are two aspects to the discussion of death. One involves your spiritual or religious beliefs about death and the afterlife. The other is physical aspects of what happens to the body. The facts are in some ways easier and in other ways more difficult to talk about. Your child, however, is likely to have a number of questions about what happens to a body and the burial. Be clear about the fact that when a person dies, the body dies and cannot live again. Anything less than the truth will confuse a child.

• Avoid misconceptions and half-truths. Certainly, we don't have all the answers or facts about death. That doesn't mean we should fill in the gaps with fantastical explanations. In explaining death to your child it is best to avoid such statements as, "Aunt Millie went on a long journey"; "Cousin Ken was old and sick"; "Grandma simply went to sleep"; or even "God took Uncle George because he was so good." As benign and well-intentioned as these explanations might seem, they can be quite frightening and misleading to a child.

Asserting that someone a child loves went on a journey is bewildering to a child. Although the explanation is meant to offer comfort, it does quite the opposite. Both children and adults often feel anger when someone dies—anger that they have been left behind. Being told that someone went on a journey adds no finality to the question. Will the person come back? Why would she go on a trip and leave me? Children need to understand that death is the end of life.

Telling a child that the person simply went to sleep can frighten a child and confuse him. It leads to thoughts of "Will I die if I go to sleep?" Be careful to distinguish death and sleep. Similarly, a child is likely to overgeneralize the statement, "Grandma died because she was sick." Children can easily associate all illnesses, hospitals, operations, and so forth with death. It takes a while for children to make a distinction between colds, measles, and serious illness. Be sure to emphasize the fact that people get sick and become well all the time.

Avoid statements that equate a person's goodness with the length of his life: "God took Aunt Sally early because she was so good." The implication is that the good die young and everyone else gets to stay for the ride. Certainly you don't want your child to see merit in being "bad." Nor do you want your child to be angry with a God who would rob him of a loved one.

Helping children to experience the finality of death is an important step in coming to terms with the concept of death. Children will often create elaborate funerals for pets. This is an important part of the bereavement process and it should be encouraged.

• Use books and films as starting points for discussion.

Even if your family is lucky enough not to lose anyone, your child will not be able to avoid this final fact of life. No matter how dear a pet, it is still far easier for your child to cope with its loss than it is to deal with the loss of relative or friend. Losses are unavoidable. Books and movies provide a natural and less painful introduction to the subject of death. While it is important to monitor the viewing of a very young child, watching *Bambi* and other children's films in which a character is very ill or dies offers a natural opening to discussion. Similarly, there are many books written for children that will help your child put into words the thoughts that he has. Many books that have stories about the loss of a friend or loved one are found at the end of this section. An excellent source of information as well as an extensive bibliography of children's books is *Talking About Death* by Earl A. Grollman (Boston: Beacon Press, 1990).

• When you are handling the loss of a loved one:

Allow your child to see your grief. A death in the family touches the lives of everyone who is left behind. Your child's confusion will be lessened considerably if he understands what is happening to the rest of the family. The tales he constructs to explain your reactions might be much more alarming than the true explanations for your behavior.

Allow your child to express his grief. Children do feel grief and go through stages of emotion when they experience the loss of a loved one. They may feel anger at being left behind, or guilt that they somehow did something that caused the person's death. Children believe in magic and may assume that a wish they made contributed to a person's death.

Sometimes well-meaning adults tell children, "Be brave; don't cry." Tears are the first and most natural way to express emotion. On the other hand, you do not want to make your child feel guilty if he does not cry.

Respect your child's feelings. There are many ways to express grief. Your child might go through stages of denial and then panic over what he will do with the person gone. You need to respect what your child is feeling and at the same time offer support, love, and comfort.

Include your child in the family's ritual. Although the answer is likely to differ from child to child, do not automatically exclude your child from the mourning rituals and the funeral of a loved one. The death of a mother, father, sibling, or close relative is one of the most profound events in the life of child and a family. In the case of a parent or sibling, it forever changes the family. It might not be appropriate for very young or very sensitive children to attend the funeral, but by the age of seven, most children should not be automatically excluded from this important event and need the experience to provide closure. Even if a child does not attend the burial ceremony, he might visit the grave later or help welcome guests to the home after the funeral. Just as children should not be isolated during happy occasions, they need to be and feel part of the family during times of sadness.

Books for Parents

Explaining Death to Children. Earl Grollman. Boston: Beacon Press, 1967. Discussions of how to present the concept of death are provided from numerous points of view and religious orientations.

On Children and Death. Elisabeth Kübler-Ross. New York: Collier Books, 1983. From the preeminent authority on death and dying, a thoughtful discussion.

Tough Topics. Sara Wilford. Stamford, Conn.: Longmeadow Press, 1989. Includes a bibliography of books to use with children on this subject and many others.

Books for Children

Badger's Parting Gifts. Susan Varley. New York: Lothrop, Lee and Shepard, 1984. A story about the memories a special friend leaves behind for those who cared about him.

Bridge to Terabithia. Katherine Paterson. New York: Crowell, 1977. Leslie and Jess are from different backgrounds, but they form a close friendship. The girl's tragic accidental death marks the end of childhood for Jess, but their shared experiences help him deal with the loss.

Coping with Childhood Traumas. Joy Berry. Chicago: Children's Press, 1988. A factual discussion of the feelings children have when someone dies.

The Dead Bird. Margaret Wise Brown. Young Scott Books, 1938. For a child who has recently lost a pet, this is a good book that deals with children and a bird that has died. They have a funeral in the woods.

I'll Always Love You. Hans Wilhelm. New York: Crown, 1985. A child's sadness about the death of a beloved dog is tempered by the remembrance of saying every night, "I'll always love you."

It Must Hurt a Lot. Doris Sanford. Portland, Oregon: Multnomah Press, 1986. A sensitive book about a mother telling her child that their dog was hit by a car.

Learning to Say Good-bye: When a Parent Dies. Eda LeShan. New York: Macmillan, 1975. A supportive book in language children can understand about dealing with the death of a parent.

Nana Upstairs and Nana Downstairs. Tomie de Paola. New York: G. P. Putnam's Sons, 1973. A warm story of a boy's love for his grandmother and how he copes after she dies, written and illustrated by an award-winning children's author.

The Tenth Good Thing About Barney. Judith Viorst. New York: Atheneum, 1971. With some help from his parents, a boy recalls all the good things about his cat Barney who has died.

To Hell with Dying. Alice Walker. San Diego: Harcourt Brace Jovanovich, 1988. Alice Walker relates a very special friendship.

15

GROWING UP LESS FEARFUL IN A FEARFUL WORLD

How many times have you said that you are glad that you are not a child growing up in today's world? With the proliferation of drugs and crime and the looming presence of AIDS, the world certainly seems to be a more dangerous place than it was when we grew up. From a kid's-eye view, alarming images of guns and crime and the increasing divorce rate offer an ever-present threat to a child's personal world—his family. It has been estimated that in the inner city, 70 percent of the children personally know a victim of violent crime.

The scenes are not isolated to inner-city districts; instant replays of death and disaster constantly flash on the television screen and across the front pages of the nation's newspapers. It is easy to understand how a child can develop a heightened sense of vulnerability.

How do you educate your child about the world without traumatizing him? How do you teach her to be "careful out there" without creating a child who is scared of the world?

There is a trade-off between shielding your child and presenting the facts about the world. In a media-driven society, it's impossible to protect childhood innocence and simultaneously fear-proof our children. You will not be able to totally control the images and situations that confront your youngster. Perhaps a little fear is a healthy thing to have in today's world.

Too much fear, though, is not healthy. Maybe the carefree period that we like to imagine as our childhood never existed. Children in the fifties grew up with bomb shelters; in the sixties, televised views of riots at home and distant jungles with bloody fighting invaded our homes. Whether the world is actually a more dangerous place now than when we grew up is debatable. It cannot be denied, though, that it is a more frightening place—we know too much and are bombarded by confirming facts everyday.

Studies of children's fears through the years indicate that although the basic fears remain the same, fears of kidnapping, war, and crime have increased. You cannot pretend that the world is a safe place. Consider the way most adults go about their daily lives. You keep your doors locked at home and avoid dark empty streets when you jog. You look behind you as you search for your car in a crowded parking lot, and you lock the doors and rarely drive with the windows wide open. You've learned where the fault lines lie and know the tornado belt, and you've identified a safe area in your house should a natural disaster strike. You have smoke detectors, perhaps an alarm system in your home, and maybe a weather radio sits by your bed. And when you watch the evening news, you know you are right to be concerned.

Like most parents, you probably alternate between alerting your child to the dangers that truly exist and protecting her childhood innocence. Often, adults are much too casual about the images and scenes we introduce to our children through the media. Perhaps we have become so hardened ourselves that we are immune to headlines about serial killers, rape, riots, and natural disasters. This is not old news to children, and it does not go over their heads as much as we like to think. If an Academy Award–winning movie has adult themes, it is probably wise to leave the children home. They are likely to misinterpret rather than forget what they see. The violence that is so nonchalantly introduced into the story line is the stuff that nightmares are made of. Even the impossibly improbable horror movies that delight some youngsters are not for everyone. The imagination of the sensitive child relentlessly weaves these stories into daytime thoughts and nighttime dreams.

No matter how religiously you attempt to provide a safe buffer for your child, you cannot totally shield her. Nor would that be wise. Unfortunately, in today's world you can raise a less fearful child only if you provide the skills to contend with the world as it is. You will have to pierce the bubble of carefree ignorance to teach your child the safety skills she must have.

1. Discuss what your child sees and hears. Don't assume your child understands everything he hears. During the Gulf War, one young boy became terrified when he heard jets flying overhead. He knew the soldiers were bombing Iraq, but he thought that was a city nearby.

Your child's interpretation of events might not be accurate. One evening a nine-year-old girl walked past the television as footage of a woman being put into a car was aired. The child became frightened that women were being pulled off the street by strangers, and luckily she asked her parents about it. The story was about a prostitute resisting arrest. That child would have had another nightmare to contend with that evening if the information had not been corrected.

We have become such a crime-conscious society that even the most innocuous items take on double meaning. Every morning at breakfast your child is likely to be confronted by another image of a missing child on a milk carton. As tragic as these stories are for the families involved, it will be reassuring to your child to know that most of these children have not been kidnapped by strangers.

2. Play the what-ifs. Arm your child with the facts about what to do in various situations. Rather than just telling him, role-play typical situations that might confront him. Most children think strangers are people they have never seen before. Anyone your child doesn't know very well but might see often is also a stranger. Playact how to behave when someone in a car asks for directions or a stranger offers a treat. Teach your child to be polite, but to maintain a safe distance. Give your child permission to say no to requests that feel wrong to him—even when adults are doing the asking.

3. Teach your child what to do when he becomes scared. Your child will be more confident if he knows what to do when he's frightened. Certainly the coping skills we have taught are one way to confront fear, but there are times when a different approach is necessary.

- Teach your child basic information. Every child should know his full name, address, phone number, and the full names of his parents. You'll be surprised how early your child can learn this information, but you must rehearse it from time to time during the early years or it will be forgotten. Once your child can write, teach him how to write the same information. Show your child how to use the telephone, dial his telephone number plus area code, and when to use the emergency number 911.
- Teach your child what to do if he becomes separated from you in a crowd. Before entering the mall or a crowded event, designate a meeting place in case you are separated. Help your child identify individuals who would be appropriate to ask for help. Remind your child never to leave the area with anyone.

4. Make your child aware of the safety measures you take to protect your family. As your child becomes more aware of his environment, he will find it reassuring that you have taken precautions to protect the family from disasters and crime. Explain how smoke detectors, weather-alert radio, alarm system, and other safety measures work. Draw a map of your home and practice escape drills should there be a fire. As an added safety measure, teach your child a secret code word that only members of the immediate family or someone you tell would know. Instruct your child that any messenger you might send for him would volunteer this word.

5. Safety-proof your child against preventable harm. Every child should wear a helmet when she rides a bike or skates. No child should ride in a car without wearing a seat belt. Injuries to hundreds of children each year could be prevented by these safety measures.

There are other situations that have inherent danger. Make sure your child knows how to swim. Teach your child never to dive into unknown water. And always provide adequate supervision when your child is in the pool; even the best of swimmers drown.

Children and adults are bound to get hurt occasionally. Learn first aid skills and cardiopulmonary resuscitation (CPR) skills. Teach your child basic first-aid skills, too. Ideally, she will never have to use the knowledge, but you'll be glad she's prepared if the situation arises. Learning these skills will make your child feel more confident.

6. Prompt discussion of feelings. People who develop strong fears have often hidden their feelings for a long time. Encourage your child to discuss what he is feeling and give him the words to do so. At very early ages, label your child's feelings for him. When he hides behind your legs, tears up a drawing in disgust, or becomes angry over a missed turn, supply the words that express what he is feeling. During the preschool years, widen his vocabulary by cutting out pictures and labeling them with the appropriate emotions—happiness, fear, frustration, sadness, anger, pride, jealousy, and others. Use this tool to help your child find the right word to express what he is feeling.

Take the time every day to unwind with your child and review his day. After a nightly story, take a few minutes to talk together. Although some children will be reluctant to open up at first, if you are there, consistently willing to listen, your child will share his thoughts with you.

7. Provide a safe environment. You are your child's protector. With more single-parent families and approximately 50 percent of women in the work force, more children come home to empty houses every afternoon. Whenever you can, arrange to share supervision duties with another parent in your neighborhood. It is a mistake to assume that older children need less supervision than younger ones. Preteens and adolescents need help contending with the pressures in their lives. Their world is filled with competing seducers that would change their lives forever.

If you cannot arrange for personal supervision, define the rules and keep in touch with your child by other means. Clarify the way his time alone should be used and make contact by phone and note. Always leave emergency numbers in clear view.

The fact is, you can neither paint a rosy, worry-free picture of the world nor casually ignore the perils that do exist. One goal of this book is to help you better understand fear and how a child's personality and your responses influence her reaction to fear. We've presented information about common fears that most children experience and pass through. We have talked about understanding these fears, minimizing their effect, and sometimes preventing them. In addition, we've presented the steps to take to desensitize a child to fears that intensify or last beyond the expected time frame so that they don't persist into adulthood or become phobias.

Maybe the world is not a more dangerous place today than it was when we were growing up—perhaps the dangers are simply different. It is, though, a more frightening world for our children because they are so much more aware of the dangers that lurk. Certainly, they are still afraid of dogs and noises, monsters in the night, and babysitters. In most cases, they will outgrow these fears like generations of children before them have. There will still be adults who are afraid to speak in public, won't use an elevator, avoid dentists, and won't fly on airplanes. But your child won't be in that group, because you will give him the skills to overcome his fears.

AFTERWORD: WHEN YOU NEED HELP

Sometimes no matter what you might do, a fear persists or becomes a phobia. When that occurs, you must seek professional help. At the clinic we see countless adults whose phobias started in childhood and now hamper their daily existence. This does not have to happen to your child.

The research literature indicates that when fears and phobias are directly treated through cognitive and behavioral approaches by trained professionals, success rates are high. There are a growing number of therapists who specialize in the treatment of fears, phobias, panic, and other anxiety disorders. For the name of a specialist in your area, send a self-addressed, stamped envelope to

The Anxiety Disorders Association of America
6000 Executive Blvd., Suite 200
Rockville, MD 20852

You can also ask your family physician or pediatrician for several referrals to therapists who work with this problem. Check the phone book or a local college or university for suggestions. As you look for the right therapist for your child, don't be frightened to ask questions. Some questions you might pose include the following:

- How much training and experience have you had in dealing with children?
- How much training and experience have you had in dealing with children's fears and phobias?
- What is your approach to overcoming a child's fear or phobia?
- What is your success rate?
- How would you work with my child—with my child alone? with parents and child? in the office or in the feared setting?

Of course, you are free to ask other questions related to fees, length of sessions, and how long the therapist has found treatment of similar cases to take. It is important to select a therapist you trust and like as well as one who has the expertise and experience you need. Once you begin therapy, give it a chance to work. Change takes hard work and time, so be patient.

BIBLIOGRAPHY

Bandura, A., and P. G. Barab. "Processes Governing Disinhibitory Effects through Symbolic Modeling." *Journal of Abnormal Psychology* 82 (1973): 1–9.

Bandura, A., and F. Menlove. "Factors Determining Vicarious Extinction of Avoidance Behavior through Symbolic Modeling." *Journal of Personality and Social Psychology* 8 (1968): 99–108.

Ferber, Richard. *Solve Your Child's Sleep Problems.* New York: Simon and Schuster, 1985.

Grollman, Earl A., ed. *Explaining Death to Children.* Boston: Beacon Press, 1967.

Grollman, Earl A. *Talking About Death.* Boston: Beacon Press, 1990.

Ilg, Frances L., Louise Bates Ames, and Sidney Bates. *Child Behavior.* New York: Barnes and Noble Books, 1981.

Jacobson, Edmond. *You Must Relax.* New York: McGraw-Hill, 1934.

Lapouse, R., and Monk, M. "Fears and Worries in a Representative Sample of Children." *American Journal of Orthopsychiatry.* 29 (1959): 803–818.

Lipson, Eden Ross. *The New York Times Parent's Guide to the Best Books for Children,* rev. ed. New York: Times Books, 1991.

Morris, Richard, and Thomas R. Kratochwill. *Treating Children's Fears and Phobias.* New York: Pergamon Press, 1983.

Oppenheim, Joanne, Barbara Brenner, and Betty D. Boegehold. *Choosing Books for Kids.* New York: Ballantine Books, 1986.

Schacter, Robert, and Carole Spearin McCauley. *When Your Child Is Afraid.* New York: Simon and Schuster, 1988.

Wolpe, Joseph. *The Practice of Behavior Therapy.* New York: Pergamon Press, 1973.

INDEX

ABOUT THE AUTHORS

STEPHEN W. GARBER, Ph.D., is a licensed psychologist, director of the Behavioral Institute of Atlanta, and a consultant to hospitals, schools, and child-care facilities. He is the co-author and creator of "Power over Panic," a videotape program for helping individuals overcome fears and phobias.

MARIANNE DANIELS GARBER, Ph.D., is an educational consultant in private practice at the Behavioral Institute of Atlanta. The Garbers appear regularly on NBC affiliate WXIA-TV's *Noonday* as parenting experts. They are frequent speakers on parenting and educational issues and conduct workshops for parents, schools, and other professionals. The Garbers have four children.

ROBYN FREEDMAN SPIZMAN has written forty-six books and numerous articles on enhancing children's learning, art education, and crafts. For the past ten years she has appeared weekly as the Super Mom and consumer expert on kids' issues on *Noonday* for WXIA-TV in Atlanta. She speaks regularly on ways to motivate children to learn. She is married and lives with her husband and two children in Atlanta.

The authors have collaborated on the successful parenting books *Good Behavior* and *If Your Child is Hyperactive, Inattentive, Distractible, Impulsive . . . Helping the Attention Deficit Hyperactive Child* and the new comprehensive parenting program "Good Behavior Made Easy." The three co-author a parenting column that appears in the *Atlanta Journal and Constitution* and other newspapers across the United States and Canada.